THE SACRED LITERATURE SERIES

THE LIVING WAY

The Sacred Literature Series of the International Sacred Literature Trust

Titles in the series

AUSTRALIAN ABORIGINAL TRADITIONS
Warlpiri Dreamings and Histories

♦

BUDDHISM
Numerical Discourses of the Buddha: An Anthology of Suttas
from the Aṅguttara Nikāya
The Recorded Sayings of Zen Master Joshu
The Words of My Perfect Teacher

♦

CHRISTIANITY
On the Life of Christ: Kontakia of St Romanos

♦

INDIAN TRADITIONS
In the Dark of the Heart: Songs of Meera

♦

JAINISM
That Which Is: Tattvārtha Sūtra

♦

JUDAISM
Gates of Light: Sha'are Orah
Yemenite Midrash

♦

SHINTO
The Living Way: Stories of a Shinto Founder

♦

SIKHISM
The Name of My Beloved: Verses of the Sikh Gurus

♦

SUFISM
Solomon's Ring: The Life and Teachings of a Sufi Master

♦

TAOISM
Lao-tzu's Treatise on the Response of the Tao

Further titles in preparation

KYŌSOSAMA NO GOITSUWA

The Living Way

Stories of Kurozumi Munetada, a Shinto Founder

Narrated by Tadaaki Kurozumi and Isshi Kohmoto

Translated by Sumio Kamiya

Edited by Willis Stoesz
Emeritus Professor of Religion, Wright State University

ALTAMIRA
PRESS

A Division of
ROWMAN & LITTLEFIELD PUBLISHERS, INC.
Walnut Creek • Lanham • New York • Oxford

For more information about the
International Sacred Literature Trust,
please write to the ISLT at:
22 Northumberland Avenue, London WC2N 5AP,
United Kingdom

ALTAMIRA PRESS
A Division of ROWMAN & LITTLEFIELD PUBLISHERS, INC.

Published in the United States of America
by Rowman & Littlefield Publishers, Inc.
4720 Boston Way
Lanham, Maryland 20706

12 Hid's Copse Road
Cumnor Hill, Oxford OX2 9JJ, England

AltaMira Press
A Division of Rowman & Littlefield Publishers, Inc.
1630 North Main Street, Suite 367
Walnut Creek, CA 94596
http: //www.altamirapress.com

First published 2000

Photoset in Sabon by Northern Phototypesetting Co. Ltd, Bolton, UK

PRINTED IN THE UNITED STATES OF AMERICA

Library of Congress Cataloging-in-Publication Data

Kurozumi, Tadaaki, 1919–
  [Kyosoden. English]
  The living way : stories of Kurozumi Munetada, a Shinto founder
/ narrated by Tadaaki Kurozumi and Isshi Kohmoto ; translated by
Sumio Kamiya ; edited by Willis Stoesz.
      p. cm. – (The Sacred literature series)
      ISBN 0-7425-0341-0 (cloth : alk. paper)
      ISBN 0-7425-0342-9 (paper : alk. paper)
  1. Kurozumi, Munetada, 1780–1850. 2. Kurozumikyo (Religious
organization)–Biography. I. Kohmoto, Isshi. II. Stoesz, Willis.
III. Title. IV. Series.
      BL2222.K8892 K88613 1999
      299'.5619—dc21
                                    99-6244
                                    CIP

INTERNATIONAL
SACRED
LITERATURE
TRUST

The International Sacred Literature Trust was established to promote understanding and open discussion between and within faiths and to give voice in today's world to the wisdom that speaks across time and traditions.

What resources do the sacred traditions of the world possess to respond to the great global threats of poverty, war, ecological disaster and spiritual despair?

Our starting-point is the sacred texts with their vision of a higher truth and their deep insights into the nature of humanity and the universe we inhabit. The translation programme is planned so that each faith community articulates its own teachings with the intention of enhancing its self-understanding as well as the understanding of those of other faiths and those of no faith.

The Trust particularly encourages faiths to make available texts which are needed in translation for their own communities and also texts which are little known outside the tradition but which have the power to inspire, console, enlighten and transform. These sources from the past become resources for the present and future when we make inspired use of them to guide us in shaping the contemporary world.

Our religious traditions are diverse but, as with the natural environment, we are discovering the global interdependence of human hearts and minds. The Trust invites all to participate in the modern experience of interfaith encounter and exchange which marks a new phase in the human quest to discover our full humanity.

Contents

THE STORIES

A Word to the Reader

You can start reading this book almost anywhere. The Editor's Introduction gives general background and you may want to start there.

More eloquent by far, and surely more enlightening, is a brief summary of Munetada's teaching given in Appendix B. Or, begin with any of the stories and move around the collection. The spirit of Munetada is visible in all of them. Words of commendation by Kurozumi Tadaaki, the second writer of stories, or by Kurozumi Muneharu, present head (*Kyōshu*) of Kurozumikyō, might also give you your best starting point. I leave it to you.

For an explanation of the title of the book see note 18 in the Editor's Introduction. Read stories 14 and 30 to see why straw sandals appear on the cover. The index gives you a start in doing topical study.

Willis Stoesz

Acknowledgements

The Editor and the International Sacred Literature Trust are grateful to the Kurozumi faith community for their generous help in the publication of this volume.

Permission is gratefully acknowledged to quote six *waka* from *Kurozumi Shinto: An American Dialogue*, edited by Willis Stoesz. Copyright 1993 by Columbia University Press (Anima Press, 1989). Reprinted with permission from the publisher.

Permission is gratefully acknowledged to republish fourteen stories and five citations of original materials published in *The Opening Way: Kurozumi Munetada, Founder of Kurozumikyo*, edited by Willis Stoesz. Copyright 1994 by University Press of America. Reprinted with permission from the publisher.

Foreword

When one tries to get a proper understanding of someone's character it is best to see what that person actually did in particular situations and at specific times. How did that person act in relation to his family, his neighbourhood, and his community? This is better than relying only on what that person wrote, however valuable those writings may be. This is true also of Kurozumi Munetada.

He was one who grew up in the midst of the overflowing love of his parents. He responded to that love and trusted them in all sincerity, from the bottom of his heart. As he grew up he wanted his parents always to be pleased with him, not causing them any worry about anything he did. His affection and filial piety toward them was the fundamental theme of all he said and did throughout his youth. This feeling was deepened in his mature years, coming to fruition in his personal life and teachings and, eventually, in the faith of Kurozumikyō.

He taught that true parental love pervades nature itself. The power that sustains all living things on earth is parental love, the same as the love that parents naturally have for their children. What each of us has received as a result of parental love must fill us with humility and gratitude. The rising sun has traditionally been regarded as the symbol in nature of this mysterious power of love and support. We worship it as Amaterasu Ohmikami, the Kami of the Sun.

Throughout his life Munetada expressed an attitude of gratefulness and sincerity toward everyone, equally and without discrimination. Though he lived at a time when a strict feudal code of behaviour separating the classes of society was in force (the late Tokugawa Shogunate), he always treated people equally. For him, each had within them a share of the inner presence of Amaterasu, and so each had a right to equal treatment. A man with a disfiguring case of skin disease (Story 43), a highway robber who tried to rob him (Story 2), and an arsonist who tried to burn down his house (Story 1) all received his compassionate attention as fully as anyone else. He extended to them an attitude of sincerity so they might become able to cultivate their own sincerity. Munetada even felt a deep sense of thankfulness, to the point of reverence, toward the worn-out straw sandals he no longer could use (Story 30).

As we are well aware, we modern people have exploited our mother earth in order to support a style of life we have become used to. The result of our egoism is all kinds of disharmony with nature, so that our existence itself is threatened. As one of the members of modern society I am fully convinced that Munetada's almost foolishly unselfish words and actions, which are boundlessly warm and undiscriminating yet strong and brave, must say something that touches our hearts no matter what our cultural and ethnic differences may be. His deeds, as described in these stories, speak for themselves and say it the best.

1 November 1996
Kurozumi Muneharu
Kyōshu (Chief Patriarch),
Kurozumikyō

Preface[1]

In 1994 my biographical work on Kurozumi Munetada, *The Opening Way*, was published. This present collection of stories about the founder of Kurozumikyō is next in a series of publications for the English-speaking world.

Munetada was born in a household which had served as Shinto priests for centuries. From childhood on he was uncommonly filial, and as a young man he thought hard about what true filial piety meant for whatever he did or was to be. When he was about twenty years old he made up his mind to become a living kami. He believed he could reach this goal by avoiding whatever his conscience judged to be wrong. He strove hard to attain this goal until he was thirty-three years old, when his parents passed away one after the other within a week. His deep sorrow and grief made him sick and brought him to the point that he no longer knew whether he would live to the next day.

On such a morning he worshipped the rising sun and was miraculously saved from his sickness. After the recovery he started to help people who were suffering from all sorts of illnesses and life troubles. He did so making use of his own experience of recovery, and he continued to do so until the day he died at the age of seventy.

His teaching came out of this experience of recovering from what had been an incurable sickness. But, what he taught the people went far beyond just overcoming sickness. It reached also into gaining true health of the spirit through unity with Amaterasu, the Kami of the sun. He was a living practitioner of his own teaching. There was no difference between what he told others and what he himself did.

Often we are at a loss what to do when we encounter all sorts of new and unexpected developments in life. Putting his teaching into practice is much

1. In *gasshō* (with hands placed together in prayer).

harder than just studying what he taught. This collection of stories about the Founder is a precious one, helping us by allowing us to see what Munetada did in the specific situations he encountered. They give us the example he set, showing us the way our own health of spirit may be opened for us.

This book contains a hundred and twenty-seven stories. Seventy-five of them were collected by Kohmoto Isshi and fifty-two of them by me. The history of this process is as follows. A collection of them was first published during the years 1896–1906 in the Kurozumikyō journal *Kuni-no-Oshie (Teachings of the Nation)*, the forerunner of today's *Nisshin*. In 1949, as part of the Centenary Commemoration of the death of the Divine Founder (*Kyōso-shin*), these were compiled in a single volume and published as *Kurozumi Kyōso Itsuwa-shū*, or *Tales of the Founder*. However, since the style of writing was outdated, publication of a new, modern version was much desired and earnestly solicited.

The late Kohmoto Isshi (1877–1947) had already, during the years 1937–1944, provided in *Nisshin* a series of his versions of the stories under the title *Misebumi*. Compilation of his series led to the publication of *Kyōso-sama no Go-itsuwa-shū (Tales of the Kurozumikyō Founder)* in 1960.

Then, twenty-six stories that were part of the original series in *Kuni-no-Oshie* but not in Kohmoto's version were rewritten by the Kurozumikyō School of Theology in 1974 expressly for a new edition, and added to them. The title *Kyōso-sama no Go-Itsuwa (Tales of the Founder)* was kept, along with the subtitle *Misebumi*.

Now, with the publication of this English version another twenty-seven stories have been added, bringing the total to 127 (after one of the 1974 stories was combined with an earlier version of the same story).[2]

I think that the more stories we have the better, giving us more opportunity to learn about Munetada's teaching in the concrete terms of our everyday lives. It is a great pleasure for me to see this collection published in English, following on the appearance of *The Opening Way*.

12 October 1996
Kurozumi Tadaaki
Secretary General,
Kurozumikyō Theology Bureau

---

2. Editor's note: Thus, the storyteller in Stories 1–75 is Kohmoto Isshi; in Stories 76–100, the School of Theology group under Kurozumi Tadaaki's leadership; and in Stories 101–127, Kurozumi Tadaaki.

Editor's Introduction

These stories come to us from a Shinto denomination known as Kurozu-mikyō. It is a religious group rooted in Japanese culture and history, and most readers' understanding of "Shinto" will be considerably broadened by reading them. We get a direct look into Japanese spirituality from knowing these stories. Their central figure is Kurozumi Munetada (1780–1850),[1] priest in a Shinto shrine in Okayama, located on the northern coast of the Inland Sea halfway between Osaka and Hiroshima. Okayama was the castle town of the Ikeda clan, feudal lords in the Tokugawa period (1600–1867), enlightened and firm rulers of Bizen Province. To the west and south lie rich agricultural areas and to the east lies one of the most famous pottery-producing areas of Japan. The region was affected by the same social and economic trends that were bringing winds of impending change everywhere in the closing years of the Tokugawa shogunate, opening Japanese culture to new levels of development.

Shinto concerns and values were deeply involved in this history. We must, however, think not of State Shinto which began in the late nineteenth century and ended in 1945, but of something more enduring – the growth of ideals of daily life in keeping with changing economic and social opportunities in urban and rural settings throughout the country. These ideals are indeed the core values by which Japan has guided itself in its recent history.[2]

A number of Neo-Confucian scholars, and of teachers and religious figures rising from the ranks of laypeople, were involved in shaping the growth of these ideals. Shinto ceremonies and attitudes often helped in that shaping, notably so in the case of Munetada. As background we also take special note of the Ise Pilgrimage which enlisted large numbers of people in a growing cult of Amaterasu; and we bear in mind the repeated protest movements of the whole period, signalling to us the tensions under which the people lived who appear in these stories.[3]

Kurozumi Munetada was one of those who showed the way in this history. He is known to historians[4] as a faith healer and as a teacher of faith in the Kami of the Sun, Amaterasu Ohmikami.[5] But these 127 stories give us information not easily available up to now, enabling fresh perspective. They help us see the spirituality of this gifted priest as it unfolded itself in relation to those he met in daily life.[6] His inner life had been transformed by an experience of ecstatic union with Amaterasu and by dedicated cultivation of his relation to her within himself after that. Through lifelong spiritual practice he came to be so thoroughly attuned to her inner presence that his spontaneous words and actions were selfless and compassionate, apt to the needs of others. He was honoured as a man of the spirit in his lifetime; the community of faith and practice he founded continues to the present day.[7]

We can see a number of similarities between his teachings and those of others of his times. To know Kurozumi Munetada is to gain entrance to the wider Japanese religious tradition. Yet we can also see that he is an original voice founded in his own transcendent experience of the Kami of the sun.

Life of Munetada

Munetada's life and work took place almost entirely in Okayama and the surrounding countryside. He was the son of an assistant priest in a Shinto shrine in Imamura, a village on the southwest outskirts of Okayama. Near Imamura lay the hamlet of Kaminakano, or simply 'Nakano', where the family lived.[8] Stories of his childhood show him a dutiful, filial child who soon caught the eye of his teachers for conscientiousness in learning and for aptitude in calligraphy. At the age of twenty-six he married; at the age of thirty he assumed the role of priest in the Imamura Shrine (Imamura-gū) which his father had filled until retiring.

He developed in stages, building on the foundation of a strong family life and attentive parents. At the age of twenty he made a vow to become a living kami (*ikigami*), expecting thereby to bring honour to them. The form in which he envisaged this goal corresponds somewhat to sainthood in western tradition, though with important differences.[9] These are the rules by which he expected to reach this goal.[10]

Five Rules to be Followed at Home

1. Born into a family deeply following the faith, I pledge never to be without faith.

2. I pledge not to be filled with self-conceit nor look down upon others.
3. I pledge not to increase the evil of my own heart by focusing on the evil of others.
4. I pledge not to be negligent in attending my family occupation unless I am ill.
5. Since I have entered the Way of Sincerity, I pledge that my heart shall never be allowed to lack sincerity.

Standing before me
    others hold up mirrors
        as their own hearts
And there within I can see
    my heart being reflected.

The above articles are awesome. I shall follow them as principles of my religious discipline.

The kind of person he intended to become required a high level of ethical effort and constant self-examination. His was a Shinto concerned with character development and not simply with the performance of ritual. The mirror to be used for self-examination was the minds and hearts of other people and not simply the mirror traditionally present on Shinto altars.

There were in those times others who gave close attention to character formation. Such concern was in fact a salient feature of the Neo-Confucianism that informed the educational programmes of governing authorities of those times, and it was a feature also of lay movements such as the Shingaku movement which had widespread influence.[11] But his path to personal development was a self-chosen one, guided at first by "what he felt in his own heart" was good or bad to do and later by whatever was consistent with his own experience of ecstatic unity with Amaterasu.[12] Before that experience occurred he used the Five Rules as guidelines for over a decade of religious practice. During most of this time he served as an assistant to his father and as an instructor in calligraphy.[13]

But then in 1812 occurred a Copernican revolution in his spiritual attitude. It was brought on by the deaths of his parents in quick succession late in the summer of that year. The centre of his life collapsed since his goal in seeking to be a living kami had been to bring honour to them. Filial piety, that most basic of Confucian virtues, seemed to have lost its basis. All the next year and until January 1814, his health deteriorated until it appeared he would die of tuberculosis. On 19 January he made a second vow: that after death he would be a healing kami, one to whom people could pray for relief from their illnesses. He prepared for death, carrying out his morning prayer before the sun (*nippai*), thanking the Kami of the sun and his parents and ancestors for his life until then.

In the more resigned state of mind that followed it occurred to him that his parents would be more honoured if his life were to continue than if he were to die. He saw that the gratitude he had expressed to them in his dying prayer was a better basis of life than his earnest search for ethical perfection had been. With this change of attitude his health began to stabilize. Two months later he resolved to take a hot bath and to worship the sun at sunrise out on his veranda.[14] His condition now began to improve.

It was on the day of the next winter solstice (1814) that the decisive shift in his thinking occurred. Here is how he later described what happened.[15]

> The day of the winter solstice, a splendid and auspicious day when nature passes through seasonal changes, is also the day of my own birth. Having a birthday on the day of winter solstice is fortunate but this year was very special with my having experienced the revival of my life by the blessing of Kami. This is indeed an incomparably auspicious birthday for which I am most grateful. The *nippai* of that day was carried out with special care and deepest gratitude. With complete earnestness I respectfully offered up my prayers ... when, just at that moment, the sun appeared brilliant in the eastern sky, centreing on me. Fixing my mind on the rising sun, my feelings deepened and my prayers became more concentrated in their devotion. Then suddenly in a moment I felt that my heart was pierced by a ray of white brilliance that filled the whole of Heaven and Earth. I felt my full self wrapped in the great *yōki* of joyousness of the sun.[16] Elated by feelings of gratitude, my mouth flew open in amazement and I swallowed down the rays of the sun.
>
> What happened next was wondrous! The great orb of the sun soared down into my body and heart. The sun and I, I and the sun, became absolutely one. And there in the ecstasy of selflessness I realized the wonderful truth that Kami and man are never two. I had become fully enlightened,[17] knowing the Great Way of eternal immortality, the abiding life that all may share with all of Heaven and Earth.[18]

In discovering Amaterasu, the Kami of the sun, to be the origin of his life, both in body and heart, he experienced a recentreing of his personal existence. The rays of the sun entered his body with the inrush of his breath, down to his *hara* (lower abdomen), considered the seat of the human spirit. The confusion of the previous two years was replaced by a source of stability: Amaterasu as known within himself. He had gained a transcendent reference point – Amaterasu the Divine Parent – that allowed a recentreing of all he had thought and known until then. The experience is referred to in Kurozumikyō as the "Direct Bestowal of Divine Mission".[19]

What he had gained was not so much a new theory or belief as a new experience, one to which he constantly referred thereafter. It was a "chartering experience", empowering him for the rest of his life. Re-enacted daily in morning worship of the sun (nippai), it gave him a lens through which to understand all his other experience. From that decisive moment he gained a keen sense of the initiative Amaterasu exercised in each moment of his life by which the elements of each moment's actions could be drawn together as harmonious activity.

Kurozumikyō members still make nippai the central ceremony or sacrament of their religious practice. It is a ceremony with great religious power. Each morning's observance begins with the traditional Prayer of Purification (Oharai),[20] then goes on to other prayers, some perhaps written for that day, and hymns using the Founder's poetry. Worshippers express gratitude for the Sun Kami's gift of life. Then, following the Founder's example, they take into their abdomens a strong breath of air through the mouth at the moment when the sun's rays first become visible. Thus they receive Amaterasu's day-initiating light and warmth into the hara which is the seat of the kokoro (heart/mind). It is an action that replicates the Founder's decisive moment of ecstatic unity with Amaterasu. Amaterasu the Universal Spirit (honshin), made visible in the sun, makes contact with the human spirit (kokoro), reinforcing the "divided presence" (bunshin) present in all human beings. The power animating all of nature vivifies the worshipper in his or her daily life along with all of nature.[21] Nippai is the paradigmatic ritual expression of Kurozumi spirituality.

Munetada had come to understand Amaterasu as a "living-presence" (ikimono) within himself. For the rest of his life he endeavored to "practise the presence" of Amaterasu.[22] He sought to be constantly alert to that presence and to allow her divine intention (goshinryo) to be enacted in whatever he did.[23] He wished to be empty of his own self (mushin), of his own will (muga) and thought (munen). He became transparent to her divine energy and virtue (shintoku). Reliant on his sense of her presence within himself, he no longer was anxious in ethical striving as before.

In the days that followed his experience he was filled with a kind of giddy joy and complete sense of freedom, puzzling his family and friends by the apparent loss of his senses. But soon he steadied himself, finding ways to relate what had happened to the needs of everyday life. He discovered he had the ability to heal others' diseases; before long people with various illnesses crowded to his house and he performed many healings.[24] It was apparent that his vow to be a healer of others' ills was being fulfiled without his having to die. He had become a living kami in a way that included both his first vow (with spiritual understanding transformed) at the age of twenty and his second vow made at the time his death was expected.[25]

From the beginning he was clear that when these healings occurred it was not due to his own powers but due to Amaterasu's power manifested within the person who was ill. It was a person's turn toward receptivity to that inner presence, a change in attitude, that made his or her return to health possible; it was the "divided presence" of Amaterasu within everyone that was each person's basis of health and well-being. One can be unaware of that presence, one's heart and mind clouded over by concern about one's self (*manshin*, egoism). As the numerous healing stories make clear, when the Founder by his words and example brought that inner presence to an ill person's attention so that he or she could again become actively receptive to it rather than remaining self-concerned, then Amaterasu's divine virtue had a chance to work and to bring about healing of spirit and body. Munetada's own life provided the shining and guiding example of fully attending to Amaterasu's presence in daily life. These 127 stories give us access to understanding that example.

Thus, the faith healings had a spiritual basis, contingent on the ill person's gaining a grateful relation to the transcending presence of Amaterasu within. So, in addition to rituals of healing he also presented sermons (or lectures; *kōshaku*) that provided the proper understanding needed for a thorough healing to take place.[26] He was an inspiring preacher. His sermons had the effect of awakening his hearers' sensitivity to Amaterasu's presence apart from the content of what he said (Story 108).

He now embarked on a busy schedule of preaching and healing, both in his own house and at a number of locations to which he was invited. Services in his own home (called *gokaijitsu*) were held on the "two and seven" days of each month, but additional services elsewhere increased in number. Circles of followers formed in various locations, becoming nuclei of permanent congregations. In the decade that followed his chartering experience growing numbers of people became his followers and some of them made vows (*shinmon*) to Kurozumi Sensei to follow his teachings in a disciplined way. These latter were the "direct disciples" (*monjin*) who by the time of his death numbered over a thousand.[27] Those who regularly attended such meetings were called "way-companions" (*michizure*); for some years the only term used to refer to the following as a whole was *Omichi*, the sacred or great Way. Among them were townsmen and village leaders from the countryside, tradespeople and samurai in the service of the Ikeda clan. Some were highly educated, and some were energetic, talented people who gave outstanding leadership to the emerging movement, helping to give shape to the following of the Founder.

After about ten years of this kind of activity he felt a need to renew his inner relation to Amaterasu. He made a fresh vow, preparing himself to receive a second mandate from her. During 1825–8 he fulfilled a Thousand Days' Seclusion (*sanrō*), spending that number of nights in nightlong prayer before her altar in the shrine in addition to carrying out his normal daytime activities. The result was a further clarification of his spiritual sensitivity. A dream he had during this period, reported to a follower in a letter, gives an indication of what it meant.[28]

One night while in confinement in the Imamura Shrine I fell into a drowse and had a dream. In the dream I was sitting all alone when a swarm of snakes, large and small, came in countless numbers looking for a chance to torment me. The more I tried to brush them aside the more they came after me. They wrapped themselves around my arms and legs. They wrapped themselves around my neck. Everywhere, all the fields and mountains, was full of snakes. One large one flicked out its reddened tongue and tried to swallow me. I tried to escape, but there was nothing I could do.

But when I looked carefully I could see that all I had always considered important – my beloved children and wife, as well as gold and silver and everything I had ever wanted – had all taken the form of snakes. And the largest one, their leader in their midst, I saw was my own body and flesh. At the moment when I was astonished and confused I suddenly remembered Amaterasu Ohmikami and I earnestly prayed to her, leaving everything in her hands.[29]

Then it was as though everything changed. Everything that had seemed fearful returned to its normal state. My wife and my children and my valuables became real treasures once again. If we become attached to our family and the things we value and lose our hearts, it all turns to snakes and serpents. But if we surrender everything to Amaterasu Ohmikami and accept all as gifts from her, then all those things will nurture our hearts and we can live abundantly.

It is said that our daily perplexities show up in our dreaming, and I must have been in some kind of delusion at that time. However, I feel extreme gratitude for this kind of religious practice, giving nourishment for my heart's cultivation. I have told this experience to our followers, and they nodded their heads in agreement, sharing my sense of gratitude.

He also took an important step in the guidance of others, setting forth "Seven Daily Rules for the Whole Family" to be observed within the households of all followers.[30] He used the five rules he had set for himself, adding two others concerned with avoiding anger and cultivating gratitude. These Rules have remained in common use in Kurozumi Shinto households to the present day.

During the following decade and a half he maintained an active schedule of preaching and healing, and also continued his service in the Imamura Shrine. There were a number of converts from among samurai circles, and many letters survive that were written to those who attended the Bizen *Daimyō* in his alternate-year service in Edo.[31] In 1843 he resigned his priestly occupation, designating his son, Munenobu, as his successor. Two years earlier he had already deferred his role as family head to his son. These moves left him free to teach and preach more actively, and there was a distinct increase in the number of his followers.

The last seven years of his life saw several steps that provided structure for the growing religious movement. In 1846 he instituted an organizational code regulating the work of disciples who extended his work of teaching to distant locations, and guiding the organization of local groups of followers. These Six Regulations were the core of subsequent development of rules governing the growth of the Kurozumikyō denomination. Also in 1846 his followers set about to build a house that would be adequate to Munetada's role as Kyōso, or "Founder". This building was completed in 1848. All the needed money and labour was donated by followers. It was an important step for the organization, not only in supplying a more appropriate residence, but also in setting forth an expression of the importance of their Kyōso to themselves.[32]

A number of capable, dedicated followers had emerged by the time of his death in 1850.[33] We hear in these stories of two principal disciples, Akagi Tadaharu and Tokio Katsutarō. We hear also of Four High Disciples including these two and Ishio Kensuke and Kawakami Chūsho; and of Six High Disciples including these four and Hoshijima Ryōhei and Morishita Keitan. These men led the way in spreading the Founder's teachings in western Japan and as far east as Kyoto. Their abilities and their commitment to the Way taught by Munetada are a measure of his stature as a spiritual figure.

The process of defining Munetada's religious role continued after his death. He was officially accorded the title of "Daimyōjin" in 1856 by the Yoshida house in Kyoto.[34] A shrine was built for him in Kyoto in 1862; his shrine in Okayama, placed next to the house built for him, was completed in 1885. This Okayama shrine served as the headquarters shrine until 1974 when a new central shrine (the *Daikyōden*) was dedicated at Shintozan on the southwest outskirts of modern Okayama.

Teachings of Munetada

The teachings of Munetada as well as his personal devotion were focused firmly on Amaterasu, the Kami of the Sun known throughout Japanese history. Amaterasu is, of course, the mythological ancestress of the imperial family. The "divine descent" of each Emperor from her was much emphasized in pre-World War II State Shinto. However, Munetada was little concerned, if at all, with this aspect of the story of Amaterasu, or with matters of political governance. He identified strongly with the nation as a whole and he made use of the idea of the renewal of the ancient "age of kami", common in the Shinto Restoration movement, to refer to his renewal of the heart within humans.[35] Yet his recourse to Amaterasu was first of all a quest for personal (and interpersonal) well-being. Close attention to the most inner and intuitive of the movements of his heart and their expression in word and act was the burden of his effort.

He was assiduous in following devotional practices. Six times he went on pilgrimage to Amaterasu's shrine at Ise and he lectured often on the meaning of that pilgrimage. He often went on pilgrimage to nearby shrines and emphasized the frequent recitation of the Great Purification prayer. Daily he offered prayer before the rising sun (*nippai*). His purpose in all this practice was to cultivate gratitude to Amaterasu and to diminish egoism (*ga*).[36] Practice should not be mere asceticism, mere self-denial in pursuit of greater strength of mind or heart. Such a motive for practice cannot accomplish well-being because it is not focused on overcoming self-concern.

His most important discipline was practicing devotion to the inner presence of Amaterasu in every thought and action. This means accepting all that happens as the effect of divine intention; all of daily life becomes religious practice. Every apparent discomfort or setback is then an occasion for reflection about how self-concern might have led to interpreting some event negatively. The key to progress is responding with gratitude for everything and "leaving all to Kami", letting go of the self-concern that might be present in the moment.

This, of course, is not easy. Constant attention is needed and particu-

larly distressing experiences are a serious test. A salient example is the
death of family members, particularly of his wife Iku. A series of *waka*
he composed when that happened show him achieving acceptance. When
she died he first wrote,[37]

> The world of dreams
>   Is, I know, a world of dreams,
>   Yet I cannot waken ...
> For another yet to wake
>   I know I shall be longing;

and,

> Although I have heard
>   That the flowers of yesterday
>   Are dreams of today,
> Towards this storm that rages
>   I hold a deep resentment.

But then, after reflection, he wrote,

> Flowers of the world
>   Scattered everywhere about ...
>   let it then be so.
> I will bring the boundless Way
>   to bloom again everywhere.[38]

Focusing his thought on the Way of Amaterasu and its fulfilment in each
moment and every place made it possible for him to accept his loss.

The concept of the Way is indeed important to Munetada. It is a concept fundamental to Japanese worldview from its ancient Chinese her-
itage. What is real in this manner of seeing reality is a process of actions
taking place, and of countless processes of action taking place, all interacting with one another.[39] For Munetada, "Way" is the all-embracing
reality of things, the fullness of "Heaven and Earth" (*Tenchi*; *Ametsuchi*), pervaded as it is by the presence of Amaterasu, the Kami of the
Sun, within all.[40] The word also may refer to religious practice that is
intended to bring people into harmony with that universal Way. As we
have seen, the focus of his practice was to hold the inner presence of
Amaterasu in constant and grateful regard.

He bore in constant mind also her presence within others with whom
he had to deal. A Way of interacting with others results from her simul-
taneous presence within all other people. An example is the occasion
when an angry priest berated him, and he offered no defence (Story 26).

His reason was that if he had given a defensive answer, the man's own inner relation to Amaterasu would have suffered a setback. His concern was that the Way should come to fulfilment in that person, not that he should vindicate himself in a conventional sense. What guided him in his relation to others was his appreciation for the quality of sincerity (*makoto*) in them. Sincerity is the cardinal virtue in the Confucian tradition, but for Munetada it was redefined by his recentreing experience. For him it meant filial devotion to Amaterasu's transcendent presence; in every moment of life he sought to leave all to her divine intention so as to "live through" each moment in utter reliance on her. He wanted all others to have the same experience.

Total sincerity, total filial devotion, is total inner reliance on Amaterasu and total absence of self-concern. It means acting in no other way than as an expression of Amaterasu's transcendently present action. All goodness (*toku*), all well-being, flows from that total sincerity.[41] Sincerity must be present in everyone so that the Way may come to fulfilment in the world generally. Total sincerity *is* the presence of Amaterasu acting in all concrete circumstances, it *is* the principle by which the world finds its well-being. The realization of total sincerity in everyone, in a manner for which his own experience of Amaterasu was the paradigm, was the goal of the Founder's teachings. As the story of his healing of a man who had died makes clear (Story 42), this realization reaches deeper into the energies of human life than did the teachings of Confucius himself.

Universal Presence of Amaterasu

Since he understood this principle to apply to everyone throughout the world, the Shinto of Kurozumi Munetada may be called a universal religion, not in its geographical extent but in its intention.[42] Sincerity is a distinctively Confucian concept; and the Founder's understanding of it is supported by concepts deriving from Buddhism. Both traditions phrased their teachings to apply to all people everywhere, and Munetada did nothing to make them parochial; indeed, his chartering experience mobilized the universal potential of those teachings in his own distinctive way. The effect of his Shinto devotional experience (his 1814 Mandate and his lifelong practice of religious exercises) recentred his mind, setting a universalizing direction in his way of thinking. Resources from each of these traditions played a role in enabling him both to think concretely and effectively about people's experience and to extend his thought toward world-wide horizons.

Some of this universality stems from the nature of the sun itself, the object of reverence in daily prayer,[43] coursing daily over the whole earth. But there is more to sun-worship than is visible to the eye alone. Though Amaterasu is made apparent as the sun, she is not identical to it. The sun is the symbol of her presence just as sacred objects (*shintai*) in shrines symbolize the invisible presence of kami. Such symbols "partake in the sanctity" of the kami; without them a shrine cannot be a sacred place.[44] That the sun provides the occasion for energization of life at all levels, but most importantly at the spiritual level, had become apparent to Munetada in his experience of sun-worship in the winter solstice of 1814.

Munetada used vocabulary from Neo-Confucianism to refer to Amaterasu's presence in the world and in people. She is the Spirit (*honshin*) of the universe ("Heaven-and-Earth"). Wherever true sincerity is found, there she is making her presence felt. The intention of the Founder and the will (*goshinryo*) of Amaterasu is therefore that there be a network of interacting people, potentially world-wide in its extent, based on knowing Amaterasu the Kami of the Sun. Three *waka* of Munetada summarize this point.[45]

> It is our wish
>   to have Amaterasu's
>   Goodness be known
> To all the world's people
>   soon and without exception.

> True Sincerity
>   is the one thing we must be
>   most thankful for;
> With Sincerity alone
>   the Earth can be a family.

> In this world of ours
>   we have all come together
>   to form a Circle;
> Let us pray to be joined
>   by the Heart of all our hearts.

The Founder as Guide to Living

The spirituality of Munetada serves as guidance to his followers. A notable aspect of this guidance was the stability of his demeanour. When on occasion his inner feelings were disturbed he felt he had dishonoured Amaterasu, as for instance in the story of crossing a slippery foot bridge (Stories 11 and 12). But, when a lightning bolt struck in the garden of a house where he was leading prayers he was the only one unruffled (Story 71). The best-remembered instance of his stability was his firmness in facing down a drunken samurai who was threatening people with his sword; again, his concern was for the well-being of the man who faced him and not for himself (Story 72). His ability to be constant in changing circumstances often awed his followers.

In a number of stories he advised his followers about the feelings of anger arising within them. Such feelings should be completely eradicated, for the reason that anger causes an inner disturbance that is disrespectful to Amaterasu within one's self (Story 80).[46] At the same time he took individual differences into account and advised people according to circumstances. When an angry critic confronted him he bore with that person's feelings rather than return the criticism and discourage him unduly (Story 26).

He did not take a perfectionist attitude but was flexible in how he conducted himself and had a good sense of humour. Often he responded to his disciples with a "beaming smile" when they were slow to understand some point. He was not stiff and conventional but lively toward others. His liveliness shows itself repeatedly in the stories. He was able to be flexible in this way because he was so firmly attentive to Amaterasu's presence within rather than keyed to matters of precedent and status.[47] He was fully present in the moment, "living through", "abiding in", each moment in a spirit of *ikidōshi*. His was a spiritual stability, not some sort of stiffness in behaviour. Thus he could make use of circumstances as they presented themselves rather than try to force an occasion into the mould of some precedent.[48] The stories show him taking a compassionate interest in others, appreciating their sincerity and making use of the circumstances of the moment in how he responded to them.

His quality of flexibility can also be described as spontaneity. He had a rare talent, displayed in many of these stories, for knowing the mind of persons he was talking to and of responding to them with apt guidance (Stories 89 and 47). His flexibility can best be understood from the way he prepared himself to speak in giving sermons; or rather, from the absence of preparation. It sometimes happened that, on going up to the platform of a meeting place to speak, no words would come to him and he would simply explain that this had happened and step down again. He explained it this way.[49]

> When I lecture I do not rely at all on any sort of written materials. Since in each moment I speak I am following the will of heaven, I may on occasion say

"east" after saying "west" or, right after that talk about it as not being so. But, since the inner heart is the same each time, just listening is the most important thing. People with learning should discard their learning; even those people who are wise or virtuous should put aside their standards of measuring that. All need to get themselves out of an egoistic attitude and merely listen single-heartedly without attachment to the words that are said. Without that state of mind no one can understand anything I say.

His practice of the inner presence of Amaterasu, engaged in for years, had strengthened the original occasion of unity with her at the equinox in 1814 to the point that the words he used in giving his sermons were "words from Heaven" (*tengen*). On such occasions Amaterasu and Munetada had indeed become "not-two".

He sought to help others reach the same spiritual condition. Those who were freed of their self-concern became able to perform their daily tasks with full use of their skills and without tension. His advice to the elderly woman whose work was to weave *tatami* mats enabled her to work long hours without getting tired (Story 83); men skilled in horsemanship and swordsmanship were able to use their skills much more effectively after he advised them (Stories 86, 96, 120). When it is Amaterasu's inner presence that supplies the energy (*shintoku*) of action and reliance on that energy attunes all the energies of the heart/mind and body, then the various elements in any activity are put into harmonious interaction. One's ego no longer intrudes as a disruptive element, so that the skills or "arts" (*dō*) one has learned can be put to fullest expression.[50]

Such advice is familiar in Zen Buddhism;[51] what Munetada did was to apply the insight to the everyday circumstances of workers and businessmen, leading them to become more successful in their endeavours. Yet he always kept his eye on the limitless horizons of Amaterasu's presence in the world and resisted every move to be impressed with utilitarian outcomes which would trivialize the Way, as the story "Asking Kami to Catch Fish is Small-Minded" indicates (Story 112; see also 70 and 110). Any temporal benefit a follower of his Way might receive had real value only as the consequence of spiritual relation to Amaterasu. To be at one with Amaterasu is an end in itself; it is in fact the supreme goal of life.

Summary

At the equinox of 1814 Munetada discovered a new relation to Amaterasu the Kami of the Sun in which the sun was the visible occasion for him to experience Amaterasu rushing into his heart and body. The inrush of breath in that moment penetrated into his lower abdomen (*hara*) and was felt as a burst of vitality in the seat of personality. The practice of worship before the sun (*nippai*) was a constant reenactment of that moment, reinforcing his attentiveness to Amaterasu. Other rituals and ceremonies served in a supportive way to train his attention toward her and away from himself.

His most important practice was a moment-by-moment discipline, seeking to make gratitude for divine presence his governing feeling; gratitude to Amaterasu was to result in every moment of life becoming an occasion for the expression of divine vitality (*yōki*). In such a state of mind one would be able, without attachment and free of all egoism, to "savour every sight and every sound", as the *Michi no Kotowari* puts it (Appendix B). The high degree to which he achieved this goal made him a deeply respected and loved figure among those who knew him and followed him. They regarded him as their *misebumi* indeed, the one who showed them how to get across the river of life with well-being and with joy. As each moment of life becomes an occasion of sincerity, the Way of Amaterasu moves a step closer toward Munetada's goal of a universal harmony of everyone in the world.

How These Stories are Used

Kurozumi Tadaaki has described the process by which these stories reached the stage from which this translation was made (Preface).[52] All of them are in active use in the religious life of Kurozumikyō. They represent the group's authorized understanding of its Founder and express his continuing importance to them. Japanese publications of them are part of the working library of all priests and preachers of the denomination.

An example of how they are used may be seen in a sermon to a local congregation transcribed by Helen Hardacre.[53] The heartfelt discourse of the preacher drew on five different stories. The sermon focused on family relationships, citing with particular effect the Founder's love for his wife Iku. Another example is a short presentation to an American audience made by The Reverend Kurozumi Muneharu in 1985;[54] he made use of four stories in a short period of time. The official biography published as *The Opening Way* is peppered with them.

Kurozumi Muneharu has said that his group has no written canon. The life of its Founder is its point of reference[55] and that life is made present in the telling and retelling of these stories.

Thanks and Acknowledgements
I want to thank the Reverend Kurozumi Muneharu and the Reverend Kurozumi Tadaaki for asking me to undertake this editing project. It is a rare act of trust and I hope the published results will be worthy of it. I have appreciated their hospitality at Shintozan on several unforgettable occasions. Kamiya Sumio and Kurozumi Tadaaki have been indefatigable in furnishing draft translations, and in responding to round after round of Englishings of stories and to questions about particular points. This English edition is a true team effort. Together the three of us have been a trans-Pacific translation team of the most pacific sort imaginable. The drawings illuminating the text were prepared by The Reverend Kumamaru Ken-ichi, a Head Lecturer at the Kurozumikyō Seminary at Shintozan.

On this side of the ocean, Professor Harold Wright of Antioch University clarified a number of terms and was a source of encouragement to the project from the beginning; David and Kazuko Stoesz illuminated a number of usages on a wonderful summer afternoon in Dayton. I appreciate the material and personal support of Dean (now Provost) Perry Moore and Associate Dean (now Associate Provost) William Rickert of the College of Liberal Arts and of Paul Griffin, then Chair of the Department of Religion, at Wright State University.

Altogether the process of developing these stories into the form in which you have them in your hand has been long but enjoyable. For errors and obscurities that remain I accept all responsibility.

Willis Stoesz
Emeritus Professor of Religion
Wright State University

Kurozumi Munetada

Kurozumi Muneharu (*top left*); Kurozumi Tadaaki (*top right*); and group showing Kurozumi Tadaaki, Willis Stoesz and Kamiya Sumio (*above*)

The Stories

The Living Way

1. Praying for the Arsonist

One morning some of Kyōso's neighbours happened to notice that the roof of his house was scorched at several places.[1] One of them went up to take a closer look. Soon he came down with a half-burned torch he found up there.

"What a terrible thing! Look at this torch! In seven places your roof has been scorched. Someone tried to start a fire up there! The fire died out in all the places and didn't keep burning, fortunately. Clearly, some bad person has tried to burn down your house. How awful! It's hard to imagine there could be a person who would try to commit such an outrageous crime." With these words he handed the torch to Kyōso.

Taking it in his hands, Kyōso gave his sincere thanks to the neighbour who had gone up to look at his roof. "Yes, this really is outrageous. I do thank you for your courtesy and for going to such trouble to help me." After thanking his neighbours and sending off the curious who had gathered, he was seen pondering alone over the incident, quietly thinking to himself.

"This really was an awful thing. Maybe it does not matter so much that my house could have burned down. But think of the person who tried to do this. Whoever it was tried to do something really bad. What will happen to him if the crime is revealed and the authorities come to know about it? Arson is a serious crime. There is a heavy penalty for it … one is punished by being burned to death. What a frightful act this person has thought of, and then he has actually done it! How did his heart become so wretched? It is hard to understand how a person who has the gracious *bunshin* within him, received from Great Kami herself, could commit such an offence. It is fortunate for me that he did not cause serious damage. But, for him, it was even more fortunate.

3

Thatched roof made of *cogon* grass

"And, come to think of it, it must be a great sorrow to Great Kami that this person did such a terrible thing. I must pray for him so that his heart will be converted and returned to its original pure condition. Without question, if I offer my wholehearted prayer to Kami this fellow's heart will be restored to purity. Yes, that is exactly what I will do. I will offer this torch to Kami, and pray for the well-being and good fortune of this man so he will regain his true inner heart." Kyōso carefully washed the half-burned torch in clean water, purified it with salt, and placed it on an offering tray on his altar.[2] For a period of about three weeks he prayed singleheartedly that the arsonist would correct his heart, and be blessed with a return of his good fortune.

One day a stranger came to pay Kyōso a visit. To his delight and pleasure, this person began to give him a confession. His body was shaking with fear and his voice was trembling. He spoke in a voice that was low and hard to hear.

"I must confess to you that about twenty days ago I had a horrible delusion, and I tried to set fire to your roof. I know there is no way I can apologize and be forgiven for committing this crime. Still, I must beg your pardon. Over and over, I tried to set fire to the roof. Somehow, each time I tried I couldn't do it.

"Everybody knows a thatched roof of dry straw will easily burn and quickly become a big fire, but I could not start a fire anywhere. I moved around to seven places on the roof looking for a place to get it going. Wherever I went, it would not start burning. Then I remembered what neighbours have been saying about you, that you are a truly saintly

4

person. Then, in my fright, I dropped the torch on the roof and hurried back home. I must apologize to you for my foolish and terrible conduct. Since that day, I have spent every night repenting what I did, accusing myself over and over with pain and regret. Until today, I could not do anything more than that.

"It is only this morning that I resolutely made the decision to come here and extend my apology from the bottom of my heart, and to seek your pardon. I do swear that from now on I shall never again commit such an evil. Please do forgive me." Drooping down and bending his head, in such fashion this fellow offered his sincerest apology to Kyōso.

Kyōso was happy to know that his prayers had been answered by Kami. He took the opportunity to teach the fellow the essence of the Way, using what had happened as his starting point. "Let us follow the true Way together!" he said to the man. In this way, in all kindness, Kyōso encouraged the man's heart and gave him new life. The fellow's heart had been in such a wretched condition, but now he was deeply moved and his eyes flooded with tears. Eventually he submitted his believer's pledge (*shinmon*) and became a very faithful follower of the Way.

This man had been by profession an itinerant faith-healer who had gotten very discouraged and angry that so many of the people he had been taking care of were losing their confidence in him and becoming followers of Kyōso.[3] He feared that if he lost his popularity, he would also lose his income. His jealous, envious heart had filled him with anger, enough to attempt such an arson. Kyōso teaches us this gracious lesson: "Pray for those who curse you and try to bring evil upon you." This incident shows vividly that he practised what he taught.

2. Keeping His Promise to a Highwayman

The sun had already set and Kyōso was still walking home from some missionary work in Bitchū Province (to the west of modern Okayama City). He was walking alone through a very lonesome area where there were no houses and no one else walking. The location was perhaps close to Yonekura, a hamlet about two and a half miles from his home in Kaminakano. Suddenly a man jumped out from behind some shelter and stood in the middle of the road, blocking the way. He demanded, "I am in desperate need of ten *ryō*.[4] Lend it to me or else!" The fellow was a highwayman, a robber.

5

After hearing what he said, Kyōso looked closely at the robber for a moment and then calmly responded,

"Are you sure you by all means need the money? It does look like something has happened to you that leaves you no choice but to stop someone on the road and ask to borrow money. I would like to lend you what you are asking, but, unfortunately, I only have five *ryō* with me now. I am sorry, but for now please take what I have. As to the remaining five *ryō*, I will bury it in the ground beside the washing place in front of the Imamura Shrine.[5] I will leave a small stone there to mark where it is buried. Please be sure to come to the shrine tomorrow night and pick up the money. I assure you, you will find the five *ryō* buried where I said it would be."

The highwayman stood there for a while with nothing to say, staring back at Kyōso. Then he quickly said to himself, "This old man looks very honest. But he might be good at telling lies. Still, he is very polite. When I demanded ten *ryō* he took that for serious truth. He gave me five *ryō* and promised to give me the rest tomorrow." On one hand he was much impressed, and on the other, he was really puzzled by Kyōso's sincerity and uprightness.

When the robber showed up at the shrine the following night, half in doubt, the five *ryō* was there as he was told it would be. "After all, the gentleman was truly honest. Today, there is nobody like this in the world." The fellow was much touched with Kyōso's sincerity and kindness, and at the same time he found himself feeling ashamed of his wretched heart and bad conduct. It is said that before too long he joined in the pursuit of the Way, and proved himself another faithful and devoted follower.

3 Paying the Same Debt Twice

Towards the end of one year, Kyōso received a request from one of his relatives to return the six *ryo* he had borrowed. He had actually borrowed this amount, but he had already repaid it to the lender. Something seemed to have gone wrong. Six *ryo* in those days was by no means a small amount of money. Still, Kyōso gave him that amount for the second time without saying anything further. This is the *waka* he composed at that time.

> The eye of Great Kami
>   always sees sincerity

> Never should others
> wear my wet and dampened clothes
> however heavy they are.[6]

Kyōso thought that if he came out and said that he had already paid back the money, then someone might be suspected of wrongdoing. That person could be accused, or at least suspected, and then caught up in the trouble and difficulties that would follow. This is why he dared to "wear the wet clothes".

4 Accepting the False Accusation of an Embezzler

Kyōso was a most benevolent and humane person, and often loaned or even gave his own money generously to those who were in need of it. In some cases, he went out of his way to help people who were in need. Once, when he found out that a near neighbour of his was in desperate need of money, he went with him to visit a wealthy Bizen clan samurai who was a private money-lender, to borrow the sum of *ryō* that was needed. But, when the term of the loan was up, the debtor did not repay the money. Each time the samurai's assistant came to collect what was owed, the man made up some excuse or other. Finally, the samurai himself came to see this neighbour, strictly insisting on repayment. At that time the samurai class usually had people at their mercy, and could do anything they wanted to enforce their will.

The debtor was stricken by the menacing attitude of the samurai, but then the name of Kyōso flashed into his mind. Maybe, he thought, by this means he could get himself out of a tough situation. Although he knew it was a bad thing to do, he said, "Um, as to that money, well, I have to say that I have entrusted Kurozumi Munetada with it. I asked him to pay it back to you on my behalf. As you remember, Sensei is the gentleman who first introduced me to you."

On hearing this, the samurai thought it a little strange, but he saw how very humbly the debtor was speaking and he thought it might be true. But, to be doubly sure he asked again, "So you have entrusted Kurozumi Sensei with this money? Are you sure?"

The neighbour replied, "Yes, sir. Definitely!" With this confirmation, the samurai creditor left satisfied, saying, "If that is the case, there is nothing more I need to say to you."

On his way back home he dropped in at Kyōso's house. He explained the

7

nature of his visit. "Today I have been to your friend's house, the one whom you recommended to me, to urge him to settle up his debt with me right away. It's something you know about. He told me that some days ago he had entrusted you with the money, and you would forward it to me. Is this true?" Kyōso, who had been watching the samurai carefully from the moment he came in, said, "Oh, ah, yes, sir. I certainly received the money some days ago. I wanted to bring it to you the first time I had a chance to see you. It's too bad that I didn't have the opportunity. I have been quite busy, and didn't get the time. Have you had to go to all that trouble to go see my friend to get your money back? Well, well, what a big trouble and great inconvenience I have caused you. I am very sorry. But please wait here. I will be back in a few minutes."

So saying, he went to his room to see how much he had, and returned with some money, as much as he had. "Well, I must explain the true story. The other day something came up I needed some money for, and, er, I borrowed some from what I was entrusted with. And so I can only give you half the amount today. I will be sure to pay you a visit in a few days and bring the other half. May I ask your further patience for a few more days?"

Hearing this apology, the samurai thought that what the debtor had said was not wholly a lie this time, and responded with some feeling of relief. "I am sorry I did not know that, and I have nothing to worry about since Sensei is entrusted with the money. That is perfectly all right. This unpleasant affair only happened because that fellow always makes some excuse or other to delay his payment." So, the samurai went back to his house with half of the money he had wanted to collect.

Seeing the guest had left, Kyōso's wife, Iku, said, "Oh, my dear, is that the true picture? Did you really receive the money and then you spent some of it?" "Well, well, as you can guess, what I said is not true. This is a business I really don't know much about." "Ah, then, if it was a lie, why did you lie? Being considerate of others' worries and troubles might be a good thing. But that depends on circumstances. That a person like you who teaches the Way should spend some of the money you were entrusted with! This was not your own personal matter, and what you did is a disgrace to the Way.'

Hearing his wife spill out this earnest, reasonable piece of advice and regret, Kyōso replied,

"Well then. You could put it that way. But please listen to me. When the samurai came in he had such a threatening look. He was furious, and he had a smell of murder about him. I saw right away it was not a trifling matter. And alas, when he began speaking it showed me right. It was a dispute about money. If I was going to say that I had nothing to do with this business, he would surely have left here heading right back for our neighbour's home to cut and kill the poor old fellow with his sword.

"When I saw what might happen, I decided instantly to accept the responsibility, and take the blame on myself. Of course, I had to lie because the amount of money I had in my room was not enough, and then also I had to make an apology to the samurai. So, coming now to think it all through, how good it was that we were able to save the life of our neighbour. When a sick person who is at the verge of death is cured it is a gracious thing. But let's consider what a pity it would be if a person who is healthy were cut down to death with a single sword stroke. That would be a more terrible pity than when a person dies of illness. What a sorrowful tragedy it would have been! But, his life was saved. How gracious Kami has been! Concerning this matter, my name really has nothing to do with it. But, Kami knows everything about it, and what I did is according to the rightful and true Way. Do you understand what I am saying?

"Have you heard the story about a certain Buddhist priest who was unjustly accused of fathering a baby with his neighbour's daughter?[7] This priest accepted the false and groundless charge, took the baby in and raised it with the help of a neighbour's wife who nursed it for him. This is what I'm talking about. This is the true pursuit of the Way. And, by the way, do you think I am not of the same calibre as that priest, not able to do a similar thing? It is not so. Perfect pursuit of the Buddhist Way is actually the same as pursuing the Way of Great Kami. It is of the very essence and secret of Great Kami. There can be no reason why I can't do the same. What a gracious day it is today! What a gratifying gift of a day!"

5. The Bad Luck Day (*Unkoh-nichi*)[8]

One day a lady who was a regular visitor to Kyōso's house and who worshipped at his shrine said to him, "Sensei, you have added some years to your life and you also seem to have gained some weight. Please excuse my being forward, but I am very concerned that you might some day have a stroke and be paralysed. The other day I learned a moxa treatment that is said to be very good for preventing such an illness.[9] Wouldn't it be good for you to have a treatment?"

Then Kyōso, his face showing his usual friendly smile and now starting to beam, replied, "Well now, that is very considerate of you. Thank
you so much. We have a saying, 'Make no delay in doing what is good'.
The sooner the better. Why not try out this treatment on me right away?"
The lady was very happy that her suggestion was so promptly accepted.
She put the moxa ball on the proper spot on his body as she had been
taught, and started it burning.

While this was going on, another lady, who also was a faithful and frequent worshipper, came in and happened to see Kyōso receiving the
treatment. She was shocked by what she saw, and burst out shouting in
a high voice. "Oh Sensei, think what you are doing! Sir, don't you know
today is an unlucky day? They say moxa treatment on this day has to
bring some big trouble. It could bring you to suffer a high fever. You
should know better, and not have moxa treatment on this particular
day." "Is that right? Thank you for telling me. Oh, my. In my great carelessness, I did not know today is this kind of day. Well, well." Instantly,
he had the treatment stopped.

The second woman left soon after that, having recited the purification
prayer two or three times. The lady who had proposed the treatment sat
there humiliated and embarrassed, not knowing what to do. She apologized meekly. "Sensei, I really put you in an awkward position. If only I
had some knowledge of what today is, and had more sense ... ! What a
terrible thing I have done! Please forgive me." Kyōso quietly removed the
clothing covering the spot on his body that had been treated, and said,
"Why not continue the treatment, and put on some more moxa?"
Stunned to hear this, the lady said, with hesitation, "But today is *unkoh-
nichi*?" Not allowing her to finish her words, Kyōso said, "Well, it may
be so, but *unkoh-nichi* has left for home."

Kyōso was not the kind of person who carried worries around. He was
absolutely not the kind of person who would worry about this and that,
or whether his weight increased with his age. Even though the thought of
a possible attack of paralysis at his age might have occurred to him, he
was confident that he would be able to recover from any hard-to-cure illness by using his own *majinai*. Although this was his nature, when the
lady proposed moxa treatment as a means to prevent paralysis, he raised
no objections in order not to abuse the lady's kindness, and then, after
the interruption, to prevent the lady from losing face.

We believe he accepted her suggestion, and received the moxa treatment quietly, as something that Heaven intended. He was much more concerned with his followers' feelings and with encourageing their faith than he was with moxa treatments and beliefs about bad luck days.

6. "Fortune in, Devils out"

The bean-throwing ceremony known as *Setsubun* has always been observed throughout Japan.[10] There is a traditional ritual for it that everyone knows. Here is a story about one year's observance that Kyōso's family enjoyed.[11] After Madame Iku with her maids' help finished purification of all the rooms of their house, throwing beans and shouting, "Fortune in, devils out", she went to her husband's room and told him in friendly fashion, "My master,[12] I must report to you that we have duly and properly performed the *Setsubun* ritual. I wish you many happy returns."

Then, Kyōso said with his usual beaming smile, "Well, well, O-Iku, many thanks for your trouble. Now with your help we are ready to welcome in the spring season. The auspicious bean-throwing has a special meaning this year, don't you agree?" These words puzzled his wife, and she asked, "I did the ritual just as we usually do it every year. I don't see any difference. Was there something we left out, my master?"

"Oh, no, nothing was left out. But there was one unusual point. That is why I said it was especially auspicious." "Is that so? I didn't notice anything. Are you telling me there was something different?" "Ha, ha, ha, oh yes, there was a difference, a really significant one. O-Iku, you started out throwing the beans, shouting, 'Fortune in, devils out', as we do every year. But after a while, without noticing it, you turned it around and said, 'Fortune out, devils in, fortune out, devils in'. Ha, ha. That was the unusual point, so funny and interesting. I was really happy to hear it."

She was dismayed to hear this, and immediately gave her apology. "Oh, my goodness, what a blunder I have made! Is it true? I didn't notice what I said. I am terribly sorry I was so careless. Should I go over the ritual again?" "Oh no, O-Iku. You don't need to do it again. The part where you made the mistake was so very gracious and welcome. What I thought while listening to your shouting, 'Fortune out, devils in', was that this is funny. Well, but let's think about the point. Tonight every family is chasing out the devils and the demons with the bean-throwing ritual. Everywhere they are shouting the same thing, 'Devils out, devils out' to shut out the devils.

"If you put yourself in the devils' position, you will easily understand it is more than any devil can put up with, chased out from here and from there. There is no home that will tolerate them. Would it not be good that there is at least one home that will accept them? And also, when every family keeps on shouting 'Fortune in, devils out', only wishing and hoping to bring good fortune into their own houses, then every family must share good fortune with the other houses. Then each home will be blessed with only a small portion of fortune. Your shouting 'Fortune out, devils in' was really good. It was really good, and a blessing. I think this year's bean-throwing was especially good and gracious."

"But, I should have been more ... ."

"Oh, no. It was really auspicious. In this connection, this *waka* flashed through my mind. What do you think of it?

> Not chasing devils
>   nor seeking our good fortune,
>   what I pursue is
> But to bring the chased devils
>   to the way of good fortune.

Oh, O-Iku, there is nothing to worry about. If the devils come, let them come. I will make them happy and help them enjoy good fortune. Ha, ha, ha."

7. Repairing a Bridge Wearing His Best Formal Clothes

Once Lord Ikeda, ruler of the Bizen *han*, bestowed on Kyōso a magnificent suit of clothes. Because of his honest and sincere nature he was much impressed with this gift and joyful about it, and he took very good care of it. He wore it only on special occasions such as being received in audience by the Lord, or on visits to the houses of his highest retainers. On these limited occasions he dressed himself in this formal attire to show his respect for the dignity of the persons he was visiting.

One day, wearing this attire, he set off for Okayama City. On his return he was caught by a sudden shower. Soon the sky cleared up, but when he was close to his house he noticed a hole in a small mud bridge crossing the stream running from the direction of his home.[13] The shower had made a hole in the bridge, big enough that it could catch someone's foot. Without going any further he stopped at the bridge. Still wearing his fine clothing, he started picking some weeds in order to fill the hole. Then he gathered up some dirt to fix the hole more carefully.

After checking to see whether his repairs were satisfactory he went into his house. Madame Iku, who greeted him at the entrance, was surprised at how he looked. "Oh master, what have you done? Take a good look at yourself! Your clothes are all dirty, covered with mud. Look, see what you have done to the precious clothes the Lord has given you!" After seeing the mess he had made of his clothes, Kyōso admitted, "Oh, my goodness, you are right. But I just saw a hole that the rain made in the bridge. I happened to think how awful it would be if someone would catch a foot in the hole." "But you should have come home first and changed your clothes. If you had done that, it would have been so much better."

"But, once I saw the problem, I did not feel I should let any time go by. Not even a second. Otherwise, someone might have got hurt. In the worst case, the person might break his or her leg. The clothes may be important and precious, but never could they be more dear than a person's leg. A living person's leg is worth so much more."

8. A New *Haori* for Kyōso

The village of Sanban is well-known for its location at the mouth of the Asahi river that flows through the city of Okayama. The head of the village in Kyōso's time was a man named Fujiwara san. In those days the position was passed down within the family from one generation to the next. This man revered Kyōso and held him in high esteem, and often invited him to his home to give a formal lecture. He liked to share with his neighbours the pleasure of hearing such a lecture.

On one such occasion Fujiwara san noticed while Kyōso was giving the sermon that his *haori*,[14] dyed with a kind of dye made from the areca nut, had quite worn out. Its original deep black had become a rusty or liver colour. He thought it was high time for a new coat, and he ordered a new one. When the meeting was over, ending with the sermon, this village head went up to Kyōso to present him with the new *haori*, asking at the same time to be forgiven for his forwardness. Kyōso responded, "Oh my, how considerate of you! Thank you so much. I will accept your thoughtful present with pleasure. I will take off my old *haori* and start wearing

13

the new one right now." He expressed his gratitude and was as delighted as a child. He took off his long-used *haori* immediately. Putting on the new one, he said again, "It is very kind and thoughtful of you. Thank you, thank you."

He seemed very delighted and satisfied, but when he saw a shabbily and dirtily dressed old man in the back row wearing neither a *haori* nor a *hanten*, Kyōso said to him, "Let me present this to you." He handed the old man the old *haori* he had just taken off. Then Dai Sensei left for home satisfied, at a brisk pace and full of smiles.

Thereafter the Fujiwara family made it an annual festive custom to have a new *haori* tailored for Kyōso. Always he was as happy as a child to wear the new coat, and always he passed the old one on to whoever happened to be there.

9. Walking Serenely in a Shower of Rain

This was when Kyōso was walking with some of his followers from Ohgashima to Sōsan, both in Oku County, Bizen Province, while on some missionary work there. Suddenly, they were caught in a severe evening shower at a place where there were no houses or shelters near by. Caught in such a sudden and severe shower, those who were with him were thrown into some confusion, and raised cries. Finding no shelter to hide themselves, and having no other solution, they suggested, "Let's run out of this rain."

Kyōso said, "How can we get away from the rain when it is falling all around us?" With this remark, he continued walking calmly in full self-possession. Everyone soon was wet to the skin. When the rain stopped, they took a brief rest beside the road. Kyōso said, "The farmers must surely be happy for this rain they waited for so long. Look around. See everything growing around us, the rice and the vegetables. Aren't they all looking so happy to have the fresh green life the rain has given back to them?"

10. The Facial Features of a Fool

Once a famous physiognomist who had great renown in the Kyoto-Osaka area came to the town of Okayama. He was a man who claimed to be able to tell a person's character just from the lines and shape of his face. He had won a high reputation from the public for his judgements and predictions. People believed that what he said was really true. Kyōso had gone to Okayama at this time, and he had this specialist look at his facial features to hear his judgement and prediction. He did this just for fun, and for his personal information. The famous physiognomist looked at his face thoroughly, and said nothing for a while. He only tilted his head a little to one side.

Kyōso urged him, saying, "Well, come, come. Give me your verdict." "Er, I am sorry, it is hard to tell you", the man said, as he seemed really to be in a puzzled situation. "Come on. I am ready to listen to what you have to say. Please feel free to give your frank and candid diagnosis and comments." "Well, since you insist, I will tell you the truth. Your face shows the features that, according to the theories of physiognomy I have studied, are those of a fool (ahō).[15] I am very sorry. Please accept my sincere apology for being so rude." "Oh, is that so? What a blessed and welcome thought! As a matter of fact, I have long been practising religious exercises with the hope of becoming a fool. If your physiognomy really reveals that my features are those of a fool, it means that my wish and my effort for many years have finally been realized. No other joy can surpass this. Thank you so much."

11. Apologizing for Disturbing His Heart

Once, while on his way to see Mori san, village head at Komoto Village, Kyōso was crossing a one-plank bridge over the Sunagawa stream. This was just after a heavy rain and the bridge was almost flooded over by the rushing water. When he was halfway across, the plank lurched with a sudden wobble. Without his intending it, the inner heart (bunshin) within Kyōso was ruffled by the sudden jolt. After he had crossed over and gotten up on the bank, he sat down in formal fashion on the grass, wearing his hakama.[16] He offered a formal apology to Amaterasu Ohmikami for the way he had lost his inner calm. Though it might seem a small thing, he thought he had behaved badly.

It is quite natural that a plank bridge would be unsteady in the midst of a flood of water like that, and that a person crossing over might be startled, even for just an instant. Even so, Kyōso offered an apology for allowing his heart to be disturbed. If that is what he did, what should those do whose hearts have been disturbed and dismayed with sufferings over a long period of time? What sort of apology should they offer? When we ponder on this experience of Kyōso, it leads us to revere him with awe.

12. Giving the Same Sermon Seven Times

Soon after the incident of crossing the plank bridge across the Sunagawa, Kyōso described his experience to those attending the Ohmoto meeting group. This was the group that met in his own house. All the worshippers listened earnestly and thankfully to what he told them. Wasn't his experience a natural thing? Wouldn't anyone's heart become alarmed, wouldn't anyone's heart lose its inner calm, when the plank on which one is crossing a rushing stream suddenly wobbles? The water under the bridge was rushing and turbulent. It's human nature, and it is quite reasonable. Although Kyōso's heart was disturbed, it was just for a moment. It is something no one would criticise or even comment on. Yet, in this reasonable matter so free from the need for ordinary comment, he offered his heartfelt apology to Amaterasu Ohmikami for what he considered misconduct.

As for us, how often should we offer our apologies for our many unpardonable misdoings and faults that we commit in our daily life! How often do we become irritated and angry, and spend our worry on trifling things, and so bring pain to our inner *bunshin*? For these things we truly should offer our apologies to Amaterasu. Those gathered in worship at Ohmoto were given the chance to give thought to this point and to reflect on it carefully, and at the same time to give due reverence to Kyōso. They could understand and respect the effort he had made through religious exercises to elevate his heart and his personality to a point where his heart could remain unmoved and undisturbed by his surroundings. And, thinking of it this way, his followers did in fact show him their respect and admiration.

Then at the next meeting of the group Kyōso told the same story a second time. Then again he did so, and yet again, at successive meetings. Finally, Madame Iku spoke to him quite pointedly about it, telling him, "The sermon was indeed very good. It was very welcome to us. But this is the seventh time you have given the same subject in your lectures. It was really a good sermon, but don't you think it is about time to change the subject? I am thinking it is about time to leave off talking about that experience." Hearing this, Kyōso said,

"Oh no. What you are saying shows just why I have to keep telling them about my experience. We must not have our precious inner hearts disturbed, we must not harm our hearts in the very least. These points should always be borne in mind and observed much more than we usually do. What a foolish thing and good-for-nothing it is to keep track of numbers, and get all concerned about the thought that the same sermon is being repeated for the seventh time! You are saying 'this sermon is troublesome to our hearts', but you should have a better understanding than to say that. Now I see that other people must be listening to my sermon in the same way you are, and I am all the more convinced that I must continue telling about my experience." In this way Kyōso admonished Madame Iku.

Iku's thoughtfulness was a becoming attitude on her part, as his wife. The attitude we on our part bring to hearing a sermon or following a lecture is a key to how we can understand this matter. We are left pondering what a great many lessons can be drawn from his repeating the same sermon.

13. Throwing Away His Walking Stick

This was when Imada Sōjirō of Shimoyamada Village, Oku County, Bizen Province,[17] had his servant bring a letter of invitation to Kyōso. As he had done before, Kyōso accepted the invitation and set out for Imada's along with Morikane Tamezō sensei on the agreed-upon day. Imada's male servant escorted them and carried Kyōso's personal effects on his back. When they were passing by Nishifurumatsu Village (about a hundred yards east of Ohmoto), the servant started talking to the two gentlemen.

"Sensei, I have had an experience that has meant a great deal to me. Sir, when I got to the age of sixty-four I started using a walking stick. Sometime after that I heard your sermon on the topic 'not to allow one's heart to get old, and as long as one's heart stays alive and active, one's bodily form (katachi) will also remain vigorous'. I felt that this was exactly true. So, one day when I reached the age of seventy, I took courage and completely stopped using my walking stick. During the time I was using it I would leave my master's place early, before dawn, in order to cover the fifteen miles to your house. On my way back, by the time I got as far as Saidai-ji it would usually be after sunset, and I could not get back to my master's house before ten at night.

"But, to my amazement, sir, after I decided not to use a stick, and up to the present when I have reached the age of eighty-five, I don't need to start as early as I did before. I am able to cover the whole trip with no special effort needed to get home by four in the afternoon. Today I feel much more healthy, and you can see that my legs allow me to travel faster. This is just a small thing, but I do feel very grateful. Sir, I now understand the true meaning of your sermon that everything depends on the work of one's heart."

When the old man had finished his story, Kyōso stopped in his tracks. He just stood there for a little while. "So that is how it works?" With that, Kyōso threw his stick far out into the field with all his might. Then, as if talking to himself, "I have been using a walking stick without any reason to do it, just following along after other people's fashion. I did it without thinking about it, without giving care to what I was doing. I have allowed my heart to add years to itself and to get old. Oh dear, what a wrong, what a sacrilege I have done!" After that day, no one ever saw him using a walking stick.

Morikane sensei, who was with Kyōso at the time, recalled the incident some years later. "Up to this very moment I can remember vividly the stick flying with force out to the field, giving a big whirling sound as it went, and finally sticking right into the ground. It made a lasting impression on me. I won't ever forget it."

14. *Geta* and *Zōri*[18]

This story happened in Kyōso's early childhood. One day he was about to leave the house to play outside. He heard his father, who was inside, telling him to wear his *taka-geta*s (high clogs) on his feet. Just as he started obeying this instruction, another came from his mother who had not heard what the father had said. She advised, "The rain is over, and the ground is not so wet. It would be risky to wear those big clogs. You should wear your *zōri*s" (sandals). Although the boy replied, "Yes,

Geta and *zōri*

mother", he found himself at a loss as to which shoes to wear, the *geta*s or the *zōri*. As the story goes, the boy, after some thinking, put a *takageta* on his right foot and, on his left, a *zōri*.

The different instructions from his parents confused the child, who finally found a solution to please both of them. The innocence, the singlemindedness and modesty of the boy, move us to smile, but the more we think about his pious conduct the more it touches our hearts and brings tears to our eyes. No one is sure how old the boy was at the time. It does not matter whether he was five or six according to the traditional age-counting system, but according to one account this happened when he was seven.[19]

15. Taking Cold Water Ablutions
Wishing to Prolong His Father's Life

When Kyōso grew a little older he overheard two or three people talking about his father's health one day, saying that he looked older than his years. This shocked the boy, making him feel sad and lonely. It is said that he made a firm decision to do cold water ablutions early every morning at a nearby stream, and to pray that his father would enjoy a long life.

The wholehearted filial affection he held towards his father, which we on our part think of with much esteem and respect, are well demonstrated in this story. The mere thought of a little boy dipping and splashing cold water on himself with his small hands, praying and worshipping out of concern for his father's longevity, truly cleanses and purifies our own hearts. It is a thought that leaves a refreshing impression on all of our hearts, living as we do in a world full of people who are dirty and lacking in honour. We picture to ourselves an innocent child's pious deed. He was praying not for some theoretical reason but for the benefit of his parent, from pure feeling and genuine sentiment from the bottom of his heart. It presents us a pure and reverent picture of a little angel sent from Heaven.

16. Practising Calligraphy under Ichimura Sensei

This is another story from which we can well appreciate the innocent filial piety and affection of Kyōso for his parents. At the time of his childhood there was a man named Ichimura Sanzō serving as one of the secretaries of Lord Ikeda, feudal ruler of Bizen Province.[20] He was widely respected as a talented calligrapher. The quality of his work was excel-

Learning calligraphy

lent, but more than that, there was a special dignity about it. There was a divine quality about it that people held in high esteem. For example, the signboard which he wrote for the gate of the local Tōshō-gū Shrine was so superb that a common saying around Okayama was that even the birds would not make it dirty.[21]

Ichimura also was a schoolmaster, taking boys into his home for instruction. As a young boy, Kyōso went every day to this school, located about three miles from his home. There Ichimura sensei taught reading and calligraphy. Kyōso may have been born with potential talent, but it was his innocent and earnest personality and the great effort he put forth in school that led him to the brilliant skill with India ink and brush for which he was to become so well-known. His enthusiasm of course exceeded that of the other students. He quickly attained such a high level that his mentor said to him when he was thirteen, "My boy, you have learned everything that I can teach you. From now on, you are qualified to teach others. I want you to teach the boys in your neighbourhood." This is what Ichimura sensei told the boy.

While studying in this man's classes Kyōso kept a calm demeanour, devoting himself to his studies. But when evening approached and the time drew near to go home he seemed to lose his calm. He would grow uneasy and anxious to leave. Ichimura sensei thought the boy's late afternoon restlessness somewhat strange, and one day he asked him about it. The boy, who in his adult years would become the Founder, replied with shyness, his face downward, "Sir, I must apologise for how I am acting. To be frank, when it is getting time for me to return home my mother comes out to the gate to wait for me, even when I am still far away. She does it even when the weather is freezing cold. When I am a little late, she still stays there waiting for me. Then she gets very worried. Sir, that is why I am so anxious to get home as soon as possible."

This explanation impressed the mentor so much that, as the story goes, he mused to himself, "This boy is much more unusual than I had thought!"

17. Returning Home after Watching Half of a Hunt

East of the Asahi River that flows from north to south through the town of Okayama lies a hill called the Tatsunokuchi yama. It is over 800 feet high, the highest elevation in that area. At this place the Lords of the Ikeda clan held an annual wild animal hunt. The year Kyōso was seventeen years old he was invited by some youngsters in his neighbourhood to go with a group of them to watch the hunt. They went off happily and he joined them, though without feeling much interest. He didn't share their enthusiasm for the occasion, but he went with them, not having any reason not to do so.

When the hunt came close to its climax, various wild birds and animals both large and small, including pheasants, wild boar, deer, rabbits, hares, and badgers, came rushing out of their hiding places and ran around, finding no place to get away. It was a lively, spectacular scene. The excited youngsters couldn't contain their enjoyment of it, clapping their hands and shouting with delight.

At this moment of great excitement, Kyōso had a very unhappy look on his face. He told his friends standing nearby, "I'm leaving." They were quite bewildered to hear it. Some of them went up to him and said, "What's this! What's the matter with you?" They said, "The hunt is just now getting interesting. It's just getting to the high point. Don't you have enough sense to know it's silly to leave now, and not wait for the best part? Are you sick, is there something the matter with you?"

Kyōso said quite seriously, "No, nothing is wrong with me. I am all right. Actually, I didn't feel like coming to start with, but because you invited me so specially I decided to come along. As soon as I got here, I realized this event is not something the Lord and his samurai do just to enjoy themselves. They do it for weapons training. They are improving their skills in shooting rifles and bows and arrows. It is something they have to do for that reason. As for us, we are here just to have a good time. We are following and watching just to have fun. And, what we are seeing is a lot of birds and animals being shot and killed, one after another. Many are trying to run away in every direction, crying out and screaming in hopeless fear.

"Still, we can get some value and meaning from what is happening. We are seeing a picture that reminds us of Hell. That is the meaning of it. And in spite of that, the crowd is jumping up and down, full of joy and delight to watch it all. This is what I cannot stand. I cannot stay here and watch this scene anymore. A few minutes ago I began to feel lowdown about it. I am feeling too sad, I can't watch the hunt anymore. This is why I asked you to excuse me to leave early." Then he started walking home alone. His friends were all quite surprised to see him go, but all of them stayed to watch the whole thing to its end anyway.

18. Crossing the Asahi River in a Calm State of Mind

This was when Kyōso was on his way to Okita Shrine in Shinden, Jōtō County (in present-day Okayama City), on the other side of the Asahi River, to give a sermon there. As usual, he took a ferryboat across the river. It was the kind of ferry that had a long oar fastened at the back, and the boatman would stand there, moving it back and forth to push the boat across the water.[22]

After he had got in, the boatman, who seemed to be a person of a sarcastic nature, said, "Sir, am I right, that you are Kurozumi, the Great Teacher? I hear that you preach to people not to care about things, to leave everything to the Will of Heaven. Leave everything to the course of

Ferryboat with oar at the stern

Nature. Should we really let loose of everything that way?" This is what the man asked Kyōso, just that abruptly.

Kyōso replied with a smile, "Oh yes. You are right. That is just the way you should conduct yourself." Hearing this, the boatman said, "Well, and is that so?" With all his might he gave a push with his oar to shove the boat off the bank and out on the river. Then, pulling his oar back into the boat, he threw himself down, rested his head on the edge of the boat, and looked idly up into the blue sky. At this point the river formed rapids, running fast enough for the boat to start drifting quickly downstream.

The man's rude behaviour prompted the anger of Hachiya Shunzō, who happened to be going along with Kyōso that day. He was a logical kind of person who liked an argument, and he was just on the point of hurling words of thunder on the boatman. But then he noticed that Kyōso was signalling him silently with his eyes, "Calm down. Keep quiet. Don't say anything." Hachiya kept silent. Meanwhile, the boat was floating quickly downstream. It was coming to a point that if nothing was done, they would soon be offshore from Sanban and entering the sea at Kojima Bay. Hachiya now felt he had enough. He thought it was about time he should say something, and looked back at Kyōso to seek his approval. But seeing him with his smile still on his face, seeming to ask him to keep quiet, Hachiya still kept his mouth shut. He felt a little helpless but not a word did he say.

By and by the boat floated with increasing speed, to the point that some decision seemed to be needed. If the two had been on some private business it might not have been a problem whether or not they got where they were going. But the case was something different. They were going to Okita Shrine, where many followers were gathering to hear Kyōso's sermon. If they were to drift on out to sea the consequences would affect a large group of people. There would be no words that could be given as an excuse to them. It would be unpardonable. Pondering in this way, Hachiya felt he could not resist scolding the boatman. But still, Kyōso was saying with his eyes to keep quiet.

On the other hand, the boatman kept on with his nonchalant and unconcerned pose, lying down with the edge of the boat for his pillow, smiling sarcastically and staring up at the sky. We can easily envisage even today how helpless Hachiya felt, how much he was at a loss between these two men so different from each other. One maintained his calm, the other kept his provokingly cool posture.

Meanwhile, the boat was not actually drifting straight down the river but was going on a slant towards the left bank. Suddenly there was a crunching sound as the boat went aground at the river's edge. Kyōso looked around and said, "How fortunate! We have arrived on the shore at Ichiban-no-Itaya. This is just where we needed to go. Skipper, thank you so much for your trouble." Kyōso stepped out of the boat lightly, with Hachiya following after. The one who was most surprised was the ferryman. "Oh, are we at Itaya?" In a second he was up, looking around with surprise. "Oh yes, you are right. We are certainly on the shore at Ichiban-no-Itaya. What a terrible thing I have done!"

Regret always comes afterward. Regret never mends matters. When the boatman went back to his place up the river, he had to get back over with the unnecessary trouble of oaring his boat strenuously through the rapids upstream for a distance of several miles. If the man had gone straight on his normal route across the river in the first place, and allowed his passengers to land at that point, they would have been the ones to travel that distance. Instead, the walk became unnecessary and they were able to rest in the boat to get where they were going. Since the boat took them just to that place, they travelled easily. The person who had to go to needless trouble was the boatman, who had to go back through the rapids, and the one who was in a fever of impatience was Hachiya. In contrast to both of them, Kyōso never lost his calm posture, either mentally or physically, throughout the whole time crossing the river.

The ferryman, whose name has not been recorded, is said to have become ashamed of himself and so enlightened by the incident that he became a diligent follower. Some even say he eventually became one of the instructors of the Way.

Kyōso preached *maru makase*,[23] that is, to leave everything totally to the hands of Kami. One should observe the Way of Heaven (*Tendo ni shijun*) fully in everything one does. This is different from *sute makase*, that is, to throw everything away and neglect everything. At the same time, he reminded us that we should never neglect our responsibilities to others. The boatman, whose responsibility was to take people across the river, neglected his duty by doing nothing, laying his oar aside, and lying down in the boat. By taking no heed of his boat and his passengers and allowing them just to drift, he was intentionally neglecting his responsibility in a way that Kyōso called *sute makase*. The fellow's conduct was out of joint and irresponsible. That is why he ended up spending his energy and time for an unnecessary purpose.

And we can see that Kyōso's conduct in this circumstance had an entirely different meaning. He never allowed things to take their course in an irresponsible way, but left all in the hands of the Way of Heaven, untouched by his own hand. When asked by the boatman whether it is good to leave and forget all, Kyōso answered that this was absolutely right. For him, that was the true and apt answer, in harmony with Heaven's Way. But the way the skipper of the boat acted did not make use of this aptitude. Kyōso found this very funny and accepted it as an expression of the special Will of Heaven, the course of things that the Divine Kami felt to be good in that particular moment. He allowed this event to take its "natural course." This was the *maru makase* that Kyōso preached to us.

19. The Core of the Way

After listening to Kyōso preach at one *gokaijitsu* meeting, Hachiya commented, "Oh, today's sermon was so welcome and gracious. Even though I am so humble and unworthy I would like to 'go to *miyako*',[24] to the core of the Way. Oh indeed. That is the thing I should not fail to accomplish." Hearing Hachiya speak so enthusiastically, Dr Miyata Shō,[25] a physician living in the town of Natsukawa (within present-day Okayama City), responded, "Twenty years have passed since I entered the Way. However, the more I listen and hear the sermons, the more wide and deep I find it

25

to be, and the more I realize it is a goal that is very far away. I feel as if I am on a boat drifting in the ocean, not knowing which way is east or west, nor even knowing in what direction the boat is going. Excuse me for being forward, but it is just a few years since you entered the Faith. It is not so long that you have been pursuing the Way. Your discernment and your feeling that you wish to go to the core of the Way are nothing but admirable. But may I have the liberty to ask you this question? Would you please tell me in which direction lies the core of the Way? Is it in the east, in the west, or in what direction? I will surely appreciate your giving me kind and good instruction so I can clearly understand it."

Hachiya could not keep silent when he heard this sarcastic challenge. "Please do understand that after pursuing the Way for only two or three years I am not trying to say that I know in which direction the core lies. I only expressed my desire to go to the core. I just said that is my ultimate wish. It is taught that at the very start when one begins learning a religious practice, the first thing one should do is to set a high aim. One should orient one's life with a fixed purpose. This is how you determine what you are doing, how you make a decision about your purpose. This is just common knowledge." He continued his argument, "Despite this well-known fact, are you trying to tell me it is wrong to express one's aim in life this way?"

Hearing Hachiya offer this view, Miyata replied, "Oh well, would you please listen to me. What I am driving at is that it is important not to look ahead unnecessarily, but to pursue the Way and observe it day by day with gracious thanks and gratitude." This angered Hachiya, and he responded, "What I am talking about is in no way an unnecessary looking ahead. Determination and resolution could never be unnecessary. Let's go to Kyōso, present our argument to him, and hear his judgement as to who is right."

With Dr Miyata's consent to this proposal the two went together to consult Kyōso's opinion on the two different ideas. On hearing them, Kyōso gave a beaming smile.

"How admirable are the heights of faith of the two of you. Both of you have attained the utmost limit of your faith. The core of the Way lies neither in the east nor in the west. It is not a place to which we can go, not a place that we should try to go to. You two must understand that in this very moment we are resting peacefully in the core of the Way. The teachings of the Shingaku by Ishida Baigan tell us that 'As a fish does not know the water it lives in though it lives in the water, so we humans live in air without noticing it or seeing it'. We are living in the divine virtues and blessings without being aware of them. We live in the Way peacefully with no notice of its presence.

"Despite this fact, we sometimes try to discover it and to locate it somewhere apart from ourselves. Where could the core be, if we were to depart from the divine virtue and blessing that fills Earth and Heaven? We try to do this only if we have a wrong idea about the location of the core of the Way. To say it is hard to find one's way to the core is as wrong as to say one wishes to reach the core by great effort. Now do you two understand what I am saying?" In this way he gave his admonition and remonstrance, by which the two were enlightened to the truth.

In connection with this anecdote Tokio sensei added the following comment.[26] "We were also present at the time and we all listened to Kyōso instructing Hachiya and Miyata with care and sincerity. They both seemed really enlightened by it. The 'core of the Way' is a word used by the Confucians, and it must mean what is preached about as Takamagahara in Shinto."[27] Tokio ended his remark with the following *waka*:

From the ancient days
　　up to our own present day
　　　　it is always true,
That those pursuing the Way,
　　they all are divine kami.

20. Warning of a Second Fire

Once a resident of Mimasaka (the province to the north of Okayama) was feeling very downcast because his house had burned down. Then he came down with an illness that would not respond to treatment. Finally, he decided he needed a divine blessing and he went to Ohmoto and explained the whole thing to Kyōso. Kyōso gave him this quick response, a flat warning. "If you are not careful, and keep on taking no heed to yourself, you will suffer a second fire." Then, having said this in a rather imposing and dignified tone of voice, he went straight back to his study. His visitor was left quite puzzled.

Since this despairing man could not understand what was meant, and since he was completely heartbroken by the fire that had led to his illness, he got all nervous and frightened that another fire would break out where he lived. Not knowing what to do, he brought his perplexity to

27

one of the leading disciples, Matsuoka Kiyomi sensei, who had been present at the consultation. Matsuoka sensei composed two *waka* on the spot by way of answer.

The poor fellow read them again and again, and this got him to thinking. Before long he slapped his thighs in sudden understanding. Then, his face started to regain its colour, showing that his vigour was coming back. "Oh please, forgive me. Kyōso is right. I now see that my whole state of mind was all wrong." With this change of mental attitude, his condition improved quickly and soon he was blessed with a complete recovery.

These were Matsuoka's two impromptu *waka*:

Fire that burned your home
    still is burning and threatens
        to burn down your heart.
If you take no heed or care
    your heart will turn to ashes.

One loss in the past
    is provoking another
        trouble in your heart.
Loss of your health will end in
    total loss of everything.

Indeed, this is true. The fellow who was in this deep distress acknowledged the truth of these improvised *waka*. As may be expected, they cheered and enlightened him. The moment he recognised the truth in Kyōso's dignified and reverent words he was impressed and moved and his face showed vitality. This revitalised the *bunshin* within his heart so that he was blessed with divine virtue.

Kyōso's demanding admonition, "If you are not careful, and keep on taking no heed to yourself you will suffer a second fire", was indeed put rather strongly, though it also was gracious and auspicious. It is true that having one's home burn down is a serious loss and disaster. We must, however, understand Kyōso's teaching that disasters and troubles should be accepted with a thankful heart. Getting to the point of being able to accept everything thankfully, even great trouble, is nothing but an expression of the deepest and truest faith in the Way. The man's house had burned down and he had lost valuable belongings, but he was not injured and his body was sound and healthy. This was the first thing, above all, for which he should have been grateful.

Instead, what a thoughtless reaction! This victim of fire was so full of despair that he thought the loss of home and property was the greatest misfortune life could offer. It distressed him, hurt his heart, and worst of all, injured the *bunshin* bestowed on him by Great Kami. Sometimes people who suffer losses turn to cursing the world, bearing grudges against Heaven and even saying faithless and unfaithful things against the kami. Distressed conduct such as this led the fellow to the added distress of being seized by an illness.

All of this lacks reverence, it is a sin against Heaven. How dreadful it is! This is why Kyōso gave him such stern words of warning. What he meant was, "the fire will burn your heart", and, "the fire in your heart can burn you up completely." This is certainly a lesson every one of us should always bear in mind. The warning, of course, is not limited to fire. It applies also to such things as business losses, illness of family members, or someone's passing. We must be very watchful when such things happen, or else there is the possibility of double losses. How awful that is, and how much we should pay attention to the lesson. We must recognise the deep significance of Kyōso's words about the "second fire", and always be attentive and prudent in everything we do as in deep devotion we pursue the practice of the faith.

21. The Father's Extravagance Reforms the Son's Prodigality

In the main business district of Okayama there was a dealer in herbs and drugs who had a large business. He was an earnest sort of person, one whose enthusiasm and devotion to his work helped him build up quite a fortune. He had made his way into the top rank of the wealthiest, most successful merchants in the busiest shopping district of the city. But his son, his eventual successor, was a carefree and spendthrift youngster who felt no cares and had no worries. Not long after he came of age, at least officially, he was inveigled by some of his no-good friends to spend his days in the entertainment quarters. He squandered his money like water, and this became a matter of grave concern to his father.

This prudent but so-cautious merchant had made money his most important concern in life. His anxiety grew day by day, to the point he could not stand it any more. He began to think that if this went on much longer the fortune he had worked so hard to build up would all be gone, long before he came near to closing his eyes in death. His fears made him restless. He tried to think of some reasonable and effective way to deal with this serious problem. He tried various approaches. He threatened and scolded his son harshly, he coaxed and wheedled him, he gave him advice, he expostulated to him about his careless behaviour, he gave him a good talking-to. He pestered his friends and relatives for advice on what else he could try.

Alas, to his disappointment, nothing he did had any effect. Like "praying to the ears of a horse", or "ploughing in the sand", or "water off a duck's back", nothing he tried had any effect on his son's indifference. It seemed hopeless. At a loss, he finally thought of Kyōso. Since he had been a faithful follower of Kyōso for many years, he came up with an idea. "Kyōso is the right person to ask for advice. I have no other means left but to consult him about it. First I must ask him for a blessing. Then, if possible, I must ask him to admonish my son."

Kyōso listened attentively to the merchant. Then he said, quite deliberately, "So, that is the situation? It certainly must worry you. Indeed, I do see what is troubling you. It is quite natural that it keeps you worrying. But, please listen to me carefully. Usually, wealth and fortune can be a big help in leading a life that is free from all care. I have always believed this. Wealth can be a source of reassurance and give freedom from anxiety.

"But after hearing your story, I can see that in your case, it is your large fortune that is the source of your anxiety. So, if your money is the cause of your worries, I suggest you spend it all. Get clean rid of it. That is the very thing you should do. However it comes about, your fortune is destined to be spent. Your son is set on enjoying himself in the red light district till not a penny is left. So, why not go to Miyauchi yourself and use it up on having a good time there? Get started on your own life of merrymaking!"[28] Kyōso's advice puzzled the merchant. He spent that night at home thinking about it.

Then, the following morning the old man hurried out to Miyauchi on a palanquin. For days he gathered all the geisha girls of one of the lively houses, and there he held a big, extravagant party. It was the first of many that were to follow. The singing, dancing, music, and noisy laughter prompted the curiosity of his son, who had been enjoying himself at this same house. He began to wonder what vulgar and unrefined person would have the bad taste to make such a noisy disturbance. He thought he should take a good look at whoever it was. With the help of one of the maids, he hid in an adjoining room and took a peek through a gap in one of the sliding doors (*fusuma*). Who could this person be?

30

To his utter surprise, the merchant having this uproarious party was no one else but his own father! He had always believed his father to be so sincere, so humble, so gentle and courteous. Heavens! The scene really frightened the boy and created terror in his heart. He was taken aback and totally astonished. After a while he said to himself, "Oh no. I can never beat him at his own game. In comparison with this, my extravagance is modest. I have spent a great deal, but it is a sure bet that if my father is going to join me, it won't be long, it can only be a matter of days, before his whole estate is wasted and ruined. How horrible! This can't go any further. Something has to be done to save the family fortune." With these thoughts in his head, he immediately took himself away from the scene of merriment and hurried home.

His father spent more days in Miyauchi, but since he had been brought up as a man with strict morals, he had never acquired a taste for this kind of good times. He could not enjoy himself very heartily. Since this was his nature, he gradually lost interest. He returned home feeling discouraged. But, at first to his confusion and then to his joy, he found his son formally dressed up for business. He was wearing his dark blue work apron and stiff sash, tending to dealers and customers courteously and properly.

Needless to add, the young merchant continued to work diligently after that. His father was really satisfied with him. Soon he proved himself another earnest merchant, winning the respect of the public and his fellow merchants. Besides that, he gained a growing prosperity for himself.

22. Watching How Anger Hurts People

Once Kyōso was passing by Daiku on his way to a regular meeting in Okayama City. Just in front of a store called the Omote-ya there were two groups of men, cursing and shouting. They were swinging sticks and clubs at each other, beating each other up. They were having an awful fight. One could hardly bear to watch it. At this spot Kyōso stopped quite purposefully. He watched the fight with close attention.

Going with him to the meeting was Kurozumi Shōsaku, one of his relatives. He revered Kyōso very highly, holding him in such high respect that he would spend his free time listening to his lectures and sermons. On that day Shōsaku was going with him at his own initiative. The fight made Shōsaku feel anxious. He kept his eyes on the turmoil timidly and nervously. As he began to think of the possibility that Kyōso might get hurt he grew more uneasy and afraid. He began to look for a way to get him away from that place.

What concerned him next was that Kyōso remained rooted to the spot, seeming to watch with excitement as if following something entertaining. He paid no attention to anything else. Watching this strange behaviour, even good old Shōsaku began to have some critical thoughts. "This is the Kyōso who always teaches us a gracious Way and encourages us to approach others with the full round spirit of sincerity. How inappropriate it is now that he stands here amusing himself, so carefully watching these good-for-nothing young fellows people fight. What a bother it would be if someone who knows him well should see him! It is scandalous! It would hurt our reputation!"

Later on, during the meeting they were going to, Kyōso brought up the topic of the fight in his lecture. He described briefly what he had seen on the way. Then, after a brief but impressive pause, he began sharing with the audience the lesson he had learned from what had happened.

"As you are aware, I have been teaching you and advising you every time I come here not to be angry. Acting in anger is truly a dreadful thing. This I have preached to you. The fight I have just told you about also has its cause in anger. If anger had not risen up there would not have been a fight. Once a group begins to feed on anger it leads to a frightful consequence. Then a really big fight like this one can get going. Well, in the first place, such conduct can't be permitted. It offends the laws of the government. And then also, sometimes our precious bodies may suffer an injury. One may have to live with it the rest of one's life. There is no guarantee that a stick won't be the means of killing someone. There is nothing more meaningless than to lose one's life, especially this way. And, if you kill someone, you will be treated as a criminal and you may be sentenced to death.

"Oh my. All these unhappy and dreadful things stem from anger. Although this is true, people still are apt to upset their hearts through anger and lose their peace of mind. What we must comprehend very thoroughly is the divine blessing of the Way in daily life. The Way must be revered in each moment. We must learn to accept everything we may encounter thankfully and graciously. We must realize that Great Kami is constantly, at every moment, guiding and leading us towards the right way. Never should we lose patience and rise up in anger.

"As humans we have the special grace of a sound, determined heart and a healthy and energetic body – we all do. The vitality we put forth when we are engaged in a fight is one of the expressions of these gifts. If only we take care of this vitality, and not use it for unworthy purposes. If only we use it just for emergencies, when pure and worthy goals are at stake. Then it can help our actions be meaningful. When this vitality and energy are used for the world's benefit it will help us save others. I ask you all to think about this carefully and to follow my advice."

Word after word rang out from Kyōso's inmost heart into the hearts of the audience. All were most impressed and moved by his wholehearted sermon. The person among them who was most moved was Kurozumi Shōsaku, who had seen the fight. He had witnessed the details of it himself, and this is why he felt the more grateful for the sermon. How noble was Kyōso's prudence and attentiveness while he was watching the fight. His thinking has its basis in his belief that everything we do should be based on the Way. In every deed and in every word, attention should be focused on how to revere the Way and how to restore it from whatever deviations might occur. This was how he was viewing these angry men fighting.

Furthermore, though he did not know those vulgar fellows and had not even seen them before, he showed such an impressive pity and sympathy for them. When Shōsaku understood better how much the Founder was concerned about what was going to happen to them, he also realized how little he had understood the worthy ideas of Kyōso's philosophy. He regretted the fears he had felt while the fight was going on. He felt deeply ashamed of his critical attitude towards Kyōso, however mild that feeling had been.

It is reported that Shōsaku kept on talking with his close friends about this experience for many years, long after Kyōso had ascended to Heaven.

23. The Cat that Fell in a Well

This also happened when Kyōso was walking past Daiku on his way into Okayama. It was at a different time, but again while he was on a religious mission. Again there was a big, excited gathering of people along the road just there, and he stopped to see what was happening. With him this time was Hishikawa Ginjibei, his personal attendant. Looking more closely, Kyōso saw they were trying to rescue a poor cat that had fallen into a well.

When they lowered a bamboo basket tied to the end of a long piece of rope, the cat quickly got into the basket. As the old saying goes, "a drowning man will grab even a piece of straw." They carefully and slowly pulled up the rope to lift the basket. But, when the basket was almost all the way up, the terrified cat tried to save itself by scrambling out too soon. It fell back in the well with a splash. They tried the same thing again, but when they were about to succeed, the cat in its fear and haste did the same thing again. Their third and fourth attempts also ended the same way. The rescuers started mumbling to themselves about what a stupid brute the cat was. "What do you expect from such a dumb animal!" But the poor cat was showing signs of weakening.

It isn't clear at just what point Kyōso's eyes began filling with tears. Ginjibei, in his own straightforward way, urged him to keep walking but he kept looking back. Suddenly Kyōso came to a stop, saying to himself with tears running down his cheeks, "Oh, my, what a pity and what a sorrow!"

Then Ginjibei grumbled, "It really was a sad scene, sure enough. But though it is a pitiful sight, it was only something happening to an animal. I don't think it is worth the Sensei crying over it." Hearing this, Kyōso replied sharply,

"Gin san, you are wrong. It's not a matter of just a poor cat. It applies also to us humans. People might look intelligent and smart, but they keep on repeating the same mistakes. Kami is always stretching out her hands to us, trying hard in various ways to tell us, 'Now is your time to be saved, now you can be cured'. If only we had more patience, if only we would stop moving away from the help she is giving. Alas! So quickly our selfish heart comes to the fore. We rely too soon on our smartness and cleverness. When all we can do is just try to be clever when we are doing something, all we might gain is lost, each time over again. We put ourselves deeper and deeper into a hole.

"Oh, how compassionate Kami must feel on seeing that happen, and how frustrated she must be. When I think about it this way, how can I keep my tears from falling? Oh, our gracious Kami! Today again you have taught me a gracious and precious lesson. I extend my sincere and humble thanks to you."

24. The Lesson of the Live and Dead Twigs

This is an anecdote from a sermon given at a meeting.

"The other day I happened to look out and see many children flying kites high up in the sky, and I learned a lesson from Kami for which I am very thankful. Now and then a kite would be caught on the twigs and branches of trees. I saw one boy pulling with all his might to get his kite off again. I watched carefully. I saw that most of the kites that got caught on live twigs could be got off the tree easily, and when they were off they were still intact and undamaged. But those that got caught on dead twigs and branches were hard to get free and could hardly be saved. Such efforts mostly ended up in cutting the string and losing the kite.

"With this, I came to a new understanding. When your heart is vigourous and active, communication with others goes along smoothly and every problem gets a clear solution easily. On the other hand, when your heart is dead or inactive and you feel gloomy, it is quite different. You damage parts of the kite, or maybe you can't even untangle the string or the kite from the stiff twigs and branches. Anything that comes up can provoke a problem, and then the whole thing becomes more and more complicated. Everything gets all tangled up, going haywire and causing a big commotion, all confused. What a mess it all becomes!

"This is exactly the Way of the Great Kami. She revives and saves a person's heart by means of the living divine heart. There is no other way than this. I had watched the children playing, but what a great and gracious lesson I learned from Heaven, in accordance with the rule of Nature. Oh Kami, thank you so much!"

25. Kyōso's Wish that Everyone's Heart be Lively

Kyōso's calligraphy was well known for its grace and elegance. The excellence of his work was widely recognized. One of the senior members once commented, however, that he had sometimes noted differences within Chinese characters Kyōso had written. The colour of the ink in the left half of a character in a letter he had written was sometimes of a slightly different shade from the right half.[29] Part of the outstanding quality of his art was due to the special care he took with the colour and shade of his brush marks. When writing on small-sized paper, as well as when writing letters, he always dipped his brush in the inkwell at the end of a sentence or a line. Part of the elegance of good calligraphy is seen in the way the shade of the ink changes only at the end of a line. The colour and shade changes in his writing are superb, and have always been admired by experts in calligraphy.[30]

So, Kyōso was never the sort of person who would through carelessness put his brush in the inkwell in an *ad lib* fashion so as to have the left and right sides of a single character differ in shade of colour. When that happened it was for another reason. According to this senior person, when a visitor would come in while he was writing a letter he could not by nature have that person wait until he had finished the letter before beginning to talk. He would immediately lay his brush aside. Always he did this, leaving aside what he had been doing instantly so that the visitor would not have to wait even for a moment.

Thus, it happened often that Kyōso would leave half of a Chinese character unfinished, laying down his brush at that point to attend to his guest. The second half he finished later. This senior said that was why his writing sometimes showed differences in tint between the left and right sides of individual characters.

There is a saying, "Put yourself in the place of the person who is waiting." To wait for someone or something can be boring and unpleasant. Kyōso was always most careful about having others wait for him, even briefly. He did not want to cause the other person any tedium or discomfort at all. His intention was not to bore the *bunshin*, the divine heart residing in a person's heart, even for a second. To bore the divine heart would weaken its presence. It was for this reason that having someone wait for him was not permissible.

This is such an admirable story. Many dignitaries and authorities who keep people sitting idly in their waiting rooms for a half-hour or more for no reason, or who think that not keeping their visitors waiting would be to lower themselves in status, should use this story as a lesson and example.

26. Revitalizing the Heart of an Angry Man by Avoiding a Dispute

The teachings of Kyōso spread quickly and vigorously within a short time after he began his work. Soon, reports came in one after another from many who claimed they gained deep insight from hearing his sermons and lectures, and from many who were blessed by his *majinai* in overcoming their pains and anxieties. Since this raised him up high in popular opinion, there were various traditional faith-healers – *Norikura* healers, *yamabushi*, Buddhist exorcists, and others – who lost many of their clients.[31] Some began to fear they would be put out of business entirely.

Accordingly, one such group of practitioners went to their headquarters, located in Kojima County (today a part of Kurashiki City), to explain their problem and to present an urgent request. They wanted their leader to take strong action to persuade the Kurozumis to stop their preaching and missionary activities. Hearing this, the leader wondered what some person who looked like an ordinary Shinto country priest really could do anyway. He decided to set out to see this priest in person, to refute him and humiliate him to his heart's content, so that he would never preach the Way or do *majinai* again. It was with this firm determination that this man proceeded bravely toward Kyōso's home.

This man, whose name remains unknown, began his discussion with Kyōso in a very sharp, menacing tone and with anger and threats. Noting that Kyōso listened carefully, with head bowed, he decided that this fellow was practically ignorant of the difficult and comprehensive theories of Buddhism, and even of the teachings of Shinto. He did not know anything. This made him despise and disdain his host even more and made him think this priest an easy fellow to handle. Giving himself yet more airs under shelter of this belief, he presented his ideas even more firmly. Finally, thinking his scolding had quite defeated Kyōso, he heaped abuse on him, saying, "Quit your silly preaching of the Way, stop your performance of *majinai*, and all your silly religious activities from this instant on!" Shouting out these harsh words, this man left Kyōso's house feeling quite victorious.

Waiting for the guest's departure and making sure he was well out of the house, Madame Iku came into the study, shedding bitter tears of sorrow and reproach. "Sir, I had no intention of listening to that man's words and his threats. But his voice was so loud I couldn't help overhearing him. Oh my! What terrible things he said to you! I am a woman, but I feel so miserable and chagrined. And yet you said not a word during the whole time. This is not an attitude for a man. Particularly not for you who are a preacher of the Way. That person said such despising and offensive things. Oh my, it makes me shudder that you didn't even have a single word to give back to him. Your attitude made me feel so sad and disappointed."

Kyōso quietly opened the outer sliding door of the house. The man was returning home in triumph, feeling all elated, walking along with big strides. Pointing at him, Kyōso clapped his hands.

"Oh my dear. Look at that fellow. See how happy and proud he is as he goes back home. It gives me great delight and pleasure to see his triumphant mood. Well, if I had defeated him in debate, how miserable he would feel, how disheartened he would be! When he got home he would find his dinner would not taste good, and in the night he would not be able to sleep a wink. He would have to spend tomorrow and the day after that, at least for several days, feeling low and sad. What a pity that would be for him.

"If the problem were only that, it would not be so serious. His *bunshin* granted to him by Kami would also be affected. Then the true intention of the Divine Heart would be masked and covered over within him. That would be a serious offence against Great Kami, and a lack of proper reverence. Oh, just take a look at him! His *bunshin* is now filled with victory. What a gracious scene!" With this, Kyōso clapped his hands again as he offered his gratitude to Great Kami.

27. The Angry Priest at the Buddhist Temple

In Kanaoka, Bizen Province, there was a popular temple known as Tenjinbo (in today's Saidaiji area of Okayama City). The devout followers of Kyōso in that vicinity once made plans to invite Kyōso to give a sermon. Unfortunately, those who were organizing the occasion could not find any house that would be a good place to hold a meeting. Since one of them was a leading member of the village, and, as it happened, one of the leading supporters of Tenjinbo, they proceeded to use the temple as a place for the sermon. The priest was not at home at the time and they did not ask his consent.

They made a platform from where Kyōso would give his lecture. To decorate the platform and make the occasion more ceremonious, they went into the temple storeroom and borrowed a gold-braided satin damask altar cloth that was one of the treasured possessions of the temple. This too they did without asking the priest's permission. Of course, Kyōso had no knowledge of any of this. He was not a person to go around asking trifling questions. He was just happy and pleased to see the devout and thoughtful arrangements the followers had made for him. When the time came, he went up on the platform to perform his service as preacher.

During the sermon the priest of the temple returned. The scene provoked him to anger, since he had not received any word of the meeting in his temple, and certainly had not given his consent. Even more serious, he had given no consent about the use of the precious altar cloth. Although he saw that many of those attending were people he knew, this large gathering of followers of Shinto, a different faith, was causing him to feel quite angry. When he first arrived he kept his temper and stayed outwardly calm. He thought it unworthy of the dignity of his status to express his anger and make a protest. But, when his eye fell on his very precious satin damask altar cloth, to be used only to decorate the grand altar before the Buddha in his temple, he flared up in anger despite his good common sense.

Up he went to the platform and snatched away the altar cloth, roaring in anger, "What the hell do you think you are doing?" The whole audience was taken aback with surprise and shock. Timidly and nervously they watched what would happen next. Those who had organized the occasion were about to give a response, ready to respond in anger with something like, "Do you think this is appropriate for a priest? What a foolish way to act!"

At this point, Kyōso just kept his calm and went on speaking.

"My dear followers, please listen to me. Don't you agree we have just learned a lesson we must really be thankful for? All of us can see that the head priest of this temple has just returned. He has blamed us for using his precious altar cloth on this platform. On this point he is absolutely right. What he said was exactly correct. It was very thoughtless of us. What an awful mistake! We have been lacking in reverence. The thoughtfulness and attentive care he has shown us for the treasures of the Buddha, as the head priest responsible for this temple, this is what we must observe and respect.

"Too often we tend to use things without proper permission and respect, and we need to bear that in mind. May we all remember always to treat carefully the things we use in worshipping the deities. We have received a very gracious teaching."

With this the audience returned to its original silence. The hall and all who were present were filled with strong feeling of awe and respect, and from here and there came the sounds of hands reverently clapping.[32] The priest went quietly out of the hall. After the meeting was over he came out to offer his sincere apology to Kyōso for his impolite words. Kyōso also apologized for his negligence, though it was not his fault but that of the organizers.

28. "Iku, Are You All Right?"

This is a story I heard from Madam Murata Kaneko, who was one of Kyōso's granddaughters. When Madam Iku went to the toilet while Kyōso was writing a letter or going about some other business and he would notice that her return was a little delayed, he would go near the toilet and ask, "Iku, are you all right?"

Then Iku would reply politely, "I am fine. I'm sorry, but please don't bother. I am about to come out." "Don't hurry. There's nothing I want to ask you or ask you to do. I was just wondering if anything might be the matter with you. If nothing is the matter and there's no trouble, that's fine." With this he would return to his room.

Madam Murata added, "Since this happened so often, I, who was then eleven or twelve, used to imitate him, running around my grandfather's yard, teasing and calling out, 'Oh Iku, are you all right?'"

29. Reverencing His Wife and Offering Prayer to Her

Whenever Kyōso returned home from some mission, Madam Iku always greeted him politely with cordial words of thanks, and served him a cup of tea in his room. "Oh, thank you for the trouble you have gone to. You must be tired." In response, Kyōso used to clap his hands. After holding his hands together in prayer for a moment he would accept the cup with reverence and drink the tea with thanks.

One of his disciples who had observed this so often once asked him, "Why is it that you drink the tea your wife has prepared for you with such reverence? And especially, why do this just the way we offer prayers to Kami?"

He replied, "The reason is what I always say when I preach, that in every person's heart there dwells the divine presence, so graciously and kindly. That is why I do it. Remember also that when we stop being so busy with our own heart's concerns we become one with Kami who is within us. Eventually we will, in all humility, be one of the Eight Million Kami.[33] My wife does not originally belong to me. In her origin she is another divine child of Kami like everyone else. And when we leave behind all evil thoughts and drop off our self-concern we return instantly to the divine condition in which we originated.

"Well, when I come home from outside, Iku simply tries to give me comfort, serving me a cup of tea with a sincere and whole heart. There is not a speck of evil in her. So pure and innocent! At that moment I see Kami within her. She is in fact Kami to me. That is why I reverence her, and enjoy my tea with feelings of respect and gratitude towards her."

On this point, some people use the expression "respect for the dignity of humanity". Kyōso's thinking is much more advanced. His attitude is one of "respect for the divine dignity". This is what he has taught us. If we could only advance to the level where we could respect the divinity that is in everyone else, then conflicts, differences, and disagreements all could be solved, and all hatreds and quarrels would vanish away.

30. Praying Reverently to an Old Pair of *Zōris*

Kyōso often went on missionary work to Akasaka County in the Province of Bizen, since this was where a certain Mori san had his residence. He was the leading village head in Akasaka County and he also was an important follower of the Way. Kyōso used to cover this distance briskly on foot, some fifteen miles, wearing a pair of *zōris* on his feet. This story was related, it is said, by a certain owner of a general store in Shimo Village, which is on the old highway that people used who were going to Osaka or Kyoto.

"I happened to know the Dai Sensei of Kurozumikyō. In my late teens I occasionally saw him passing by our store. Sometimes he dropped in to buy *zōris*.[34] At that time I always thought he was rather strange because every time he bought a pair he would raise up the old ones in an attitude of reverence, up to eye-level. Only then would he throw them away in the trash. But then he always followed that by a prayer to the worn-out *zōris* he had just thrown away. What this man did with those old, worn-out, dirty *zōris* seemed unusual and I was always puzzled. What in the world was he doing with them?

"So that was what I saw. Then, later on, I had a chance to talk to someone who knew a lot about the Kurozumi Way. This person once had a conversation with the Teacher about his *zōris*. This is what he told me about the lesson he had learned. 'What Kurozumi Sensei told me was this: "One cannot cover a distance of eight or ten miles without taking along an extra pair of *zōris*. The soles of your feet can't stand the pain if you aren't wearing *zōris*. If you walk barefoot, you will injure your feet. If you do wear them, you won't feel pain. You can walk pleasantly and easily. But they do eventually wear out. We can put it this way. The *zōris* take on the trouble our feet would have if we did not use them. So, we should feel gratitude to the *zōris* and we should express that gratitude. It would be irreverent of us not to do that." This is what the Great Sensei believed. And this is what makes him different from us.'

"Well, I got a different point of view from my conversation with that man. I felt completely humbled by what I learned. I also believe the Sensei's ideas and his actions were different from the rest of us, somehow or other. Maybe it is something we can understand, but maybe there is something beyond the ordinary about it. After living a long time and reaching my present age, I can understand better how Kyōso felt. Well, he really was a reverend and respected person. He was so humble and so considerate that he prayed not only for all mankind but even for a dirty, worn-out pair of *zōris* that we sometimes walk with in filthy, messy places. He was this kind of person his whole life long."

Kyōso had a prayer for everything, and he was enshrined as a Kami soon after his ascent to Heaven. Today he is worshipped graciously as an honoured Kami by several million people.[35] What a strange and wonderful world this is! How marvellous!

31. Munenobu, His Successor, Suffers a Serious Illness during the Thousand Days' Seclusion

This is what I heard happened in 1825 when Kyōso was forty-six years old, at the time he had just begun the thousand nights' seclusion at the Imamura Shrine. His only son, Munenobu,[36] who was four years old at that time, was attacked by a serious case of smallpox. His mother was deeply concerned and nearby relatives joined in her anxiety. They racked their brains, worrying what to do in helping her take care of the boy. Despite the boy's condition and the anxieties of the family, Kyōso went on with his nightly devotions, not missing a single night.

Munenobu's condition grew steadily worse. One day the family physician warned that the boy might not hold on through the night. The whole family was afraid there was no hope for him. But when the time came for Kyōso to leave for the Shrine, he got ready to go as usual. This surprised Madame Iku, and she came to him, pleading, "Oh, my. You aren't going out on this night, are you? The doctor says Sano may be called to Heaven this night.[37] And you see that so many of our relatives and neighbours have gathered and are joining us in prayer. They are with us here to help us in our hopes and our worries. I don't think it's a good idea for you to go out tonight. It doesn't make sense, it really doesn't." Madame Iku tried from the heart to persuade him to stay.

But Kyōso responded, "Sorry, I do have to leave. I am just going to the presence of Kami. I'm not going anywhere else." With these words he set off quietly for Imamura Shrine.

As predicted, after midnight Munenobu's condition grew ever worse. Ginjibei, the faithful family steward and Kyōso's disciple, was watching anxiously as he continued to weaken. Unable to sit still, he ran to the Shrine to report the boy's serious condition and bring Kyōso back home right away. Hearing Ginjibei's earnest plea, he said, "Well, if his condition is that bad and you are all so worried, let me suggest this as a way of settling it. Since I can't leave here till sunrise, would you take my place and perform the *majinai* ritual on my boy? Please open your hands and show me your palms. Now I will blow *yōki* on them."[38]

When he blew *yōki* firmly on Ginjibei's hands, Ginjibei immediately felt the force of gracious power. As instructed, he quickly went back to the house. At the sickbed he performed *majinai* on the boy with his hands. To everyone's surprise, this was the turning point. The boy was very soon on the way to getting better. He showed steady improvement, and at dawn he was sleeping peacefully. Before long, it is said, he was blessed with a complete recovery.

32. Kyōso Goes on a Missionary Journey in Spite of Munenobu's Illness

Munenobu, Kyōso's son who was later to be the Second Patriarch, later experienced another wonderful blessing. I want to tell that story also. This happened about ten years after the story just related, when Munenobu was about fourteen years old. It was on the day that Kyōso was to set off on some missionary activities in the province of Mimasaka.

Munenobu was again seriously ill at this time. His condition was so serious that it had become the grave concern of the high disciples, sharing the concern of the family. On the morning of this day escorts from Mimasaka had arrived to accompany Kyōso on the mission. (Some say it was the first time they had visited him, asking him to work in their area.) Since Munenobu was so ill, Madame Iku along with all the disciples and followers pressed Kyōso to postpone the journey. However, he answered, "Oh, listen to me. There is nothing I can do that might be of any help, if I were to stay home. It is completely dependent on the divine will and power. It all depends on the faithfulness[39] of our inner hearts. Well, well. There is no worry. If others are to be blessed with the divine virtue, why can't our boy become well by the same power?"

As if to make his point decisively, with these words Kyōso left on his missionary journey, along with his hosts who were escorting him.

After about a week (some report it was on the sixth day), Kyōso found on his return that while he had been away the boy had been showing surprising improvement. "Sano, how are you doing? Won't you have some of this?" He showed the boy some of the leftovers of his own lunch. Munenobu was happy to see them, and he enjoyed having some of the hard-cooked regular food he had missed during his days of being bedridden. From that day on his appetite improved daily (so goes the story), and so did his physical vigour.

33. Madame Hoshijima Receives Blessings

Madame Hoshijima Miyako was highly respected, even regarded with reverence, among the followers of Kyōso. She had a strong character and was among the top three women leaders in his group. Once she was attacked by a serious illness, and so she asked him to come to her house to perform a *majinai* ceremony. Since he was very busy, he was unable to respond to her request for some days. During that time her condition became critical. Those who were taking care of her drew their brows together with anxiety as the time went on.

One day they did hear the call of a visitor from the entrance (*genkan*) of the house. In response, they heard Madame's calm inquiry, "Who is it?" followed by a voice saying calmly but strongly, "This is Kurozumi Sakyo, in person." When this voice came to her ears she got up abruptly and ran to the entrance to greet him. "Thank you so much, sir." She had no other words after that, but just kept her head down to the floor, touching the mat with her forehead in welcome to Kyōso.

Seeing her, he said, "But, have I heard you were in a serious condition?" With this Madame Hoshijima recovered consciousness. His words had startled her. "Good Heavens! How in the world did I get here?" She herself was surprised. "Oh, how blessed (*arigatai*) this is! I do thank you." All those present were just stunned. Reportedly, Madame Miyako's condition kept improving from then on until she had completely recovered. Kyōso's greeting given at the entrance, so gracious and kind, and in such a tone of vigour, had made Madame Miyako forget her illness and run to the entrance. Just there, divine virtue immediately blessed her.

34. Kyōso Blesses Lord Tokura, Chief Councillor of the Bizen Clan

Lord Tokura, who was a highly respected chief retainer to Lord Ikeda, ruler of the Bizen clan, was confined to his bed with a serious illness that no medical treatment could cure. He was well known for his scholarly mind and broad knowledge, and also for his courage and his stubbornness. Now, however, he was in such condition that he could only wait for death to take him away. Since he was worsening daily and awaiting death, his relatives and friends were casting about for some means that might be taken to help him. They decided there was nothing left but to ask Kyōso to visit him. Kyōso had just recently become known as a living kami, able to perform healing rituals (*majinai*) on the sick.

Since the sick man was a great samurai and scholar, however, and since he was such a determined person, he refused to receive *majinai*. He was set on accepting death rather than having such a ritual done for him. His circle of relatives and friends was in dismay at such an attitude.

Among his retainers, however, was a devoted follower of the Way named Okada Yagoemon Katsuhirō. Okada visited Kyōso secretly to explain the situation, telling him of their worry and concern. He requested Kyōso most earnestly to let Lord Tokura receive the healing ceremony. When Okada had finished speaking, Kyōso said, "How sad! I share your sympathy. Leave everything to me." After indicating his consent to the request, he prayed singleheartedly to Great Kami for three days and three nights.

On the day after that he set off to visit Lord Tokura. When he got to the mansion he sent in his wish to inquire about Lord Tokura's health. At first the servant at the door replied that he could not comply with this request because it was against his Lord's commands. But Kyōso again explained that the purpose of his visit was to inquire about the Lord's health, and he firmly repeated his request. Finally he was ushered inside and was shown into the room just next to where the Lord was lying. Kyōso shouted loudly, as he often did, "Lord Tokura, this is Kurozumi Sakyo. Your Honour, I have come today to ask about your health."

The loud thundering voice pierced into Lord Tokura's heart and soul. He sat up instantly in his bedclothes, his feelings of gloominess and distress shattered by this thunder, and gave Kyōso words of greeting. From that moment, during their exchange of words and while listening to what Kyōso was saying, the Lord found his body and soul were being purified, and he began to enjoy refreshing breath and invigorated feeling. Though he had been believed to be on the brink of death, his condition began, it is said, to improve steadily from that moment. In a week he had completely recovered. It is also said that he was able to resume his normal duties at the castle quite soon.

35. Ikeda Sensei's Timidity and Pessimistic Nature Disappear Instantly

When it comes to Ikeda Chiyozō, we always think of him as calm and self-possessed, always keeping his clear mind and thoughtful posture. He is remembered as one of the leading disciples of Kyōso. Whatever came up while he was doing his religious exercises, he maintained the same steadfast demeanour. It is said, however, that at the beginning he was a pessimistic person who took small things far too seriously. He would become nervous and timid even about trivial things. This was, regrettably, his weak point at the time.

After joining the Way he became one of the most devoted followers and he tried in his religious exercises to correct this failing. But he was unable to overcome his problem and so he finally asked Kyōso's advice. "I feel ashamed to admit that it is my nature to be anxious and troubled over small things." These were his words as he requested guidance.

Not allowing Ikeda to finish and speaking in a strong clear voice with a stern attitude much in contrast to his normal friendly and kindly tone so familiar to everyone, Kyōso said, "If you are that anxious and troubled you cannot really say you are following the Way." With this it was as if a hundred bolts of thunder had struck Ikeda. He was moved with such strong feeling that his head just bowed down on the *tatami* immediately. All his feelings of timidity that had troubled him for years vanished instantly. From that moment he became a new man. The story goes it was this that helped Ikeda gain his later reputation as a bold and audacious samurai.

There is a saying that "One word invigorates a person." This is a case of Kyōso invigorating Ikeda to help him enjoy a more satisfying life for the rest of his years, creating a whole new individual with a strong personality. What an admirable virtue this is of Great Kami and of Kyōso.

36. Morikane Tamezō Sensei

Morikane Tamezō sensei,[40] who eventually became one of the most important leaders of Kurozumikyō, was by birth and character something of a *kujinin*, so that people looked at him askance. I want to explain how he got such a reputation and what sort of a person he later became as one of the leading followers of Kyōso. When he first joined, some of the Way-followers thought at first he was something of a villain. That was not really so. It was a false charge.

This is what I mean. In today's usage "*kujinin*" refers to someone involved in litigation or court affairs (*kuji*). In the old days, however, it had a more general meaning, referring to someone who had a liking for instituting lawsuits or in taking legal action against others, or just someone who delighted in disputes and arguments. "*Kujinin*" were people who had a reputation for being contentious. This was not quite true for Morikane sensei. It was just that he was a very active person, the kind of man who would not budge an inch. And, he was very good at debating. He was different from most people in that even in the presence of a superior he would not hold back. This was in the days of feudalism when arrogant village officers were putting on airs and throwing their weight around. Morikane armed himself with rational arguments and logical reasons and took pride in arguing with village officers. He was the kind of person who is not easily led by the nose, but neither was he just trying to be hostile or contrary. He was actually quite a sensible person who just liked a good debate.

Under the laws of the Tokugawa government (1600–1867), when a non-samurai plaintiff instituted litigation against a government official, then that plaintiff would be punished even if he won his case. A townsman or a farmer thinking of making such charges had to be ready to be accused of being insolent and immoral. A reprimand, or even imprisonment, could result. In those days someone taking issue with government officials had to have an unusually strong personality or be a very upright public-spirited man who was a friend of the people.

On one occasion, Morikane, after meeting with a few others of congenial spirit and discussing some matter among themselves, decided to start a legal process against their village officers. After all those involved had put their signatures and seals on the petition letter, Morikane decided he would go off on foot for Okayama the next morning to submit the petition to the authorities. He tucked the document carefully into his clothing with that in mind.

After the meeting he was walking home as night was falling, half in elation and half in a spirit of tragic resolution. The next morning he would with desperate courage first ask pardon of the authorities for appearing before them and then say, "Most humbly and with all reverence and respect, may Your Honour please accept this letter of petition."[41]

Walking along, he looked up to find himself in front of the house of Nakayama Tsunejiro, the village head of Ohgashima Village next to where he himself lived. The place was brightly lighted and there seemed to be a large gathering of people. When he came closer, he heard the clapping of hands and the sounding of prayer.[42] That made him think, "Who would do such an outrageous thing as holding a big gathering so close to my own neighbourhood without letting me know or asking my permission?" It provoked his tendency to get into arguments. He

47

thought that whoever or whatever it was, he would see it with his own eyes and get into an argument with them. Without anyone's by-your-leave, he crept up on the veranda of the house to get a close look.

A gentleman dressed in the attire of a Shinto priest was giving a sermon. Morikane started to listen attentively, thinking, "What fun this is going to be. Let's see what he has to say. If he says something I don't like I will not let him off the hook." Contrary to Morikane's expectation, the content of the sermon being given by the priestlike-looking man (who, of course, was Kyōso) was of an earnest nature.

The sermon covered many subjects, from the boundless blessings of Great Kami to how grateful we should be to be born in Japan, the land of Great Kami; about how our goal should be to follow the Way of Kami; that we should strive to revive our hearts and make full use of all our resources; that sincerity is the essence of roundness and that in roundness there is no enemy, no one we should be against; and that everyone living in the Seven Seas are our brothers and sisters.

The sermon was presented in a way he had never experienced before. It was as warm and genial as springtime, so harmonious and peaceful, so reverent. Since Morikane did by birth have a reasonable and under-standing nature, he felt a great admiration for Kyōso. He suddenly found himself ashamed of his conduct in the past. As he looked back on how he had conducted himself on so many occasions he was overwhelmed with shame.

He waited until everyone had left and then went close to Kyōso's side. He offered a sincere and humble acknowledgement of his past vanity and conceit. He had so often felt that he was on top of the world, provoking arguments with others and rousing anger in them so much as to hurt them. He confessed his faults and his errors. He asked to be added to the group of Kyōso's followers and to be allowed to take part in the religious exercises of the Way. Of course, Kyōso gave his consent on the spot, fill-ing Morikane's heart with sincere gratitude.

With this, he took from his clothing the letter of petition he and his friends had prepared that day and handed it to Kyōso. Morikane explained the background of the letter and the trouble he and his friends had gone to in discussing the matter and preparing the document. Finally, it is said, Morikane burned it before Kyōso's eyes in a *hibachi* that was there in the room.

Kyōso has taught that the Way is about "how to correct our heart". How good it is to know that one single sermon had corrected the heart of such a distinguished gentleman as Morikane, who was so arrogant and fond of contention. One sermon was enough for him to accept a full conversion. He got a completely different insight, setting him onto the rightful way. Morikane deserves our sincere respect. We must express our admiration for him.

Morikane sensei has left many anecdotes worthy of our thought, but most are in connection with Kyōso, which I should write on at another time. Here, however, is one anecdote that will help understand the personality of Morikane.

On becoming a follower he devoted himself to religious practices. Correcting one's nature is not an easy task. It is achieved only with difficulty. Sometimes Morikane sensei raised discussions with his elders and with senior disciples, setting forth reasons and viewpoints that were understood by others only with difficulty. This seems to have provoked dispute with others, leading to misunderstandings and annoying them. The pleasant and peaceful times he could otherwise have enjoyed with them were diminished as a result.

So, a few of the elders of the group are said to have discussed the problem among themselves and they decided to bring up the matter with Kyōso secretly. "Sir, we are all troubled with that fellow. We fear that if he remains as a disciple he might eventually bring disgrace to the Way. We think some kind of appropriate action might have to be taken." Kyōso said in his usual gentle tone of voice, and with a full smile, "Well, I will not say I was not aware of it. Well, he is a person like a pit viper. When a viper is outside and in the wild, it might attack and hurt a person at a time no one expects. But as long as it is kept in a pot as I am now doing, there is no fear of its biting others."

Morikane was kept in Kyōso's pot for many years and was fed on the gracious food Kyōso gave him. Eventually he was relieved of his bad habits, finally displaying his excellent qualities beyond 120 per cent. After Kyōso's ascent to Heaven Morikane was acknowledged as one of the top leaders responsible for the religious activities and propagation missions of Kurozumikyō. What a gracious blessing that has been!

37. High Disciple Akagi Regains His Eyesight

The blessings brought by Kyōso's astonishing virtue were beyond number, needless to say. But while every one of them inspires reverence, the most famous is the one received by the High Disciple Akagi Tadaharu.[43] The blessing he received inspired him to faith in the Way that continued to grow deeper. As one of the Four High Disciples he spread the teachings and built the firm foundations of Kurozumikyō. His influence in shaping the basic outlook and teachings of Kurozumikyō was immense. In fact, he influenced the religious climate of all Japan during the years that followed his healing by Kyōso. Although this anecdote is well known I can't find any reason to leave it out, since it makes Kyōso's wonderful accomplishments clearer to us.

High Disciple Akagi was born in today's Tsuyama City in Okayama Prefecture. He was the second son of Suye Tarōzaemon, a village head, in 1816. In 1835, when he was twenty years old, he was adopted by Akagi Tsunegorō, then the village head of Nakamomi village. His adoptive father expected him to succeed him as head of the Akagi family.

Soon however he lost his eyesight. He spent eight years in misery and distress as a result. Finally a relative from his birth family, an uncle or perhaps a cousin by the name of Nishimura Saisuke,[44] suggested he visit Kyōso in order to seek a divine blessing. It was a compassionate piece of advice and Akagi thanked Nishimura most cordially, but he was reluctant to travel all the way to Kaminakano down in Bizen Province.

"Uncle Saisuke, your advice is welcome to me. However, before I lost my sight I read two whole chests full of blue-covered books.[45] Based on what I know from that I can't think of any way I could possibly get my eyesight back. A full eight years have passed since my eyes failed me completely. It is hard to believe that prayer would help. I find no reason to think it is possible. Sir, at this point I see no reason to move away from this conclusion." Akagi firmly declined to accept his uncle's kind suggestion.

On another occasion, Nishimura again brought up his suggestion. It was a last attempt to help. Akagi still maintained his refusal. This provoked Nishimura to such anger that he scolded him, declaring that he would cut his ties to Akagi and repudiate him as his nephew.

"Sōichirō,[46] I have had enough of this! From this day, do not think of me as your uncle and I no longer will think of you as my nephew. Take this as repudiation. We are through. I made my suggestion out of kindness and for your sake only, because I feel sorry for your blindness at your young age. But you have brought up one excuse after another. You have no ears to listen to me. You are just holding me in contempt and

Foot-powered rice polishing

making me out as a fool. You said you got your knowledge from your blue-covered books, but what you are giving me are idiotic reasons and excuses.

"Listen to me, young man. I am sure you have heard the wise sayings, 'The proof of the pudding is in the eating', and, 'Seeing is believing'. You should understand that my suggestion is based on the fact that I myself have seen many wonders happen. Those who visited the Great Sensei were cured of tuberculosis and even serious skin ailments.[47] Eyes were opened and cripples were returned to walking. I have seen these miracles with my own eyes. I have no more words and no more time to talk with you any more. Know that this is final. I cut off our relationship as uncle and nephew from this moment on."[48]

With these harsh words and angry face he scolded Akagi, and the well-learned Akagi was taken aback. He begged his senior's forgiveness for the way he had responded to the suggestion. "Oh, Uncle Saisuke, I don't think this is a matter that calls for you to renounce me. I was grateful for your suggestion from the start. I thank you warmly for it. The reason I have been hanging back is that it is hard for me to believe in such a blessing. That is why the only thing I could do is refuse what you said. Please

51

don't think I was making a fool of you. Please, sir, know I had not the slightest idea of that. Please forgive my being so hard-headed and so foolish. Please do take me to Kaminakano."

Then Nishimura escorted Akagi to Kaminakano. This was the first time Akagi had attended a regular meeting and the first time he ever heard one of Kyōso's sermons. At first he listened only out of curiosity without any deep interest, but after a while he began to think, "What this gentleman teaches is neither something from the Chinese classics nor is it out of Japanese classic literature. Neither are his words the lessons given by the Shingaku teachers. It is nothing so worldly or common. It is something different, something that makes an impression on his listeners and moves them. It appeals to the audience and it enlivens them. My understanding of this man was not correct. It is a remarkable gentleman I am listening to."

Since Akagi was an honest and sincere person himself, he was much moved by what he was hearing. As the lecture approached its conclusion, he was increasingly impressed, and gradually a hearty feeling of reverence to Kyōso arose within him. He kept his head bowed as he listened with a growing and earnest sense of respect. At this point the sermon came to the well-known story of the raft hermit.

"Once there was a man so honest that no one could compare with him in honesty. He was so honest that he might be called foolish. He was completely wholehearted and sincere in that quality. One day he heard of an island called the Isle of the Blessed where hermits live.[49] He felt he wanted to go there, and his thoughts turned more and more to wishing he could go to that island. He asked everyone he met where it was but no one could tell him, let alone how to get to that place.

"But he didn't give up, because he really wanted to go there. He kept on wandering through the country to find someone who could help him. Finally he reached the province of Dewa in northern Honshu.[50] Here there was a rice dealer who saw that this fellow was very honest and thought he could take advantage of him. He said to him, 'If you will follow my instructions exactly and completely for three years, I will show you how to get there.'[51] These words rejoiced the fellow's heart, and for three years he worked diligently polishing rice. The dealer rejoiced in his good luck in having the poor fellow work for him from early morning to late at night, and he grinned in secret satisfaction.

"Then the day came. The full period of three years was now over. The fellow went up to the dealer and asked to be instructed in how to get to the Isle of the Blessed as he had been promised. The dealer thought the poor fellow had forgotten his original wish and the promise that had been made. He was surprised to find the promise had not been forgotten. But not for a moment, night and day for three long years, while he was working at moving the treadle with his feet so honestly and diligently, had the fellow forgotten that he would be shown how to get where he wanted to go.

"Now the rice dealer, with cunning like a snake and without the slightest sense of scruples, thought the situation couldn't be escaped and he had to do something. So, he decided he had to deceive the fellow one more time and get rid of him. Since in those days the police system was not as well developed and thorough as today, he thought doing away with a fool would not be so hard. So, he lied to him, telling him he would take him to the Blessed Isle at night. And he took the fellow to a nearby mountain.

"Again the rice dealer told the fellow to obey strictly whatever he was told. Soon they came to a bottomless ravine. He told him to climb a high tree just at the edge. The fellow now thought, 'Now the time has come to fulfil my dream I had so long to visit the Blessed Isle'. Cheerfully he started right up the tree just as he was told.

"The master then told him to climb yet higher. As ordered, he climbed higher. Then he instructed him to go out on the highest branch, the one that looked straight down into the yawning abyss. Hearing that, the fellow leaped out there with no hesitation. Then he was told to take his feet off the branch, and then to let go with his left hand. Immediately he released his left hand and let his feet hang.

"Now he was hanging on to the bending and shaking branch with only his right hand clutching it. Down below was the yawning ravine. If he would fall he would be smashed to pieces. Then the cruel master told him to take his right hand off the branch, all that was keeping him on the tree. The fellow who was so incomparably honest, trusting the rice dealer with such full confidence, let go that last hold on the tree just as he was instructed. And he plunged down into the ravine.

"How sad? Yet, graciously, the moment he dropped down to be shattered to pieces a purple cloud showed up in that very moment, drifting by, picking him up. It brought the honest fellow high up into Heaven into the arms of Great Kami. This so very honest fellow is said to have become a hermit."

The shrine that was dedicated to the comfort of his soul exists today in Akita Prefecture in northern Honshu.[52]

Kyōso had told the audience this story of the hermit. Using the legend as a parable, he conveyed to them the power of utter trust and honesty, teaching that the essence of faith is utter confidence in Amaterasu. It means believing in Kami without the slightest particle of doubt. With such faith, there is nothing that cannot be achieved.

Akagi, listening carefully to the sermon, was deeply moved. His feeling of gratitude was reaching a climax. He had even forgotten that his eyes were closed, along with many other things he had forgotten to think about. In his mind was, "How gracious! What kind of person is this gentleman who can give a sermon like that?" He raised his head to take a look at the preacher. To his bewilderment and wonder he saw before him Kyōso on the platform. By attending just one meeting and listening to just one sermon Akagi regained his eyesight that he had lost for eight long years. That was not the end. It did not stop there, more blessings were to follow.

We must realize how full of grace and power Kyōso's sermons were, how vigourous and convincing and reverent they were. We should understand how limitless are the blessings of Kyōso. And especially, we should note it was through the pure heart of Akagi that the teachings of Kyōso were able to demonstrate this particularly wonderful blessing. How reverent, how gracious and blessed, are the boundless virtues of Great Kami! We must honour and respect those virtues in full sincerity.

This miracle took place in the eleventh month of 1845. At the time Kyōso was sixty-six years old and High Disciple Akagi was thirty. The mutual faith that bound the two together for life in a close and friendly tie began at this meeting. Indeed, the surprising miracle bestowed on Akagi helped him recover from his long dream in a joyful manner. Or rather, he was so happy to find himself in the very place he belonged to begin with. The following *waka* by Akagi vividly expresses his joy.

> Waking from my dream
>   looking at my dwelling place
>   all my heart and mind
> Held securely in the arms
>   of blessed shining Heaven.

The emotional impression he had here received, or rather, the serious conviction and deep faith that was initiated in this meeting, enabled High Disciple Akagi to begin his great leap to becoming one of the great religious leaders of Japan.[53] When we ponder this miraculous experience of blessing, we realize its immense importance to Akagi and to Kurozu-mikyō. So joyful!

38. "Know that We Are in Oneness with Amaterasu"

In the village of Kashino in Oku County, Bizen Province, lived a devout follower by the name of Idei Tsunehachi. Once Tsunehachi's son came down with a serious disease. The father tried every remedy that held out any kind of hope and also deepened his religious devotions. He had his son receive repeated *majinai* only to see the boy's condition grow worse. Despite his devotion to the Way, and out of his love for his son and his perplexity as to what to do, he next made up his mind to go to a certain shrine out in Bitchu Province (today's western Okayama Prefecture). Here he would worship a deity that was supposed to be able to help sick people.

One day Tsunehachi got up early, put on a new pair of *zōri*s, and set off briskly for Bitchu. Soon after he left Okayama town walking westward he found himself close to the hamlet of Kaminakano, close enough to see the houses over on his left. Then this thought came to him, "Oh, this is the way I always go when I visit Kaminakano to see the Great Kurozumi Sensei. Each time I went to him I was glad to see his smiling face and listen to his fine sermons. But today, I am going to pass by without stopping. Sir, please forgive me for not stopping by today. I have to go somewhere else."

As he walked along with this strong apologetic feeling the place where Kyōso lived now came into view. (Some who tell this story say he could actually see the banners, even the red ball on them symbolizing the Kurozumi teaching.)[54] Soon he felt he really could not pass along this way without stopping in to see Kyōso. The story goes that at the corner he suddenly turned towards the south to go to his residence.

To his good fortune Kyōso was at home, standing in the entrance just about to leave his house. Tsunehachi explained his worries about his son and asked for a *majinai* ritual. Hearing this, Kyōso said, "Oh my, what a pity. You must be really worried. But I am just on my way out to attend a gathering in Okayama. I will ask my son Munenobu to offer a prayer and perform the ceremony for your son's sake. Please be sure to receive the blessing that will come from that."

Kyōso kept silent for a moment. Then his eyes got a sparkle in them as if he was reading Tsunehachi's heart. He got up on his feet and said to him in a commanding tone, "Tsunehachi, you should know, as I have preached, there is no barrier that separates our *bunshin* from the Divine Heart of Great Kami. Kami and man are not two. They are in oneness. What a blessed Kami! You should know that."

Tsunehachi was overwhelmed with Kyōso's dignity, and in his surprise his head touched down on the *tatami* in reverence. Kyōso immediately went down to the entrance of the house and headed towards the gate. When Tsunehachi raised his head after a moment, he saw Kyōso looking back at him and telling him in a much louder tone, "Oh my dear Tsunehachi, to our great benefit we all are blessed by Great Kami with a portion of the Divine Heart. What can be more precious than *bunshin*?"

Having given these words, Kyōso turned around and went on to attend to his business. Tsunehachi felt thankful and sat behind Kyōso's son, keeping his head bowed during the ritual. Then, after a few moments, some hundreds of yards away, Kyōso stopped and turned around and shouted out in a thundering voice, "Tsunehachi, to our good fortune, always keep in mind that Great Kami is, to our deepest blessing, in oneness with us humankind."

Tsunehachi was surprised. He felt himself repenting his foolishness and lack of courage, sneaking off from the Way as he had started to do, willing to visit a useless deity, ready to beg the sympathy of such a being. He saw himself reflected in Kyōso's clear mirror. He felt ashamed. And he now recovered his strong conviction that both his and his son's soul and body are gifts of the Great Kami. He was dumbfounded in that conviction, unable to utter a word.

With his eye he followed Kyōso's figure growing smaller in the distance. He found his whole body and soul totally filled with a deep impression, the divine graciousness penetrating every corner of his body. In this way, with this devout faith in Kami, he regained his peace of mind so fully as to be free of all doubt and anxiety.

When the ceremony was over Tsunehachi gladly received the amulet (*kami-fuda*) of Kurozumikyō. By the time he got close to his house it was already dark. Nearing the gate of his home, he saw the kitchen brightly lighted and heard joyful voices. He could hear that one of the voices was that of his sick son. This gave him a surprise. "Oh, how welcome! It is you, father! Just about the time I thought you would be a little west of Okayama, I suddenly felt myself getting better. So, I got out of bed and had a good meal that for a long time I couldn't have. I decided to stay awake and wait for you to come back."

The son really surprised his father, who had considered him ninety per cent hopeless when he left home that morning. To his surprise he was now in good health. "Oh my goodness! So, my dear son was blessed exactly at that very moment. Gracious Kami, thank you!" Now he felt the full graciousness of the kind words and teachings of Kyōso. He respectfully reflected on the details of those teachings. It is said that the more he comprehended what he had been told the more he became aware of the goodness of the Way and the more he devoted himself to pursuing it.

39. Ogata's Weakness of Spirit is Healed

In a village of Oku County called Shimoyamada lived a gentleman by the name of Ogata Chōjirō. In the prime of his manhood he lived through many hardships and obstacles as, along with High Disciple Tokio, he engaged in work spreading the teachings. The two worked together in the province of Harima (today the western half of Hyōgo Prefecture east of Okayama), centring their activities in what is today the city of Himeji. Ogata gave distinguished service to Kurozumikyō and had many outstanding accomplishments.

In his younger years, however, he was a feeble youngster with a delicate constitution, infected with what seemed a hopeless case of tuberculosis. One day in those early years he was sitting on a bench (*shōgi*) in his front garden, sadly trying to warm himself in the sun. Facing the road, he noticed a procession of people on their way to worship at Kaminakano. As they walked by he heard them over and over sharing their impressions of the gracious blessings given in *majinai* and talking of the many who had been healed of their illnesses. On this kind of happenstance Ogata decided to pay a visit there.

At that moment he happened to see an old man from a neighbouring village passing by. The man stopped to say that he was on his way to worship at Kaminakano and suggested that the young man join him in receiving a blessing there. The words tempted Ogata. He saw it might be an opportunity to be drawn closer to the Divine Kami. So, he braced himself to go with the old man to attend his first regular meeting.

He saw how large a group was there to listen to Kyōso's sermon and to receive a benefit. He observed the good things that were accorded to them and saw them filled with such a gentle happiness. He returned home that night with his heart encouraged and stirred up and it seemed

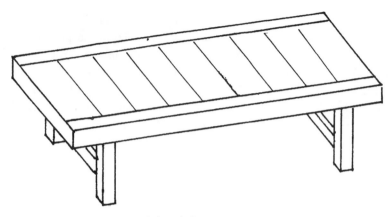

A bench for sitting on

his pain had become a little less. From that day on he was sure to attend each such meeting. This went on for a year and it proved to be good for him. Yet, despite the strong impression he had experienced the first time he went, he still felt unable to grasp the true graciousness of Kami. And he noticed his illness was not really heading towards improvement.

Though he had these thoughts in his mind he still kept on going to the meetings, not missing any. Then at one afternoon meeting he was looking on at the whole course of what was happening for others. When it was all over and everyone else had gone he went up to Kyōso to speak to him. He was full of a strong sense of grief, born of a feeling of sorrow, even bitterness. He asked Kyōso to excuse him from attending any more and he gave him a pathetic farewell.

"Oh sir, please do understand my position. I was allowed to attend every *gokaijitsu* for over a year. I feel I can understand now to some extent what the gracious blessings of the Way are. To my deepest regret, however, my illness still seems unblessed. It shows not a sign of improvement. So, I am here to ask your permission to be excused from any more meetings for a while. Please understand I have not a single doubt that what you are doing is full of divine virtue, really miraculous. I have with my own eyes seen many people relieved of their troubles and illnesses. It might be because of some really bad things I have done in the past. Sir, what sort of karma[55] can be forcing this miserable condition on me? I don't know if maybe some deity's will is being worked on me. I believe that for sure no blessings are attainable for this poor person over here. Sir, please understand what I am saying. I am afraid my lack of faith may injure the high reputation you have, or hurt you yourself, or disgrace the virtues of the Way."

Kyōso was listening quietly to what Ogata had to say. Then he opened his mouth deliberately and said to him, not in a loud voice but with strength and energy, "Ogata san, do you mean to say you have been defeated by the illness?" This is what Kyōso told him, and … .

Ogata felt as if something like a blast of thunder had pierced his body from the top of his head down to the core of his abdomen. It is said he lowered his head till it touched the *tatami* quite without meaning to do it, and that in that instant he knew that his body and soul had been made pure.

On his way home he noticed his steps were much lighter, as if he were jumping along. All along his way home this thought was in his mind, "Oh, dear me, Kyōso Sensei was right! Oh yes, I must admit I had been beaten by the illness. I had trusted that I would be enlightened. But! So *that* was the cause! It was my attitude!" He said to himself as though he were still at the meeting but now with new understanding, "Sir, I must admit that I am awfully sorry for my mistakes and misconduct. I do so sincerely ask your gracious forgiveness."

He thought and he reflected on his experience over and over as he went home. With this kind of thanks and self-examination and with his body and soul filled with happiness and joy he returned home. After enjoying a deep and peaceful sleep that night he woke up forgetting all about his disease and his worries. And from that day his illness showed such improvement that before long he forgot he had ever been sick. Such was his convalescence.

Later he distinguished himself in missionary activities, proving to be one of the nucleus of distinguished teachers of Kurozumikyō. He was to be referred to as Ogata Chōjirō sensei for a long time. He is remembered this way down to the present day.

40. Okumura Enzaemon Regains His Eyesight

An incident that has some points in common with the story of the blessing of Ogata Sensei has been passed on to us to illustrate the greatest and most miraculous blessing of all. A certain unfortunate blind man heard that regardless of the nature of the disease all patients who visited Kurozumi Sensei of Kaminakano were blessed with recovery. The poor man decided to visit this gentleman with the desperate hope of getting his eyesight back. After his first visit he attended every meeting held on the "two and seven" days of the month. He spent three full years attending and listening to Kyōso's gratifying lectures, receiving the *majinai* ritual after each meeting. But alas, he was still unable to see even a little glint of light.

When the meeting that marked the end of three full years of worshipping was almost over, the blind man waited until everyone had left and then went to Kyōso to tell him his discouragement and disappointment.

"Sir, I have come to be excused from your meetings and to bid you goodbye. That is why I stayed behind waiting for the last person to leave. Sir, it might seem strange to you but since I started coming I have not missed a single meeting. But to my disappointment, my eyes have received no blessing. Of course, I tried hard to understand what the Way is really about. I have seen myself that many people have received boundless blessings in many different ways during this time. I want you to know I hold no doubt about that at all. Sir, I have enjoyed the great pleasure and honour of receiving your personal *majinai* scores of times. But alas, my eyes are still as blind as they were three years ago. I cannot see even a slight glimmering of light.

"I am sure you will understand what a difficulty it is for a blind person to attend six meetings every month for three years. Please realize the efforts I devoted to fulfilling this desire of mine and the trouble I have gone to. Sir, it may be that my faith is not enough. To my deepest regret I can't think of anything more to be done. There is no way left but to give up all hope and to reconcile myself to my fate. And sir, in this connection, I am afraid that if I keep on coming to your meetings it will hurt your reputation and virtue and may cause an obstacle in spreading the Way. Since I worry about such a result, I will stop attending any more. From this day I ask your permission to be excused from the meetings."

He was finding difficulty in expressing himself, saying his words in a grief-stricken, inconsolable way. His seriousness reflected vividly his poverty of soul.

Kyōso, who was listening quietly to what the man said, suddenly clapped his hands (*kashiwade*) graciously. "Oh, what an immense and abundant blessing you have received! How fortunate you are and how grateful you should be!" The poor man was taken aback by these words, and responded in confusion and with some heat. "Sir, oh no, no. I said there were no blessings." Restraining him, Kyōso said, "Don't you know what you are saying? Think what you have been doing. Six times a month means you have gone to the trouble of attending more than two hundred meetings, not missing even one. Throughout these three years you were never ill, never suffered a stomachache, not even a cold. More than that, you never had to stay home in bed. That is because you spent three full years enjoying a perfect state of health. Isn't that evidence of plentiful blessings?

"Besides that, it wasn't only you. No member of your family was sick. Otherwise there would have been times you could not come. Bear in mind that you were able to attend every meeting without any hindrance or obstacle of that sort. Oh, and beyond that. If someone in your family had passed away during this time or if a relative living close to you or far away had died, it would have kept you from attending. That would have been a source of taboo, keeping you from going out to shrines and to all sorts of events.[56] So, in spite of all such things that might have happened, you were still able to attend all the meetings, every five days, all six meetings each month. What a gracious blessing you have received!" With this, Kyōso again clapped his hands.

The blind man was deeply moved by this explanation. He had listened quietly, and was startled by the sharp sound of Kyōso's handclap (*kashiwade*) as if hit by lightning. "Oh, sir, I was mistaken. Thank you so much." His words half finished, he ran to the doorway, no longer leaning on his walking-cane. Holding it in his hand, he walked out of Kyōso's place. Touched with strong, indescribable gratitude and deep emotion he passed Niwaseguchi, Kawaramachi-suji, then Saidaichō, and found himself crossing Kyōbashi bridge over the Asahi river. At this moment he felt a cool river breeze. He thought, "Oh, I am crossing a river. Where could this be?"

Then he looked around. The spacious scene of the Asahi river came into his eyes and all of the ships coming in and going out, and those in the harbour. "Oh how wonderful! I can see with my eyes! They are open! I've recovered my sight!" His voice was a sound coming up from the depth of his heart. The words coming out of his mouth were uttered so innocently, they were so spontaneous and pure, so firm, the most joyful and most grateful that any human being could ever pronounce.

The person in this anecdote is reportedly Okumura Enzaemon, a Bizen samurai who entered the faith in 1845.

41. High Disciple Hoshijima
Blessed with Recovery from Tuberculosis

High Disciple Hoshijima Ryōhei was ranked as one of Kyōso's Six High Disciples. He was called the "Sōshin of the Kokumon" of the Kurozumi School.[57] This is because he was the one who did the most to put Kyōso's teachings into order. His role was similar to that of Sōshin who as a young man became a disciple of Confucius in that great sage's later years, collecting and arranging his mentor's words and deeds.

Hoshijima sensei was a well-recognized scholar, resembling the High Disciple Kawakami in this respect. He studied under Kamoi Yūzan sensei, a graduate of the official school of Confucianism established by the Tokugawa Shogunate in Tokyo. Later he studied also under Morita Sessai sensei, who was a leading disciple of the well-known scholar of the Chinese classics Rai Sanyō.[58]

Members of the Hoshijima family had long served the Amaki clan (in today's city of Kurashiki), and thus were indirectly also retainers of Lord Ikeda, the head of the Bizen provincial government. Hoshijima sensei had lost his father when quite young and his home was in rather poor circumstances as a result. As a young man he had to walk about three miles each way every day from Amaki to attend Kamoi sensei's classes in Urata, Kojima County. We hear that he studied so diligently after returning home each evening that never a midnight would find him in bed. His fatigue and stress accumulated, and eventually he developed a critical case of tuberculosis.

One day the physician who served the Amaki clan chief came asking about Hoshijima's health. He was surprised to find what a poor condition the boy was in and he spoke to Madam Hoshijima quite sharply. "What are you going to do for this boy? Aren't you going to do something for him, Madam? According to my diagnosis young Makisaburō can't last more than another month. How dare you let him get into this condition? Isn't there something else you can do than just keep him in bed? Isn't he your only son and isn't he supposed to inherit the headship of the Hoshijima family?" He was so angry that he put Madam Hoshijima through this kind of severe questioning.

Madam Hoshijima was a woman, but she had always felt a special closeness to Kyōso. In later years, in fact, she was remembered as one of the

"Three Distinguished Ladies" of Kurozumikyō. Her sense of reliance on him was strong, so strong that she had always assumed that when her own last moment of life would come she would be blessed with divine virtue. It was because she had such a firm confidence that she had felt no particular concern about her son's illness. But when she heard the physician's words she gave another look at her boy. Then she said, "Oh, Doctor, you are right. He does look very feeble and weak. Well, I think it's about time I offered up some prayers for him to receive a divine blessing."

The following morning she told her son, "Makisaburō, today you must come with me to worship at Kaminakano and pray for a blessing. Now, let's leave together right away." At this urging, the seriously ill boy was supposed to cover a distance of almost eleven miles on foot from Amaki to Ohmoto to pay a visit in Kaminakano. The boy was a dutiful and pious son and he took his mother's words as a command not to be questioned. He went with her quietly. His condition actually was quite serious, however. He had gone through long periods of high fever and of taking no food and he was really quite exhausted.

When they reached the outskirts of Chayamachi, not very far from their home, he fell down quite unconscious. Despite the difficult situation, Madam Hosihima calmly performed *majinai* on her boy to encourage him and raise his drooping spirit. Finally they found themselves at Ohmoto, though not before he lost consciousness twice more on the way.

When they arrived at the head household of the Kurozumis they found Kyōso at home, to their good fortune. Madam Hoshijima extended her greetings. "I am here with my son desiring that he be granted a blessing of divine virtue. His condition has reached a critical stage." With this the mother and son stayed at Kyōso's for some time. (It is said that she had been staying there for periods of ten days or more on a number of occasions, as part of her obligations to Kyōso. She would come twice a year, every summer and winter, sewing and mending his bedding and his clothes. He allowed her to stay at his home this way, making herself fully at home there as he would have allowed one of his own relatives.)

Kyōso simply responded to her greeting by saying, "So that is why you are here." No *majinai* ritual was performed. Madam simply stayed on with her son, listening to the sermons and lectures. After some days Hoshijima woke his mother one night, complaining of pain. "It's so painful I can't stand it." Soon he had to go to the toilet. Some terribly foul-smelling discharges came out of him and some haemorrhaging with it. It seemed as if everything in the boy's body was coming out. He was

63

now in an extremely weak condition. All of his energy was exhausted and it seemed he was in peril of his very life. The sick boy somehow managed to crawl back into his bedding.

Now he felt very hungry, so much that he couldn't stand it. He asked his mother, "May I have something to eat?" Since it was midnight, there was nothing special to eat except some cold leftover rice. The story goes that he quickly devoured three bowlfuls of cold rice soaked in cold tea (*o-chazuke*). In later years Hoshijima sensei is said often to have reminisced, "Those bowls of cold rice were so indescribably tasty. Never in my life have I ever enjoyed anything so delicious."

Needless to add, from then on his appetite improved, his vigour returned day by day, and his condition sped towards convalescence. How gracious are the divine virtues!

42. "Know that I, Sakyō, Will Never Leave Anyone without Help Who Reveres Me as Teacher"

In Tamashima, Bitchu Province (today part of Kurashiki City), there lived a devout follower of the faith named Nakanoya Shōbei. He had a high respect for Kyōso, revering him as a true living kami. This gentleman was once infected by a disease that worsened to such a state that he was considered quite beyond any help. He spoke to his family members and relatives who had gathered at his bedside in this way.

"If this is in accord with the divine will, I believe I have no choice. But I only wish I could receive Kyoso's ritual of *majinai* one more time. Then I could leave this world and ascend to Heaven in happiness and without the least regret. If it isn't possible for me to receive his *majinai*, then that is what is going to happen to me for sure. But please listen to me. I still believe that if I could have Kyōso's hands touch me and have him blow on me the breath of *yōki* I will surely be cured. Please go and ask him to come so I can have this last request of mine fulfiled. I beg your help to reach this goal. Every effort to bring about my wish will be most appreciated." Such was his fervent and heartfelt desire.

Those who heard his wish, possibly his last wish, looked at each other with no words to say, at a loss and full of perplexity. You should know that a visit to Kyōso meant covering more than seventeen miles to get there. It would be too late for poor Shōbei, even if they set out right away on this mission to Kaminakano to ask him to come. Besides, Kyōso was always so busy and it might even be impossible for him to respond promptly to this request.

After a silence that lasted some moments, a man sitting quietly in the back thought they could not tell this poor man that he might not last until Kyōso got there. He was at the point of death. So, he explained to him that Kyōso might not be able to come right away, that the main reason would be that he was always so busy. "Oh, I can understand that completely, I am fully aware of it. But there is no time to lose, I am not just going to wait for my death doing nothing. I will do anything that gives a hope of helping me. So, what are you waiting for? Go and get a *kago* and rush me to Kaminakano.[59] What on earth would it matter if I were to die on my way there? I am a dying man in any case." So poignant, so pathetic was his request.

So everyone there decided at once it would be the right thing to do as he asked. They hired a *kago* and they chose three or four of their number to take the sick man to Kaminakano. In tears they all joined in sending him off. They knew their farewell could be a final parting, a journey to be ended by death and bereavement. The travel party left on the seventeen-mile journey quietly and slowly. They left before sunrise but they could not go very fast. By the time night had fallen they were still over a mile from Kaminakano.

At that point they heard a groan from inside the *kago*. When they put it down and looked inside they found their friend had stopped breathing. "Well, this is how far we got with our great effort to bring him to Kaminakano. So, it can't be helped. All we can do now is to go back to Tamashima." They had almost agreed on this conclusion, but one person said, "No, no. We have brought him this far already. We are just a breath from where we are going.[60] It is a real regret. But old Shōbei was asking for Kyōso's *majinai* so eagerly. So, I will quickly run to ask Kyōso's advice. Wait here till I come back with his instructions." There he left them with the *kago*, running off to Kyōso's house.

To their good fortune, Kyōso was at home. He listened to all the details. "So Shōbei was asking for *majinai* so earnestly? Even if he is dead it doesn't matter. Please don't hang back. Bring him here right away, even if he has already become senseless." Encouraged and given hope by his commanding tone, the messenger went back to his friends on the road. He told them he was instructed that even if the poor man was dead they should still bring him to Kyōso without any hesitation. The *kago* bearers rushed the sick man, or rather, the dead man, to Kyōso's place.

They carried Shōbei who had passed away some moments ago, and whose body was now dead and getting cold in the *kago*, and laid him down in the room where the Great Kami was enshrined. They paid their reverence. A Shinto priest, Matsuoka Kiyomi, happened to be present and Kyōso instructed him, "Matsuoka san, please perform the *majinai* ritual on poor Nakanoya, while I pray for him." Since Matsuoka sensei was a Shinto priest, he was in the same profession as Kyōso. He had been studying the Way under him and he was to some extent a believer and follower.

Matsuoka immediately began to perform the *majinai* ritual on the man. When he first touched his body he doubted the ritual could bring any blessing since the man seemed to be dead, already growing cold. In spite of his doubt Matsuoka continued the service, encouraged by the commanding tone of Kyōso's purifying prayer.[61] As time passed the body felt colder and the shadow of death became ever more apparent on the man's face. The point came when Matsuoka thought he might as well stop the ceremony. He looked over to Kyōso, sitting there offering the purification prayer with such poise and with a voice so pure and vital. His poise and his tone were so gracious and full of ease that Matsuoka again felt encouraged to continue. The thought of stopping came back several times, but he kept on with the ceremony for some period of time.

Then after the purification prayer had been repeated several times, and when Matsuoka thought it really would be the last time, suddenly there came a vigorous shout out of the poor man who had been given up for dead. Everyone suddenly knew that he was coming back to life. Again the virtues of the Great Kami were demonstrated through this miraculous blessing, so immense and so gracious.

After this miracle had taken place, Kyōso gave instruction about it to Matsuoka. This is what he said.

"Matsuoka san, you must be mindful of the great benevolence of the Great Kami Amaterasu. Japan, our land that has given birth to us all, is the land of kami. The virtues and the blessings of our land are truly extraordinary. Look! You have seen with your own eyes. The dead one has been restored to life!

"Now, consider Confucius. He was the greatest philosopher China ever gave to the world. He is regarded as the greatest sage. No one else can be compared to him. His kind, or another equal to him, will never again appear, not for thousands of years yet to come. The number of Confucius's disciples is said to have run to about three thousand. Among them were seventy-two disciples who were well versed in the classic Chinese arts, including etiquette, music, archery, horseback riding, calligraphy, and mathematics. Of course you know about the ten disciples who . had shown the most distinguished development in these arts, the ones known as the 'Ten Wise Men'.

"From the standpoint of virtue only four of them, Yen Yuan, Min Tzuch'ien, Jan Po-niu, and Chung-kung deserved the highest recognition.[62] Jan Po-niu was the most advanced among these four in pursuing personal virtue. But he came down with some sort of serious disease. Confucius paid Po-niu a visit inquiring about his health, taking hold of his hand through a window. 'It is killing him!' he said. 'It is the appointment of Heaven, alas! That such a man should have such a sickness! That such a man should have such a sickness!'[63] Confucius was thinking, 'Oh, I am to be abandoned by this man. This must be his fate and his destiny. Oh what sadness it is that a person of such high virtue should come down with such a disease! Oh what a sorrow! What a pity!'

"To sum up my point, it might really be in accord with the divine will that such a disease would take away such a virtuous person. Then all Confucius could do was to say with a sigh, 'What a divine will that allows no alternatives!' Even Confucius had no alternative but to wait for Po-niu's death. He did not, or rather he could not, do anything about it. To put it more exactly, Po-niu's condition was so serious that he found it hopeless and beyond any help. Confucius took leave of Po-niu with deepest lamentation and sincerest regret as one of the most distinguished three or four leading disciples, chosen on the basis of personality and ability from among his 3,000 disciples. 'What a sadness, but we must recognize that it is in accord with the Heavenly Will', was all he could say.

"As far as I am concerned, I am, needless to say, not a person with great virtue and high moral character. In no way can I be compared with Confucius. And yet, though I am a person with no particular graces, the prayer that I have offered has restored life to a man who had been pronounced dead. What a wonder! What a miracle! You must realize it did not happen because of me. I don't deserve the credit. The credit goes to the blessing of the divine land that is alive with such numerous graces. How wonderful it is! The divine blessing of bringing someone back from the dead is such a miracle.

"The more I ponder on this grace, the more I am overwhelmed with it. The ritual of *majinai* is the action that mediates our prayers and carries them to Amaterasu. Our duty is to bring people's hopes and prayers to her. What you have seen and what you have to admit is that this is the kind of grace with which our prayers are answered when we are faithful to our duty. Although I am not a person with great moral character, I was given birth in this divine land, thankfully. I was given divine instruction and I have preached the Great Way of life. It is my utmost and ultimate mission and duty to have all people in this world recognize the supreme and immense virtues and blessings of Amaterasu.

"Know that I, Sakyō, shall never leave anyone without help who reveres me as Teacher. Know that I, Sakyō, shall never leave anyone without help who reveres me as Teacher. Know that I, Sakyō, shall never leave anyone without help who reveres me as Teacher. Never shall this Sakyō forget or disappoint a person who so singlemindedly seeks and trusts this Sakyō as his Teacher, his instructor and saviour, who places his confidence and reliance in me, who relies on my guidance, my help and support."

Matsuoka sensei, who had been listening to Kyōso's explanation, was much moved and touched, especially by these last words. "Never shall this Sakyō forget or disappoint a person who seeks and trusts this Sakyō as his Teacher, his instructor and saviour, who reveres me, who places confidence and reliance in me. Never shall I forget a person who seeks me out so singlemindedly, who relies on my guidance, my help and support, so devotedly."

These commanding words struck into Matsuoka's heart so intensively and with such grace, we are told, that his head bowed down quite spontaneously. These words and the singular experience of restoring a dead man back to life evoked heartfelt respect and reverence in Matsuoka. He was in one sense a colleague of Kyōso but in another respect he had always held a special high regard for him. Now, after this had happened, Matsuoka gave Kyōso even higher reverence, and, we are told, he asked to be added to his group of disciples. That was very understandable and only natural.

High Disciple Tokio composed the following *waka* that expresses what he felt about Po-niu and this miraculous blessing of Kyōso.

Poor old Po-niu,
  In China was he given birth,
    not here in Japan;
  If born in the divine land
  Heav'n might not have taken him.

43. Performing *Majinai* on a Hopeless Patient

This is a well-known anecdote that Madame Teruko, Kyōso's second daughter, is said to have passed on.

One day a person suffering from a serious skin disease happened to arrive in the city of Okayama after years of wandering from his faraway home. He had been on a sad and miserable journey with no particular destination in mind. He had to beg for his food. He was in terrible shape with his face half gone and his physical condition gradually deteriorating to the worst, to such a point he could hardly stand it any more.

Still, there were some sympathizers who showed pity on him and gave him a kind suggestion, "Why don't you go about two and a half miles west from here where there is a village called Kaminakano. A living kami lives there named Kurozumi. They say those who visit him and receive his blessing of healing prayer are sure to be cured of their illness and relieved of their pain. Why not go to see him?"

He only half listened to this and with doubt. No, with seventy per cent doubt and thirty per cent hope. More exactly, with only a few per cent of hope. He was in a desperate situation. He had tried many things, all of which were supposed to be good for him. Nothing had worked out. Still, he was somewhat moved by the kindness he was shown and there was nowhere else for him to go. He decided to try this place called Kaminakano. Walking slowly, dragging his handicapped legs, he finally arrived at the gate of Kyōso's house.

To his good fortune, Kyōso was at home. The poor fellow asked him for a blessing of healing prayer. Sadly looking down at him from his front door and seeing his miserable, painful condition, Kyōso could not conceal or contain his compassion. He invited the man in. "Oh, please do take off your *zōris* and come up to this room. I will be glad to perform *majinai* on you."

Kyōso beckoned the poor man into the main room of his house, the special room where Great Kami was enshrined and worshipped. Most likely the poor fellow had been forced to leave his own home, rejected by his relatives and friends as well as his own family, a victim of his dreadful disease. Now he was meeting a plump, well-fleshed, kind-looking person with a respectful personality. No doubt it was a great surprise and unexpected happiness that much impressed him as he was shown into the splendid main room.

After offering some purification prayers Kyōso performed his *majinai* conscientiously. The season was midsummer. Kyôso, who weighed well over 200 pounds, blessed the patient so devotedly and wholeheartedly that he was sweating all over his body. Sweat was dripping down all over his face. The same hands he had placed on the half-gone face of the man were now on his own face to wipe off the sweat.

At that moment Madam Iku entered the room, returning from some errand outside. When she saw Kyôso's face she gave a terrible, involuntary cry of surprise. She shouldn't be blamed for that. It was quite natural. Kyōso's hands and face were covered with the man's ugly, bloody pus.

As for the patient, it was the first time since he had been infected with his horrible disease, or perhaps it was the first time in his whole life that he had experienced such a deep impression of sympathy. He forgot his physical and mental pain, worry, and despair. When he saw what he owed to Kami through the guidance of Kyōso he began to think of the divine virtue and blessings of Kami. And when he was offered a corner of an outbuilding to sleep in he was again touched with gratitude.

When the man had gone out of the main room, Madam Iku recovered her composure and said, "It was good to perform *majinai*. But please remember that in this room we enshrine the Great Kami. We must keep it clean. I don't believe it is good to stain and soil this room. I don't worry about you giving healing prayers for people, but when I saw you had made yourself so dirty, I was just overcome by surprise."

Hearing her say this, Kyōso responded gently,

"You may be right, but … . When I saw how that poor fellow looked who came here with the express purpose of seeing me, putting his whole hope and confidence in me and wholly relying on my help, I was overtaken by pity and sympathy. He looked so miserable and hopeless. That is why I could not resist welcoming him into this room. Who could be more miserable than that fellow? He is a person who exactly fits that word.

"When that thought came to me I realized I had to perform *majinai* on him so he would be blessed with the divine virtue of the Great Kami. With my whole mind full of this I forgot everything and didn't think about the bloody pus getting on my hands. I didn't even realize my hands were covered with it. Since sweat was running all over my face, I used them to wipe myself without thinking about it. I had no idea my face was getting so dirty. Well, whatever happens now, if we are to fear diseases and feel that such things are dirty and polluting, how could we pray for those who are suffering? Now let's watch him carefully. Surely he will be blessed with divine virtue."

As expected, before long the fellow was blessed with wonderful divine virtue and was able to enjoy a complete restoration to health.

44. The Amazing Work of the Happiness Spirit[64]

This is a story about Ishida Tsuruemon Koretada. He was a samurai, a highly-placed retainer of the Bizen clan with an annual stipend of 300 *koku*.[65] He was a devout follower who had shown deep faith in the Way. While he was serving his required alternate year of service in Tokyo,[66] he was infected with a serious case of scrofula.[67] Although his term of service was not over, he was given special leave to return to Okayama. There happened to be opportunity for this when the Bizen *daimyō* returned to Okayama for a visit, so that he was assigned to accompany him.

When they had got as far as Ohkuradani (in the modern city of Akashi in Hyōgo Prefecture just east of Okayama) Ishida's condition became critical. So, he was relieved of his duty to go with the *daimyō* and allowed to stay there at an inn so he could recuperate.

As it turned out, Ishida's scrofula worsened to the point that his whole throat hardened till only a little part of it the size of a finger was still soft. Even soup could not pass his throat. Because it was a tubercular infection that caused his illness, it is not surprising that his case was pronounced hopeless by a physician. Ishida expressed his sincere regret that he was unable to fulfil his obligation as a samurai to serve his lord and that he had to leave this world with his life half unlived. He maintained a calm composure as befitted his samurai pride and self-control. With his devout faith in the Way strengthening him, he kept his heart within himself.[68]

Still, he came to think that if he were in Okayama he could receive Kurozumi Sensei's *majinai*. Then surely he would be blessed with a recovery. This thought was his only regret and he offered his prayer only privately, within his heart.

Gradually his condition grew more serious. The day arrived when his people who were with him, nursing him, were helpless and at a loss what to do. At that moment, to their amazement, the patient, so seriously ill, got up from his bedding and headed towards the entrance of the inn. No one was there but Ishida extended a heartfelt farewell out of the door with his head cordially bowed. Then he soon got back into bed, repeating, "What a blessing! So gracious! What a blessing! So gracious!"[69] Those attending him naturally thought he had gone out of his mind, and they only worried the more. In their concern they asked Ishida, "What happened? Is there something wrong with you?"

Ishida answered, "Just a little while ago Kurozumi Sensei came asking about me. He said, 'I see you are in trouble. Let me perform a *majinai* on you.' With this, he put his fingers into my throat and took out a strange thing. He said it was the root of my disease. It looked like the fruit of the lantern plant.[70] He handed me a handful of these fruits. He was about to give me a second handful of them, but then I felt my illness was relieved and I could breathe easier. And then I just went to the door to bid him farewell." His words were filled with joy and gratitude, and his tears were flowing as he spoke.

Ishida's followers thought all of this very strange, not like their master at all. It was hard to credit what he said. But his condition showed a surprising improvement from that moment on, entirely different from what they had seen a few minutes before. And since Master Ishida clearly was now so vigorous they just looked at each other and joined in their joy at seeing his recovery.

Ishida then could not stay still. He thought that since his disease was completely cured, he couldn't linger in Ohkuradani any longer. He must return to Okayama to report his recovery to Lord Ikeda to relieve his lord's anxiety over his illness. The next morning he set off to complete his journey home. When he got to Okayama he did not go first to his own home but went straight to Ohmoto. There he reported what had happened, omitting no detail. In this way Ishida extended his heartfelt, sincere gratitude to Kyōso and to Great Kami.

Listening to Ishida's account, Kyōso said, "That is such a thankful thing. Of course, as to what appears on the surface, I was here at home. I have never been to Harima Province, I never flew there. But your family members did come to me to report your serious condition and asked me to pray for a bestowal of grace on you. I instantly offered my prayer for your well-being, 'Oh, Great Kami, please bestow on poor Ishida an early recovery.' I prayed with all my might, earnestly and heartily. Throughout the prayer the only thought I had was my concern about you.

"I know that my Happiness Spirit flew to where you were to bring about this miraculous grace, showing such an amazing blessing. That was such an inexpressible good fortune. It happened because of your own outstanding faith in the Way, as you have walked in this faith over the years. In those days of miserable sickness you never forgot the deep confidence you had placed in Great Kami. Never did a doubt disturb you. You had a firm confidence and belief in Kami and your sincere wish to be blessed by divine grace never wavered in any way. This belief and trust, and your faith and confidence, are in themselves proofs of your sincere faith in the divine virtues and blessings. In fact, it was your sincerity that moved Kami to accord you this blessing. How auspicious and bountiful! How auspicious and bountiful!" In this way Kyōso offered his joy and his reverence to Amaterasu.

45. The Benefits Realized through Laughter

There was a sick person living in the city of Okayama who had been suffering a serious case of tuberculosis. Kyōso was invited to his place to perform a ritual of *majinai* on him. After the ritual Kyōso told him, "I am sorry to say it, but I have been thinking ever since I got here that this room is very gloomy. It is natural that your illness would have that result, and that your heart is gloomy with all your troubles and difficulties. And the members of your family also are in a gloomy and dark mood all the time. Furthermore, the doors and *shōji* screens are kept closed, making the room even darker. It is full of gloominess.

"Although your situation is understandable and reasonable, gloominess is taboo for one who is devoted in faith. Vitalizing your life is the divine way of things. Enjoying your life is the divine way, so practise complying with the holy heart of Great Kami. Please try to get a spark of cheerfulness into yourself. The first thing you should do is to laugh. It looks like you have not laughed for years. From this very day try to laugh as much and as often as possible."

The man replied, "Thank you, sir. But it is hard for me to laugh. I am not in a mood for it. How can I laugh?" Kyōso gave him this reply, "I can only say, 'Try to laugh. Do your best.' Although you have no reason to laugh you should try anyhow. You might just have to do it on purpose. Open your mouth wide open and say, 'ha, ha, ha'. I'm sure it will be easy for you. Give it a try."

All through the night the patient kept pondering this. "To laugh on purpose might not be so hard. I think I could do that. If it really would relieve me of my illness it would be an easy way to be cured." He started trying to laugh. But since he felt nothing to laugh at he found no joy in it. He thought how ridiculous it was even to try. With reluctance, again and again, he tried to laugh. "Ha, ha, ha."

Then he happened to notice that the paper-covered lantern was reflecting his shadow on the *fusuma* screen. His face was gaunt and rawboned, no flesh was left on his cheeks, and his mouth was moving in an awkward way as he seriously tried with all his might to laugh. It dawned on him how grotesque his shadow was looking. It was extremely funny! Suddenly he saw how comic it was! No one would be able to keep from laughing! It was an unexpected experience for him, after trying on purpose to laugh for no reason at all. Spontaneously he burst into real laughter. The humour was suddenly more than he could hold in. For some moments his sides were shaking with merriment.

The unusual sound woke up the members of his family and they came running to his room. The story and the funny shadow made them all laugh. Of course, the patient in turn was provoked to join them in even more laughter. Their sides were shaking as they were laughing, all of them.

The laughing he had not enjoyed for years relieved him of the congestion of blood in his stomach. His blood circulation showed sudden improvement. With his abdominal muscles activated, his appetite was enhanced and he began to feel hungry. Best of all, his gloominess all faded away and he felt happy and joyful. Although he ate only a little at his next meal he ate it with a hearty appetite. That night he sank into a deep and profound sleep such as he had been missing for years. His condition improved from the following morning on and eventually he was able to overcome the incurable disease.

It was indeed a blessing of *warai-harai*, "laughing-purification", because the patient was able to purify himself through laughter.

46. Chant "How Gracious!" Ten Thousand Times a Day

There was a samurai of the Bizen clan, of a good lineage and with a hefty annual stipend, who was stricken with a very serious skin ailment. The disease gradually wasted away his face so that he looked really bad. Finally he decided to pay a visit to the Teacher of Kaminakano to receive a blessing. He went to Kyōso's house and listened to his teaching. Kyōso told him, "You have nothing to worry about. It is of first importance, however, to understand and believe that gratitude is the greatest of all divine blessings. So, start by chanting 'How gracious!' (*Arigatai*) a hundred times a day. Do it with all your heart."

The samurai took this as a very easy thing to do. However, his chanting brought him no rewards.

So he paid Kyōso another visit, saying that nothing had happened. He received the instruction, "Then chant these words a thousand times a day." This was the response he got. Although it was a little more troublesome and difficult to do this, the samurai carried out the assignment for a period of seven days, but he still saw no improvement. For the third time he went to Kyōso, who told him, "Please continue the same, but increase your daily chants to ten thousand times. You are sure to be blessed." Since the man was a sincere and good person he followed this counsel and did what he was told: ten thousand chants of "How Gracious!" every day.

On the seventh day of doing these ten thousand chants, suddenly his fever increased, followed by a vomiting of blood. Then he was completely exhausted, so that all he could do was take to his bed. But he was able to sleep so deeply and so well that he could not remember when last he had slept so well. When he woke up the next morning he felt refreshed. And to his surprise, the swellings and boils on his face, arms and legs were gone and all the festering spots had disappeared from his body. His face and body were clean.

As one would expect, from that day the happy, fortunate samurai became an earnest follower. It is said that for the rest of his life he never missed a single regular meeting at Kaminakano.

47. What Kyōso Taught His Two High Disciples about Their Self-Conceit

Kyōso gave spiritual admonition to both his two principal disciples, Akagi and Tokio, but the lessons he gave them were entirely different.[71] This was especially so on the topic of self-conceit, or pride (*manshin*). To High Disciple Akagi, who was always vigorous and high-spirited, he said, "Akagi san, you have to be careful about self-conceit. You must know it could even take your life."

High Disciple Tokio was much more moderate and temperate than Akagi. He was reserved in everything he did. To him he gave this encouraging instruction. "Tokio san, someone who wants to be successful in this world has to assert himself, even getting close to the point of self-conceit, up to the very verge of it. Without doing this you won't be able to accomplish big tasks."

Here we have an example of how Kyōso taught in entirely different ways, depending on the person's character to whom he was addressing his teaching. This is an extreme instance but it is a familiar story that shows clearly how he adapted his teaching to the actual people he was dealing with.[72] The form of his teaching was "people-oriented".

48. Take Care Not to Allow Others Make You Feel Self-Conceited

High Disciple Akagi, who had so repeatedly been taught how bad self-conceit was, came up to Kyōso one day and said to him seriously and with feeling, "Oh, Kurozumi Sensei, you have taught me politely, over and over, so that I know it way down in the marrow of my bones and body, how fearful a thing self-conceit is. Sir, please feel sure that neither now nor ever will there be any chance that I will be self-conceited. Don't let it worry you any more." Hearing Akagi's assurances, Kyōso said, "Akagi san, your words give me great pleasure and relief. So, let us now go beyond that. Be careful not to be self-conceited because of what others say to you. Please take heed of this."

This was truly a most kind and considerate teaching. Akagi had promised he would always keep Kyōso's teaching in mind. He would never again be self-conceited or proud. His determination about that was serious and Kyōso appreciated Akagi's serious feeling. Then he advised Akagi to take care that others should not have this effect on him. The lesson was not harsh and the tone of it was not at all negative.

We often see that people address their teachers as "sensei, sensei", out of their sincere respect and faith. For those who are teachers it's a very risky thing. Words of praise can send you right up into the sky feeling celebrated without anyone really intending that. It is just when others are expressing the most well-meaning and good-faith words that you can be raised to the highest point of self-conceit, up to the most perilous summit of it. One should be especially attentive and cautious at such a time. This possible sense of superiority is what Kyōso was pointing out as so dangerous, so full of possible destructiveness.

For this reason Kyōso advised, "Akagi san, please try to avoid letting others make you feel proud. Please do take care."

In later years, High Disciple Akagi improved his personality to such a level that many of his friends and fellow followers revered him as a living kami. Some even worshipped him with hand-clappings.[73] Contrary to his own wish and promise to Kyōso, Akagi at that time went up again to a high point of self-conceit and again he lost his eyesight. But as soon as he remembered Kyōso's instruction to him he repented, full of remorse for his failure to follow the lesson he had received. Then he was blessed with a second recovery from blindness. Surely this time Akagi sensei learned with sincere gratitude the invaluable teaching he had received from Kyōso.

49. Self-Conceit without Education

High Disciple Akagi was not the only one who was admonished by Kyōso on self-conceit. He spoke to others about it whenever he thought it was necessary. He admonished many people when he found them to be proud. Pride, or self-conceit, is probably the pit of error most people are apt to fall into, the mistake the easiest to make. Once when a group of High Disciples was discussing the Way this topic came up: "How difficult to follow is Kyōso's teaching on self-conceit", and "That is the most difficult of his lessons to live up to." Together they discussed it with care, recollecting all Kyōso had said about it.

When everyone present had said what was on their mind, Ishida Rokuzaemon,[74] a tile-maker from Futsukaichi, who was listening quietly to the discussion from the back of the room near the door, opened his mouth to say solemnly, "I happened to be listening to your discussion for a few minutes. I heard you gentlemen saying that self-conceit is the most difficult instruction to follow. That is quite natural for you folks. I am sure it is a reasonable concern for you gentlemen. You should bear in mind how blessed you are in every way. You have education, learning, knowledge, social status, good family lineage, and wealth. It is quite understandable that you would be proud of these things. Pride easily shows itself. You don't bother with the kind of trouble religious ascetics put themselves to.

"I am different from you gentlemen. Thanks to my good fortune I am a maker of roof tiles. I have no family pedigree, no status and no wealth, and I never received an education. I have almost no learning, I am ignorant and know nothing. So, there is almost no chance of my being self-conceited. Without even trying, I am absolutely free of self-conceit. For some time I have been thinking how fortunate I am not to be blessed with any education."

The High Disciples looked at each other and couldn't think of anything to say to all that. But the instant Rokuzaemon felt self-conceited this way there came Kyōso's commanding and admonishing words from outside the door in the next room, "Rokuzaemon, you must understand something about this attitude of yours. It is nothing but self-conceit, nothing but pride in having no education."

50. Fear of Leg-Swelling Overcomes a Headache

There was a lady of a wealthy family in a suburb of Okayama who was quite a self-willed and self-indulgent person. It was perhaps a result of the high social status her family enjoyed. Full details about her weren't ever recorded, but she may have been a person of a hysterical sort. She frequently complained of headaches. At someone's suggestion she invited Kyōso in to have his *majinai* performed on her. However, because she was so wrapped up in herself she didn't understand the value of the ceremony. She had no idea of how it could be a source of blessing and it had no effect on her.

After he had paid her two or three visits, Kyōso became quite familiar with the lady's temperament. On one visit he said to her, "Madam, you seem to be concerned only about headaches. It is understandable that headaches are painful and hard to put up with. You should know, however, that no one has ever lost her life because of a headache. It has never happened. Well. There isn't a chance that your life is at risk. We do have to admit it, that's a piece of good fortune for you. You have to accept it, that is a good thing.

"I have heard, though, that there is an epidemic around here of a disease called *hayachō*.[75] It is an illness that causes swelling of some parts of the body. According to what they say, once the swelling appears, next comes a high fever and eventually death comes within a few days. They say hardly anybody recovers from this disease. Excuse my being so forward about it but they also say that those who get this disease are mostly about your age. Please do take care of yourself. Swellings appear down in the lower half of the body, they say, mostly in the legs. One symptom is a tired and weary feeling in the legs. Take special care if you notice any symptom like that." This is what Kyōso taught the lady before he left her home that day.

For three or four days after that she was full of worry and fright, so much that not only during the day but also at night when she woke from her sleep she checked her legs. Since she didn't have any special responsibilities that might keep her busy she didn't have anything to think about except her fear. Later Kyōso paid her a visit of inquiry. It was on a day when she again found to her delight and satisfaction that none of these symptoms had appeared. She reported, "Oh, sir. Thank you for warning me about the epidemic called *hayachō*. Thanks to your kind advice I haven't seen a sign of it during this whole time. I am so thankful."

She offered Kyōso her sincere and hearty thanks. He gave her a beaming smile. "Madam, that is simply wonderful. What a gracious relief! By the way, how's the headache you've been suffering?" "Oh my! Come to think of it, I have to admit that since the last time you were here it slipped my mind completely. Not for a second have I remembered my headaches."

51. The Old Mother of the Hata Family

The elderly Madam Hata, who lived in the city of Okayama in the days of Kyōso, was well known for her frequent visits to Ohmoto. She was highly respected for her agreeable good nature and also for her frankness and her amusing words and actions. He seems to have appreciated these qualities and to have talked with her quite freely, but also with a lot of special care and attention. He used to preach about something we might call "living vigour and vitality", or perhaps "living things and creatures."[76] Sometimes in his preaching he said, "While I am preaching, some 'living thing' may jump out, so always be watchful and don't be taken off guard. Be wide awake during my preaching so as to catch it."

In response, Madam Hata commented, "Sir, you often preach about the 'living thing', but why is it that not a single mouse has appeared"? We are sure that Madam Hata's comment caused everyone there to burst out laughing.

One day Mother Hata said to Kyōso in a somewhat protesting tone, "Kurozumi Sensei, I notice that you are always smiling. Why are you always so happy?" Hearing this, he responded with an even more beaming smile, "Oh, that? Well, it is true that not on every day is there some happy event. But I insist on smiling anyway. Don't you agree with me that you would say the same sort of thing if I were grumbling over things that you don't think are worth grumbling about?"

Since Mother Hata was a straightforward sort of lady she would speak to Kyōso during *majinai*, pointing to her shoulder and telling him,

79

"Sensei, this is where the pain is", or, "That is where I feel sore." In this way, it is said, she was telling Kyōso how to do his ritual, pointing out parts of her body where she felt she needed a blessing. This is how she received his sacred healing ceremony. If he had been the sort of person who took pride in expressing his insight and understanding he would have given her a good scolding and told her, "You must know that *majinai* is not massage!" But Kyōso would say, when she came to his house, "Are you here again to have me massage you?" It is said that Kyōso performed his *majinai* most attentively for her, rubbing and massaging her shoulders and limbs with the greatest care.

52. What Could We See if There Were No Sun?

There was a famous millionaire of Ajino Village, Kojima County, Bizen Province, named Koyano Buzaemon. He was also known as Tadaya after the name of his store. He was a devout follower of the Way, as we know from the fact that his name was recorded in *The Register of Disciples* as having entered the membership of the disciples in 1846.[77] Buzaemon often invited Kyōso to his home since he appreciated his sermons as an incomparable pleasure and a matchless delight.

Once he spent not a small sum of money to buy a Dutch telescope and he showed it proudly to Kyōso. "Sensei, the other day I bought this amazing telescope. With this powerful piece of equipment you can see places that are sixteen or seventeen miles away as though they are right up close. Depending on the weather, you can see the province of Sanuki.[78] I would like you to take a look." Kyōso said, "Well, that is really very kind of you." He took the telescope into his hands and with it he had a good look at the scenery. He was very happy, beaming with smiles like a child. Seeing him take such pleasure in it, Koyano said, "Sensei, don't you agree with me that this instrument is very useful? To tell you the truth, I paid fifty *ryō* for it.[79] I think it is really worth the money.

"This reminds me of something else. Sensei, you have been preaching that gratitude to the Sun Kami is all that is important in life. But money is also important. And sometimes the almighty dollar (*O-kane-sama*) is what it all comes down to. Money is the bottom line." Nozaki was saying this with a good deal of pride. Kyōso said, "Well, I am sure you can see quite well with this at night when it is dark." Koyano replied, "What makes you think you can use it at night? That doesn't make any sense." Kyōso responded instantly, "So it is because of the blessing of the Sun Kami that you can see so well with this telescope in the daytime."

It is said that the millionaire owner of the Tadaya store found himself at a loss. He had not a word to say in response.

53. "Paste This Poem on the Back of Your Navel"

There was a certain townsman who had been poor for years and he felt very discouraged about it. He was often in a gloomy mood, easily provoked to anger, his mind filled with evil thoughts. Though he didn't act on those thoughts, still, no matter what he did it came out badly. His fortunes gradually dwindled, he was going downhill. Finding that he didn't know what to do to change things, he decided to invite the well-known Kurozumi Sensei to his home. He would have an opportunity to listen to Kyōso's preaching and to be graced with a blessing, he thought. And his request was answered by Kyōso's taking the trouble to visit him.

After the sermon the man said, "Sir, the sermon I just heard was so impressive and taught me so much. May I offer my sincere gratitude to you? An idea came to me while I was listening. Would you be willing to write some of your fine *waka* for me? I would be much obliged. Although I am not very good at my religious practice, I would at least make some effort to do whatever you will write."

Here was Kyōso's answer to this cordial request. "You have thought of a very good point. I will be glad to write something for you. Please bring me some paper."[80] Kyōso quite willingly accepted the request and wrote the following *waka*, a well-known one that goes,

Do not be angry
nor let worry upset you
never do evil
Let all your prosperity
come from Heavenly blessing.

He wrote it quickly and easily ten times on ten sheets of paper.

Seeing this, the poor man said, "I know this must be a wonderful *waka* but I'm sure others could be added. I hope you won't mind writing a few others also?" "Oh, no, I will write the same *waka*. Paste these papers up in your house wherever you can see them easily. Just one poem is enough, teaching, "Don't be angry!" "Don't let worry upset you!" "Never do evil!" Be attentive to it and devote yourself singlemindedly to following this lesson. Within a few moments his famous calligraphic talent had shown itself on twenty more sheets of paper with twenty more copies of the same *waka*.

Satisfied, the man happily began pasting up the sheets of paper, starting at the entrance of his house and going back to the kitchen, wherever he thought his eyes would easily fall on them. He even put one up in the toilet. He thought that if he didn't have enough he would ask for more copies. There were exactly thirty of them and he pasted them all around, but when he was done he had one sheet left.

The honest man came back to Kyōso and said, "Kurozumi Sensei, thank you so much. But I have to return one of them to you because I couldn't find a place for it." "Oh, there isn't any place for it?" "Sir, I can't think of anywhere else to put them up. I'm pretty sure every sheet is just where it is needed." "Well, all right. If that's the case, paste the last one on the back of your navel."[81]

54. "You Are Not to Become a Kami! You Are Not to Become a Kami!"

One of Kyōso's prominent disciples was Nonoue Tatewaki. Before that he had been a Shinto priest from Mimasaka Province, north of Okayama. As regards priestly rank, he was a colleague of Kyōso at that time and enjoyed a similar social status, or perhaps somewhat higher. He was a learned man and in his community he had a high reputation for outstanding discernment and insight. Once when he was ill a friend suggested he go and listen to a lecture of Kyōso's. It was the first time he had done so. He had his own ideas, however, and he could not accept the content of what he heard. This made a kind of obstruction blocking his heart like a plug, so that he was not able to understand the gracious quality of what he was hearing.

When the lecture was over, Kyōso performed on him a ritual of *majinai*. He pressed Nonoue's stomach and recited the following *waka*.

> May our attachments
>   and every cloud of craving
>   all be blown away;
> Kami wishes our spirit
>   in this original state.

The instant Kyōso finished reciting, and at the point when he blew his *yōki* on him, Nonoue's learning and discernment were all cleared away.

All the hindrances and stumbling blocks that had filled his breast were gone. He was put into a state where he was able to accept the gracious blessing of Great Kami.

Before very long Nonoue submitted his written pledge to accept Kyōso as his Teacher in pursuing the Way devotedly and profoundly, and in spreading it further. After a time he gained a reputation as one of the prominent disciples. Once on a visit to Kyōso he showed him the following *waka*:

> Good it is to know
> through *shugyō* I become
> a divine kami
> Greater then my joy becomes
> enjoying this truth divine.

After reading it, Kyōso placed it in his left hand and slapped his lap with his right hand, strongly admonishing him, "You are not to become a kami! You are not to become a kami!"[82]

As might be expected, Nonoue instantly grasped what was meant, and went out of Kyōso's presence into the next room to rewrite his poem. Soon he returned with this.

> How blessed to know
> that our origin lies in
> oneness with Kami.
> Greater then my joy becomes
> enjoying this truth divine.

Then, giving a special smile to show his delight in seeing that Nonoue's thinking was now in full accord with his own and met his approval, Kyōso remarked, "That is exactly where the core of the Way is!" Then he showed him a *waka* of his own:

> No barrier can
> separate us from divine
> Amaterasu
> What a delight in knowing
> we always are in oneness.[83]

It is an incomparable pleasure always to live in oneness with Kami.

55. Be Humane, But
Don't Drown in Your Humaneness

There was a devout follower who was feeling very great sorrow at sending his parents up to Heaven. He had so much pain from his experience of their death that he could not get over it. He went to Kyōso looking for help in overcoming the bitterness he was feeling. At the same time, he also confessed that his religious practice was not very mature. Kyōso listened quietly to his follower's story and then offered him a ritual of *majinai*. He placed his hand gently on the man's stomach.

Soon he said, "Yes. I surely understand that you have gone through a great deal of trouble while you were nursing your parents over such a long period of time. You must feel very tired and fatigued. From what you said I was concerned that your stomach would be hard and stiff, but, to the contrary, there is no feeling of hardness or stiffness. None of your muscles is stiff at all. They work as smoothly as usual, and your *hara* is full of vigorous *yōki*. You speak of your immature practice, but, to the contrary, your level of practice is admirably high."

Then he added the following words of teaching.

"When death takes parents, or takes children, the sorrow we experience has such misery in it. This is human nature. Those who cannot feel it are lacking in humanity. Recently I heard of a person who boasted how much progress he had made in ascetic practices. He had developed himself to such a point, he said, that he had no need to shed even a drop of tears on the loss of his parent. I thought, 'What a miserable thing to say!' I felt very sorry to know there are people who so misunderstand my teaching. I had to admonish him because I don't remember any time I might have taught the Way in such fashion. How could anyone be so lacking in humanity and fail to understand the true meaning of gratitude! Someone who is like that is really cold-hearted. Remember something about rice paddies, that only when you can see weeds growing in them can you expect them to yield a rich harvest. When even weeds can't grow, then the land is unproductive and no crop of any value can be expected.

"It is most important that you cultivate your humanity, and strengthen the warm feelings of your heart and your sense of pity. At the same time, of course, you must be careful not to let these feelings flood you out. In a rice field we need just the right amount of water. Finding the right balance may seem difficult but this is what our kind of religious practice of the Way is all about." In this considerate and attentive way, it is said, Kyōso instructed his followers.

56. Changing a Man's Heart from Malicious to Merciful

In those days, in the village of Yamada, Oku County, Bizen Province, there dwelt a cotton merchant by the name of Kamezō. By nature he was fastidious, crabby, and hard to please. He had the sort of personality easily tempted to evil. So, his fellow villagers avoided him, even despised and hated him. The village head, Tsunetarō, was a sincere and courteous man. A modern expression that would fit the kind of man he was is "sterling character". From his youth he had felt affection for Kyōso and was familiar with his teachings. So, he kept looking for a way to guide this merchant towards becoming a better sort of person.

On occasion he would invite Kyōso to his home to give a lecture. He wished that the man would come to listen and he urged him to attend. In spite of Tsunetarō's frequent invitations that would give him a chance to hear Kyōso speak, Kamezō wouldn't do it. He said he had no interest in religious beliefs and he hated sermons. He had no ears with which to listen. Since the fellow wouldn't come to a meeting, Tsunetarō could only lament at finding no way to work it out.

As they say, however, it takes time for opportunity to ripen and finally the right time arrived. His daughter was suddenly taken ill with a serious pain in her stomach. Every possible treatment was tried but the pain went on for three full days. So, Tsunetarō thought nothing else could be done but to ask Kyōso to perform *majinai* for her. Then his next concern was whom he might send on the errand to Kaminakano, asking him to do it. At that moment the thought of Kamezō flashed into his mind. The village head thought, "That is the very person I should send on this errand as my messenger. What a good idea! This is such a divine blessing." He entrusted Kamezō with a letter and sent him off to Kaminakano. In the letter he included a line explaining the sort of person Kamezō was and asking that he be given the kind of guidance he needed.

After the ceremony, Kyōso beckoned Kamezō to come close to him. He said, "Thank you so much for your trouble of coming so far. Please feel sure that both the prayer and the *majinai* were offered singleheartedly. In this connection, may I ask you a favour? When you get back, would you please, on my behalf, perform *majinai* on the sick girl? If you do, she will surely be relieved of her illness. I do ask you to follow my words."

Kamezō was much impressed and moved to receive this kind of request directly from a person who was known as a living kami, and in such a polite and respectful fashion. He was completely taken aback. It was not how he was used to being treated. "Oh, no. I am not a worthy enough person. I have no faith in any religion, none at all. And I'm a little ashamed of it, but I must admit I have never worshipped any of the kami. Oh, no. It would not be the right thing for me to do at all. It isn't suitable. I can never do such a thing." With his face blushing beetroot-red, Kamezō asked to be excused from this task.

Hearing this, Kyōso said in an even more friendly way, "Oh, no, Kamezō san. That is no reason to hold back. Please know that it is for my own sake that I am asking you. I want you to take my place." With this, he gave a strong breath of *yōki* on the palm of Kamezō's right hand.

Kamezō bid Kyōso goodbye and set off for Tsunetarō's house with his heart embraced by a reverent emotion he had never felt before. He reported the details of his mission, to the great joy of the village head. The attitude Tsunetarō showed to Kamezō, however, was very serious and polite. He gave him full observance of every courtesy.

Kamezō was helped to dress formally in *haori* and *hakama* and ushered to a high-position seat. Then he was requested to perform the *majinai* in the way he had been instructed. Helplessly, Kamezō closed his eyes, prayed, and performed *majinai* with full attention and sincerity. Then, when he was through, it was found, to everyone's amazement, that the young girl's pain had subsided.

The miracle amazed not only the patient but everyone who was there. We needn't doubt that the person most surprised was Kamezō himself. What a remarkable thing, how full of meaning for us all! What a demonstration of the marvellous power of divine virtue! What a tribute to human sincerity! Kamezō was so impressed and moved and full of shame and regret for his maliciousness in the past. This feeling came gushing out of his heart, there were no means to suppress it. Needless to say, he soon showed himself to be an enthusiastic and devout follower.

As a wise saying has it, "Extremes in wickedness make for extremes in goodness." From then on the deep and intensive faith of Kamezō was quite astonishing. Many miracles resulted from his *majinai*, it should be noted. An important one concerned the mother of Tsunetarō who had been bedridden for a number of years with some kind of paralysis. Kamezō's prayer relieved it completely. Tsunetarō was truly surprised that this could happen and also he was puzzled by it.

One day he went to see Kyōso and discussed his perplexities with him. "Sensei, let me tell you what has happened" – and he told the story. "I must admit my gratitude for divine blessing has been deepened because of how my mother has been helped. But I am baffled. There is a point I don't understand, something I'm not sure about. I have often thought about it but I haven't been able to find an answer. Sir, I'm sorry to be so forward, but would you allow me to ask you?" "Of course, whatever the problem may be, please don't hesitate to say what your uncertainty is."

"It really is a source of doubt to me. Sir, as you know my mother had been bedridden for ten or more years. I asked your *majinai* several times, but unfortunately she showed no sign of improvement. I was prepared for the worst because of the nature of her illness and the fact that the many ceremonies had no effect and also because of how old she is. Now, to my surprise, she was cured after a single *majinai* was performed by Kamezō. I am just amazed that while the many prayers of Sensei showed no effect, only a single one done by Kamezō who was regarded as wickedness itself was effective on my mother. This is the point that completely bewilders me."

"Oh, so that is your doubt. Well, 'The Way is One', and, 'The Virtue is One'. It is difficult to say for whose *majinai* the blessing may show up. We don't know who will bring it out. That is why the divine virtue and blessing is so gracious. Further, suppose that I am the trunk of a tree. More beautiful flowers and larger ones bloom on new branches than on an old trunk and on old branches. You must know that trunks, branches, even flowers originate from Heaven as divine blessing in that form and they grow from roots that spread under the ground.

"We don't always see them, but the divine blessings become the roots which in turn make it possible for the tree to flourish. When I say in my lectures, 'The Way shall prosper like a tree', it is exactly this point I am making. It is such a gracious and thankworthy thing. Everything has its origin in the divine virtue. All comes forth from Kami. I know that words and reasons don't make it very clear. But, I am sure that once you have had the full experience it will be easy for you to get the full insight."

After this earnest and thoughtful admonition, Kyōso opened the sliding door (*shōji*) and asked Tsunetarō to look at the plum trees in his garden in full bloom. The blossoms were so vigorous and they extended out so strongly. When the two of them looked closely, they saw that the largest numbers of flowers were blooming on the newest twigs.

57. Kyōso Was Able to Pay Double What He Owed and the Fish Peddler's Wife Was Blessed with an Easy Delivery

One day the fish peddler who served Kyōso's family came to collect his account, which amounted to one *bu*.[84] "I know what you owe is such a small amount and I shouldn't ask you to pay a bill before the usual time. But the fact is that my wife is very sick. She is about to deliver a child and her labour is going very slowly. She is in some pain and I can't leave home to sell my fish. So, I have no cash on hand to buy rice for our house. This is why I've come to you."

Since Madam Iku was not at home and he had no money with him at the time, Kyōso said, quite thoughtfully, "So if your wife enjoys an easy delivery your mind will be put at rest?" "Yes, sir. If only her delivery goes smoothly I will be able to go on my regular round peddling fish." "Oh, now I understand what kind of trouble is worrying you. Let's go to your home to do a *majinai* for your wife."

With this, the two set out with lightened hearts for the fish peddler's home. Since his wife was lying groaning in the house, which was small and all disordered inside, Kyōso was unable to go in to see her. He gave his *majinai* at the entrance and then called inside, "Now you are sure to be blessed with an easy delivery." With these words, said in a rather commanding tone, he left the house. Not long after that the woman did have an easy delivery of her child, just as Kyōso had said.

That evening one of Kyōso's disciples came to him, reporting on the results of some missionary activity they had done on his behalf. "We were really blessed with divine virtue. It was such a bountiful time and so gracious!" With this, the disciple handed Kyōso three *ryō* he had received as a thank offering. Kyōso accepted it with a reverent attitude, but then he took out two *bu* from the three *ryō*, and said, "Since I have a need for two *bu* I will accept only that much. I accept them with thanks."

He returned the rest to the disciple, who replied, "Sensei, I can't take this. The followers gave it for you, sir, to thank you for your service and for your virtue." The disciple refused to accept the offer and tried to give the money back, but he was forced to take it. At that moment the peddler came to Kyōso's house to offer his gratitude for the easy delivery his wife was able to enjoy. Kyōso handed him the two *bu* he had just received and gave an apology for the late payment. When the peddler tried to return one *bu*, saying, "Your account was just one *bu*", Kyōso answered, "No, no. Please take the extra one as interest." The man was rather embarrassed, but, it is said, he returned home with a reverent feeling about Kyōso's virtues and filled with gratitude and happiness.

58. Ginjibei's Sermon

At Kyōso's recommendation, Ginjibei once went up to the platform to speak. Since it was his fidelity and devotion he was noted for, he was truly a man of deeds, not of words. Presenting a sermon was by no means something he was good at. Even more, it may have been the first time he ever did such a thing. Anyway, his presentation was a failure so awful it would be better not to talk about it. If it had been short or if he had stopped sooner it would have been better. But alas, the lecturer was no one but honest Ginjibei and he kept right on going.

With Kyōso's strong recommendation backing him up, he gave his presentation vigorously, with all his strength. Whenever a topic seemed to come to an end he would go on with "Er, er, well, well, as you know, ..." The whole audience got fed up listening to his long-winded and boring speech.

Needless to say, not only those who had come to worship but also the High Disciples, so confident in their own ability to give presentations, were feeling quite depressed about it. So, when the service was finally over and the audience had left, these talented people discussed Ginjibei's lecture. They completely picked it apart. Then they went together to Kyōso to give their comments.

"Sensei, we were struck dumb by Ginjibei's lecture. It was bad. It was really aggravating. Good or bad is not the point. But what a long lecture! The minute we thought it was over, he would start up again with an 'er' or a 'well', and on he went to another topic. He kept going and going. We didn't know what could be done about it. The way it went, everyone was losing interest and no one could be open to any graciousness in it. Sir, we sincerely request that Sensei never again consider Ginjibei for giving a lecture."

Kyōso listened quietly to this appeal, then said with a beaming smile,

"Come to think of it, you are right. It certainly was a long lecture. It was tedious and tiresome to hear him harping on the same old strings. But did he ever say, 'Do something wrong or evil?' No. Absolutely not. He neither said any such word nor even hinted any such thing."

With this word from Kyōso, it is said, the disciples looked at each other. Then they excused themselves from his presence, feeling ashamed and despondent.

59. Put Yourself in the Position of the Seller When You are Buying Something

Madam Iku was not at home one day when the fish peddler came to sell his goods, so Kyōso went out in the garden in her place. The peddler had some small fish called *ina* and *tsunashi* which he offered at their average prices, quite reasonable. Kyōso nodded his agreement with the price and bought some ten or twenty fish.

When the peddler had left, one of his disciples who was quietly watching all this came over with a grin.

"Listen, Sensei, I was watching you buy those fish at the price he was asking. You bought them without any haggling over the price. But that's not what I'm concerned about. You were checking the fish and choosing

Fish pedler

them very carefully and I thought you would pick out only the big ones. But instead, you only took the small ones. Excuse my being forward, but I have to admit I think what you were doing was quite peculiar. This is what I mean. When prices are given at the average, everyone picks the biggest ones and those that look good. The seller knows this, and he knows the larger ones will go first and the smaller ones will be left unsold. Sooner or later he will only have the small fish left. Then he will gradually lower the prices to sell them off. So, at the beginning he raises his prices.

"These are things everybody knows, and this, Kurozumi Sensei, is why it seemed very peculiar when you carefully took the smaller fish, one by one. Even if you had left the picking to the peddler, he would have mixed big ones in with the small ones to balance the sizes and get the price at the average for you. But you have taken the trouble to choose the smaller ones on purpose. At any rate, if you don't mind my saying it, that was not reasonable of you. It was actually quite silly."

When his disciple was finished, Kyōso said, "Well, that is the point. I am always teaching, 'When you are buying, put yourself in the position of the seller'."[85] This is said to have been his reply.

60. Performing *Majinai* with the Back of the Hand

Kobayashi Kenzō hailed from Ohzasa Village, Tōhoku County, in Mimasaka Province. He was a well-known follower who submitted his *shinmon* and entered the Way in 1848 together with Ikeda Chiyozō and Komoto Taisuke. Before that, Kobayashi was a physician by profession but he came to have confidence in the miraculous blessings of the Way. One day he asked Kyōso, "May I have your permission to perform *majinai*, just as others have permission?"

Kyōso responded, "Oh, yes, you may. Please don't hesitate to perform the *majinai* ritual whenever there is a request for it or when there is need for it. You must remember, however, that you should never perform it with the palm of your hand, but only with the back of your hand." This is what is said were his instructions.

It seemed very strange to perform the ritual with the back of the hand. It was awkward and quite inconvenient. Dr Kobayashi thought it odd, but since that was Kyōso's instruction that is how he always performed it. After three years had elapsed, further instruction came from Kyōso. "Kobayashi san, from now on you may use your palm." With these words, Kobayashi was for the first time given permission to perform *majinai* in the same way others did it.

Why was it that only Kobayashi was forbidden to use his palm? Why was he told to use the back of his hand? These questions need some explanation. Here is what Kyōso told him.

"Kobayashi san, since the practice of medicine is your profession you already have the habit of putting the palm of your hand on a patient. It would be your ordinary way to find out whether he or she had a fever, or if the pulse was normal, or of seeing whether a spot on the body was affected badly. Your observation of such things would lead you to a certain sense of caution as you use your hand with a patient. That is what worried me most when you first asked permission. I thought it would not be appropriate to doing *majinai*. The caution involved in thinking, 'Oh, this person is in serious condition, is there anything I can do to help?' would be a hindrance. If the one who does *majinai* has even the slightest hesitation or doubt it surely makes the ritual less effective."

Kyōso had the ability to perceive subtle things like this, and this is why only Kobayashi was instructed to use the back of his hand. Of course, the back of the hand is less sensitive than the palm. After three years had passed the doctor's faith had risen to a higher and firmer level. Kyōso saw that the time was ripe. The doctor was ready to perform *majinai* with the palm of his hand.

61. Let Heaven Approve Your *Majinai*

When Ikeda Chiyozō sought approval to perform *majinai*, Kyōso gave him this advice. "Ikeda san, you should realize that *majinai* is a ritual that mediates the grace of divine virtue. It is intended for the good of other people. Therefore, approval to do it is not in any one person's power to give. You should ask Heaven itself for such a grant of authority. You should understand when it is that Heaven gives that approval. It comes when someone has gained a deep faith in the Way, and when fellow-villagers and others have come to hold that person dear as a sensei out of their ordinary experience with him. This is what the words 'Heaven has no mouth except the mouth of the people' actually mean.[86] The time will come when your wish will be granted."

Ikeda was not from a family of any special note nor was he a person with high social status, and he had no distinguished learning or knowledge. He came from an ordinary farming family. And he was a person who used to say things without having much basis for what he said. His fellow-villagers did not hold him in any special regard. I believe Kyōso's comment was a very thoughtful, caring word of instruction. It came from his intuitive insight, spontaneously.

Yet, as might be expected from the superb character Ikeda was born with, he took insight from the way he was advised.[87] He was inspired by it to work ever more devotedly at growing in the faith. He began to act more prudently and to be more attentive in whatever he said and did. Without anyone remarking on the change, he began to be called Ikeda sensei instead of "Chiyozō san", or "that Chiyozō", or even "Chiyozō don" as before.[88] His *majinai* was rewarded with divine grace. Later on, at the time the divine title of Daimyōjin was accorded to Kyōso (1856) after his ascent to Heaven, Ikeda devoted his efforts in earnest missionary efforts in Kyoto, working side by side with Akagi. After he died he was given the posthumous title of Great Preceptor (Dai Kyōsei) to recognize his diligent devotion. A small shrine, the Tadatane Jinja,[89] was built for Ikeda sensei in the village of his birth.

Though it isn't very big, it shows the high respect in which he came to be held. He had established himself as one of the leading direct disciples. Ikeda had elevated himself to such a point that he has been revered by Kurozumikyō down to this day as one of the great teachers of the Way. Needless to say, Kyōso's words to him were so very thoughtful. But we must not forget Ikeda's own earnest diligence. His full devotion, inspired in him by Kyōso, led him to realize such outstanding accomplishments.

62. "Oh, Iku. I See You Are Here"

On the main street of Nakajima, which consists of two islands in the Asahi River that flows through the city of Okayama, there was a large dyehouse known as the Nanashimaya. The proprietor of the dyehouse, a man named Goroēmon, invited Kyōso to hold a meeting one night. Not only people from Okayama but also villagers from near and far who heard about this event gathered at this meeting wishing to see the *ikigami* (living kami) and to hear his sermon for themselves. After the purification prayer (Oharai) the time came for Kyōso to go up to the platform. He went up quietly and everyone was eagerly waiting, wishing not to miss a single sentence or word. Everyone's hushed attention was on him, everyone's eyes and ears were open and alert.

Just at that moment Kyōso's wife arrived at the scene. Since many who knew her offered her their seats, Iku could not decline the offer. She had to go up in front and take a seat in the first row.[90] After Kyōso had solemnly enjoyed the sip of consecrated water (*shinsui*) served to him on the platform,[91] he started his sermon, saying, "Oh, Iku. I see you are here. You have gone to a lot of trouble to come to the meeting. I am very grateful to you. I know you have finished your housework for the day and all you do every day to take care of our children and oversee the kitchen. In spite of your hard and busy day, you took care of everything quickly so you could walk this long two and a half miles to join us at this meeting. It is so commendable, so full of devotion!"

Without first giving a single word of greeting to the audience, he began by greeting his wife. And he spoke to her with full regard, conscientiously. After a moment, he glanced up at his audience, and then came these words. "Well, now, my dear followers."

Everyone present now waited happily for the sermon. They had been looking forward to hearing it. Now it was beginning. "As you all have seen, Iku is with us here tonight." In spite of her busy and heavy daily tasks, she has finished them all and has walked in the darkness for two and a half miles. I am sure you will agree with me it is such an admirable thing for a woman to cover that distance alone in the dark night. Doesn't it show devotion to the faith? Doesn't it really warm our hearts?" It is understandable that the audience was surprised to hear this kind of cordial praise.

For some moments Kyōso kept his mouth closed. Then when he finally did open his mouth to speak he said just one short thing. "Oh, folks. I am sorry that a subject for tonight's sermon does not float up in my mind. Now you will have to excuse me." And he descended from the platform.

This is an anecdote in which, I am sure, there are many important lessons. As I have written elsewhere,[92] everything Kyōso said in all his sermons and lectures was given "as it floated up spontaneously" (*ukabi no mama*) in his mind, absolutely free of ego or selfishness. That is, what he said in his talks was something independent of his own wisdom, removed from what he knew from his own ideas and his reasoning. When he gave his sermons he was free from any connection with what might be called "Kurozumi Sakyō." He handled any matter he was talking about in a way that was completely free from conscious intention or any kind of self-concern. Free from all thoughts and ideas of his own, he gave his sermon directly and spontaneously. He referred to his lectures and sermons as "words from Heaven" (*tengen*).

Here we find a spirituality that is truly superlative and reverent. We have here his own example of what he taught us about the secrets of all faiths and of all the arts and skills.[93] So it was on this evening, that at the moment he went up on the platform he had not the least idea of what he would talk about. Then he noticed Iku had arrived and he thought how faithful and admirable her action was in coming so far. Then he followed this with the words that next came to mind. That was all. There was nothing more. Nothing else came up in his mind. So, he simply came down from the platform.

This anecdote vividly and clearly illustrates my belief that Kyōso was a person who had not the slightest tincture of self-concern. His character was such that he gave not the slightest consideration to what he would say in his sermons, nor did he have any attachment to any one way of presenting them.

63. It Was Kyōso's Gratefulness That Prevented His Lecture

This is what he said at a meeting held at Ishida Rokuzaemon's place in Futsukaichi. "On my way here I worshipped the sun setting in the west. It was so beautiful and so solemn. Words could never describe the splendour. I just stood there among the rice-fields, completely absorbed and caught up. I just worshipped the sun. The splendour overwhelmed me. It flooded me with tears. It filled me completely. Gratefulness fills me even now. The grace of it still holds me speechless in this moment. Tonight there seems to be nothing more I can say. I can't find anything to tell you tonight." Thus his sermon began and so it ended. Thus he was moved to come down from the platform.

Kyōso's attitude was so truly filled with the spirit of gratitude (*arigatasa*) that his audience was deeply impressed. Not one of them was able to utter a word.

64. Coming Down from the Platform after Saying "How Gracious" Five Times

This was at a meeting held at the house of a man named Aguro, who was a village head at a place on the outskirts of Tsuyama, about fifty miles north of Okayama.[94] Kyōso had been specially invited to this place in the mountains so far from Okayama and some of those who attended had come from long distances. This was the content of his sermon.

"My dear followers! So gracious this is! The Great Way is indeed so gracious. In all truth, the divine virtues of Amaterasu Ōmikami are so gracious, they cannot be described in words. The more I ponder, the more I find them so gracious. Oh, it really is so gracious."

He had repeated the words "so gracious" five times. It took just seconds to say these few words, and then he came down from the platform. The whole audience was so deeply impressed, however, that the eyes of many were filled with tears. Although the presentation was so brief, the background out of which it came was full of graciousness, full of thankfulness and gratitude. Kyōso's whole life was full of it, every day of his life. That is why the audience was so deeply moved.

Well. We can put this in a more straightforward way. It was Kyōso's immersion in graciousness that moved the audience in their hearts when they heard this brief sermon with its five repetitions of "so gracious!"

65. "Whenever I See Young Wives and Maidens"

The High Disciple Morikane Tamezō was a man who liked to put the intellects of others up against his own sharp intelligence. We have seen this in a previous story. He was the kind of person who found it hard to keep from arguing people out of whatever thoughts they might have had. On one occasion Morikane had made arrangements with the village head of Oh-hashi, a man named Nakayama Tsunejirō, to hold a special meeting to hear Kyōso, different from the usual sort of occasion. At this meeting people from the educated classes would be invited: neighbouring village heads, town officials, Shinto and Buddhist priests, rich farmers and wealthy villagers. It would be a meeting in which the intelligentsia of the area would have a chance to hear one of Kyōso's sermons.

According to Morikane's belief, the people who came to most of Kyōso's meetings were "religious folk", elderly men and women without much education. He feared that the gracious virtue of the Way was too hard for the general public to understand in any short period of time. It would take years for it to become properly established if only such people attended. Nakayama had a similar idea and he held it quite boldly and openly, that the lectures and sermons Kyōso was giving in his own commanding and dignified way were meaningless to such people, like serving caviar to the masses. He thought it was without much effect or even lacking in reverence. He believed that if people with more learning and insight could be in the audiences that heard the Dai Sensei's gracious teaching, they would turn to him in great admiration.

Both men felt sure that those of higher status would learn to admire Kyōso after listening to him and it would bring these leadership groups in. As a result, the Way would prosper more quickly. With high hopes and expectations they carefully laid their plans. All proper arrangements were made. The nature of the meeting and the objectives they had in mind were explained to Kyōso and he gave them his approval and consent.

The day for the meeting arrived. Filled with excitement and pleasured expectation, Morikane called for Kyōso and escorted him to Nakayama's home. The time was ripe and the meeting was opened. Morikane looked around the audience and saw that the place was filled with distinguished people with high reputations. We can imagine how he puffed the air, filled with immense pleasure.

Kyōso appeared on the platform and began his sermon with a beaming smile. Since for many in the audience it was the first time they had experienced his preaching, they welcomed him attentively and with enthusiasm. And as you can guess, no one was more enthusiastic than Morikane himself.

Kyōso opened his mouth to speak in this way, saying in a deliberate way, "My friends, on my way here we passed by Shinden in Jōtō County. The weather was so fine and beautiful. And the autumn sky was so blue and so high, I felt the warm weather as comforting as a day in spring. Then I noticed around me many young wives and maidens in their teens. Their heads were covered with bandannas. They were picking cotton and with joy they were singing beautiful songs. When I saw them I felt my spirit roused up and refreshed. My steps became lighter and the walk felt very pleasant. In this way I enjoyed my trip here. Well, as you all know, it is always inviting and pleasant to see many attractive young women and girls. It was the sort of enjoyable scene that never fails to enliven you."

To those who had looked forward to the commanding sort of gracious sermon Kyōso was known for, his words sounded vague and trivial. It seemed petty to the audience, quite different from what they had been expecting. They didn't know what to think. Still, they expected that a more earnest and deeply considered sermon would follow these remarks about his journey to the place. They had looked forward to an instructive and grace-filled sermon that would in careful, clear steps explain the very essence of the Great Way. But what then followed was the same story repeated: his trip to Nakayama's house. And soon the lecture for that night was over.

Of course, those who were attending one of these meetings for the first time found it quite skimpy. It was quite unsatisfying. And who could be more disappointed than Morikane? His special hopes and plans had been shattered. For him it was an awful failure, entirely contrary to what he had been hoping for. The special efforts he had so carefully made to arrange a fine evening's meeting were all to no avail. Already at the very beginning of the lecture Morikane thought what he was hearing was strange, and he ended up thoroughly disheartened and miserable.

Oh, what a disappointment. "How can a person like Kyōso, who always delivers such an impressive lecture full of such graciousness, pick such a subject for tonight's special meeting? How could he have chosen a topic so dull and so worthless?"

Nevertheless, Kyōso came down from the platform in an excellent mood and with ever-beaming smiles.

66. Words from Heaven are beyond Sakyō's Control

This happened one evening when Kyōso was on the platform. As he usually did, he first enjoyed with thanks a cup of consecrated water that had been offered to him. But no word followed. He took another drink from the cup. Still no word came from him. He took a third drink. But no topic for discussion came up in his mind.

There was someone in the audience who knew full well that sometimes he left his audience without saying anything, and who knew that many would not understand and be disappointed. He made this request, "Sir. It could be anything. May we at least hear something from you? Even if it is only a word." The person who said this said it with a certain emphasis.

Instantly, back came Kyōso's thundering voice, "You must understand that the words from Heaven are beyond the control of this Sakyō." With that, he came down from the platform.

67. Ah! My Sermon is Now a Poem!

This was also at a meeting, but on a different occasion. Kyōso's lecture proceeded smoothly and enthusiastically, covering the essence of the Way, and the time had come when he raised his tone to offer his gratitude for the divine virtues of Amaterasu Ohmikami.

"Amaterasu / kami no mitoku wa / ametsuchi ni / michite kakenaki / megumi. ..." The words came smoothly. And at the instant the next word came out, "*narukana*",[95] Kyōso added this, still in a spontaneous way. "Well now! My sermon has taken the form of a *waka*!"[96]

The content of these words may be translated, "Amaterasu, your divine virtues filling Heaven and Earth, extending blessing everywhere with nothing lacking ...". Then at that point his habit of composing *waka* showed its effect, with the emphasis word "*narukana*" being added. The words that came out of his mouth turned out to be poetic in *waka* style.

Amaterasu!
  In all the Heaven and Earth
    your divine virtue
filling all things overfull
    granting blessing unrestrained.

In ancient times as well as today many *waka* have been composed praising and revering the virtues of Amaterasu. But none is as clear and easily understood as this one. It is so excellent that it should be passed on to the whole world. No other *waka* surpasses this one.

In addition, the fact that it never underwent polishing or elabouration must be mentioned. The words came out just as they are without any need to be improved. No choosing of diction was involved in its composition. The words came out spontaneously in the form of a *waka*. No, it was an expression of Heavenly virtue that Kyōso spontaneously composed this poem as one that would be sung and recited over and over by millions of people in their praise to Amaterasu. Even today it is sung in Kurozumikyō churches after the regular morning service.

Amaterasu had appeared in the form of a *waka*.

68. The Gathering of the Kami

One day Takeuchi Raizō sensei of Sayama Village, Oku County, Bizen Province, paid Kyōso a visit. Kyōso was very happy about it and said, "We have not met for a long time. I would like to hear you deliver a sermon." Takeuchi felt much honoured by this request and presented a very fine sermon. Then the occasion was completed with Kyōso's own sermon. It was not a regular meeting day, so no others were present. Only the two of them were there: Kyōso and Takeuchi. Still, Kyōso went on preaching for more than two hours. We are told it was a splendid, vigorous, and instructive lecture.

Takeuchi listened gratefully and earnestly. When it was over he said, "Sir, thank you so much. I have listened to many lectures of yours so attentively, but this one today was special. It was the most instructive and gratifying I have ever experienced. It was such a privilege for me to preach and then to hear you preach also. What you said pierced into my heart and soul for more than two hours. The meaning of the Great Way became clear to me in instant flashes of insight as I listened to your lecture. Sir, I do have a question I would like to ask you. I was the only one listening here today. It is hard for me to understand why you delivered your lecture in such a loud voice and resonant tone. This is the only point I don't understand. I did find it a little strange."

Kyōso replied in the same commanding and firm tone, "Takeuchi san, although you believe you were the only listener, you must see with all awe and reverence that the Eight Million Kami come to hear the divine teachings of Amaterasu Ohmikami.[97] They come to hear the Heavenly words (*tengen*) so freely given and they receive them with pleasure." This was all he said, but he said it firmly.

We are told that Takeuchi was so touched that he fell flat on the floor, unable to move. Kyōso's words struck home to him, into his very bones and muscle. In later times, whenever he recalled this incident, he felt his face redden with shame, as though he had been splashed with cold water.

69. No Rain on Meeting Days

When rain seemed to threaten while a meeting was taking place, some of those who didn't understand the Way very well used to get ready to hurry quickly home. It would cause a great rush and commotion. On one such occasion, a regular meeting day, there was a large number of people attending and many who were devoting themselves to worship. When rain seemed to be approaching, signs of unrest were beginning to show in the audience.

Kyōso noticed this and said, "May I have your attention, please. I assure you there is nothing to worry about. Let me tell you that from this very day, there will be no rain on days of *gokaijitsu*. Never will it rain on such days. I assure you of it. Please be relaxed and calm yourselves." This is what he told the audience. To their surprise and wonder, the weather did improve. It is recorded that from that day onward, for a period of several years, on not one of the six days of meeting each month did it rain. The weather was always fine on those days.

Then someone or other began to call the weather on those days "the fine weather of *gokaijitsu*". The use of the expression spread to neighbouring villages and towns. Those who knew of the incident and used the expression had a firm confidence in this saying. One of the main crops in the Kaminakano area, along with rice, was the kind of rushes used to make the *tatami* mats commonly used in Japanese homes.[98] Rushes must be dried carefully after they have been cut so they don't deteriorate in colour and quality and good weather is needed for that. Rain falling on drying rushes can cause serious damage to the material. But after that on *goikaijitsu* days when it was cloudy in the morning, farmers didn't worry about rain when going out to their fields to work with the rushes.

Some years after that particular day (some say it was exactly five years later), Kyōso was recalling the event. He came to realize that when he said, "There will be no rain on days of *gokaijitsu*. Never will it rain on such days", these had not been words he had said out of his own intention, but they were "words from Heaven" that had floated up in his mind spontaneously. Since then it had never rained on a meeting day. He believed that to be one of the excelling graces of Kami. Kami was able to control the weather. Such virtue and power is gracious and gratifying.

But Kyōso felt it would be a fearsome thing for such power to be attributed to him personally. He considered it, then reconsidered it, and finally declined to be thought of this way. Though the words had been the words of Heaven, he realized it was also true that he had himself held the wish that it would not rain on such days. He then realized, quite humbly, that having such power was too holy a thing for him to have for himself. From that day on, after he realized he ought not to have such power, the weather returned to normal. It would sometimes rain on *gokaijitsu* days.

Still, on most meeting days even today, those who attend do enjoy fine weather.

70. Never Shall I Reveal the Trade Secrets of Pottery Menders

This is a story that a certain samurai family in the city of Okayama experienced. When a maid of the household was dusting one of the rooms of the house the end of her duster accidentally brushed against a ceramic ornament. The ornament was in the shape of a horse and it was standing in the *tokonoma*.[99] To her great dismay an ear broke off the horse's head.

This was a fine piece of Bizen pottery,[100] inherited by the family head and his wife as one of their family treasures. Since the maid was well aware of its value, what she had done set her heart pounding in worry and concern. She was at a desperate loss. What in the world could she do? There was no way to make it up. What would the master and mistress of the house say? When they came to know of it, what a fierce scolding she would receive! Scolding and punishment might be tolerated, but how could she ever be excused for breaking such a fine, valuable piece of pottery?

Nevertheless, she got around to accepting the fact that her own carelessness was the cause of the damage. There seemed to be no way to fix things. On considering various possible solutions, she finally had this thought. "I should follow the teachings of Kyōso. He always preaches that when one offers one's sincerity to Kami, then, whatever it may be, one's wishes are heard and they will come true. More than that, I know he has taught us gratitude for the divine graces. Yes, that is what I should do. I will pray to Kami with all my heart and I will ask Kami to put the ear back on the horse."

With this firm thought in mind she offered her prayer. With utmost sincerity of spirit she purified the broken-off piece of ear with consecrated water (*shinsui*) and put it back on the horse where it had broken off. To her great surprise and joy, the ear stayed back in its place. Not a single wiggle or jitter. What a delight! The maid's heart was now fluttering with joy and the deepest relief.

The next morning she checked the horse to see if the ear was still on. Yes! The ear that had broken off was still on the horse where it belonged. Not a single crack or joint was visible, to her added delight. She was so happy about it she went straight to her mistress to report what had happened the day before and to offer her apology. This surprised the mistress and she checked the horse herself. Both of them were deeply moved by the divine blessing, and then told the rest of the household about it. Since the master was a person who was well known for his deep faith and reverence to Kami, he also was much moved by this blessing. He renewed his recognition of the divine power of *shinsui*, coming as it does from the shrine of Kami for worshippers to take home. He reported the story to his close friends. So, the news of this happening caused a big stir, and of course it came to Kyōso's ears.

This is what he said about it. "Nothing is more prodigious and more wonderful than the heart that is in each one of us. The wishes one holds with wholeness of heart certainly do reach the Kami of Heaven to be answered."

When in course of time Kyōso preached about the holy power of *shin-sui*, he referred to this story. He explained that it was the singleminded, heartfelt sincerity of the maid that had caused the broken-off piece of ornament to stay back in its place. He added, "That is not cause for surprise. What does surprise me is the fact that so many of you were surprised. Never had this person[101] any intention of revealing the trade secrets of pottery menders. The divine virtue gives life and vitality (*ikashi*) to all beings in Heaven and Earth, but we should not trouble Kami with such trifling requests as having pottery mended.

"Please make sure this story does not spread any further. Let me remind you, and do you make sure to remember, that this Kurozumi Sakyō has not the slightest intention of opening a pottery mender's shop."

71. Offering Purification Prayer while Lightning Struck

This happened at the spacious residence of a wealthy family. Some say it was the home of the Honourable Ikeda Iga, then the top councillor to Lord Ikeda, ruler of Bizen Province. Kyōso was invited there to offer purification prayer (Oharai) before the kami enshrined in the main room of the house. The season was midsummer and the weather was humid and hot. He was offering the graceful prayer in his usual calm, resonant tone.

On that day there was no prediction of any change in the weather. No one saw anything that might indicate a change. But suddenly came the thundering blast of a lightning bolt. Bam! Everyone was completely shocked and startled, it was so unexpected. Since the house and its garden were so large the lightning had found a place just outside in the garden to hit. Not only was the disturbance great among those chanting the prayer along with Kyōso but even those in the kitchen or busy with other tasks were affected. Whoever and wherever they were, they flattened themselves down on the ground instantly, frightened out of their wits. After a moment they all got up again, glad and grateful to find themselves still alive. They looked around, relieved to see that no one had been injured.

Then the way Kyōso was sitting struck them. His posture and position were just the same as when he had started the prayer. He was chanting in the same ringing tone. They all looked on in wonder at the sight of Kyōso going on offering prayer as if nothing had happened.

72. Facing a Drunken Samurai

In the *Chronology of the Founder's Life* the following is recorded for the year 1838.[102]

On the twenty-third day of the third month, Matsuo Chozaburō, an Okayama clan retainer who was under the influence of alcohol and out of his head, walked into the castle town of Okayama. After injuring about twenty-three people with his sword he went so far as to threaten to attack Kyōso, who happened to be approaching the West Gate of the castle just then. With Kyōso's word of remonstrance the possible attacker repented, regretted his misdeed, recovered his sobriety, and came to himself again.

This event is worth telling in more detail.

The West Gate of the castle was commonly referred to as the Nakano-chō Gate after an important section of the city just in front of it.[103] It was a section reserved for the homes of high-ranking samurai, living near the castle to be ready to serve when needed. Today the gate no longer exists and the area has become a part of downtown Okayama but a sign has been put up in memory of this historic spot. This retainer, Matsuo Chozaburō, was a decent and honourable samurai. We know that from the position he used to hold under Lord Ikeda. But despite his high position he had a weak point. He was given to drink and he was quarrelsome when under the influence. Because of this weakness he often had strayed from virtue, risking his position.

That day, the twenty-third of the third month, was when spring was at its height of arriving. Cherry blossoms were in full bloom and in many places people were enjoying themselves at blossom-viewing parties, exchanging toasts of *sake*. This was what was happening when Matsuo's weakness hit the town of Okayama up and down with a most unwelcome and most untimely commotion.

It was also the day one of the leading Buddhist temples of the area, Hōkkai-in located in a northern suburb, was holding a grand ceremonial event. They were displaying a treasure of their temple to the public, a likeness of a group of Buddhas centred around Gautama Buddha. It was something done only once a year. Matsuo had gone to pay his respects at the temple and afterwards dropped in to a blossom-viewing party at the house of a friend. Since he was so fond of alcohol he drank more than he could handle and left his friend's house very drunk. This was the condition he was in when he came back to the castle area. He was walking with a staggering gait, reeling down the street, swaying from one side to the other. It was only a matter of minutes before he began bumping into people as he went. These small encounters led him to start picking quarrels. Because of his status as samurai the commoners were at his mercy.[104] It seemed certain that before long he would draw his long sword and injure somebody.

What a great trouble his condition was causing! The whole neighbourhood began to scatter in confusion in all directions, both people who lived there and those just passing by. The excitement sent a rush of blood to Matsuo's head. He began attacking anyone who came into his path, not just one but several people. The sight of blood set him off even more. His drunken reeling took him up and down several streets in just a brief span of time. The number of his victims up to this point came to an alarming total of about twenty-three, it is said.

Now the setting sun saw him approaching the Nakano-chō Gate. At that moment Kyōso also happened to be approaching the gate, but from another direction. He had just set out for home from Uchisange, about a hundred yards to the east. The two were headed for each other in the area just in front of the gate and it looked like they would surely bump into each other. At the next moment it appeared that Matsuo, with his sword held high above his head, was about to cut Kyōso down. Those who saw what was about to happen raised their voices. They called out in panic. "Help, help! That gentleman will surely be cut down by that rascal!"

Kyōso, however, to their amazement and puzzlement, just kept his pace, still heading past the Nakano-chō Gate as though there was nothing unusual. In the moment when he raised his head to look, what he saw was a samurai about to swing his blood-covered sword down on him. Whom would he attack? No one but himself. When Kyōso grasped the situation, what he thought was this.

"Oh my. What has happened to this fellow? What's wrong with him? He is dressed as a samurai, but doesn't he realize where he is now standing? Of all places, this is the middle of the castle town. Inside the gate are the actual premises of the castle itself. What a thoughtless thing to do! That anyone would draw his sword without taking account of how important this place is. Furthermore, he is going as far as cutting others. Never will he be pardoned for it. He will be punished by being ordered to commit ritual suicide.[105] And his whole family will be sentenced to death. Has this fellow gone mad? What a pity!"

This was the situation as Kyōso instantly understood it in his mind. Then came his brief words, said in a normal tone of voice, but calmly and ringingly, "Don't you know where you are?"

The area outside the gate was not part of the actual castle premises, but just inside the gate the broad streets were lined on both sides with magnificent mansions of higher-level retainers. It was also where the various agencies of the Bizen clan were located. The gate commanded an important site in the castle town, connecting all of that with the city. It was indeed an important, solemn place.

Matsuo Chozaburō, whose behaviour had been like a person half-crazy, was brought up short by these words of sincerity (*makoto*). He was suddenly unable to swing his sword down upon Kyōso. The anxious crowd who had thought, "That gentleman is going to be cut down", now were amazed. They held in awe the sight of Kyōso walking briskly straight towards the drunken man.

At the instant Kyōso saw that the drunken man was about to attack him he had not the slightest thought of his own safety and life, but only of the fate the samurai would meet. With his sole concern the drunken man's fate, the spontaneous words he spoke were full of sincerity. This sincerity had the power to move Heaven and Earth, to say nothing of the possible attacker himself. It is quite understandable that the drunken man was brought to a standstill, unable to bring down his sword. It is an amazement that is not really amazing.

We have so much to learn from this revered lesson. Some phrases to be remembered are, "Utmost sincerity, devotion, and wholeheartedness", "Kyōso's most revered poise of soul", and "Kyōso is our *misebumi* in setting an example of poise of soul."

This incident aroused a lot of attention at the time. A few days later there was a person who paid a visit to Kyōso's house to express his pleasure that it had ended without his being injured. This man asked him what mental attitude someone should have who might find himself in such a situation. Kyōso, just then sitting on the veranda with his legs hanging down, responded by slapping his legs lightly, saying, "It is a long time since I have thrown these away." This is what we are told he said.

A well-known *waka* starts this way.

My body, my self,
  also my heart departed,
    just sincerity ...[106]

Sincerity, indeed, is the virtue that brings about the true poise of the soul.

73. "Please Go to Osaka to Do Missionary Work"

Misawa Sahei was a leading Bizen clan retainer who held the important position of Bizen Clan Rice Manager in Osaka. He was also a devoted follower of the faith. Misawa revered Kyōso's teachings and always held a strong belief that the citizens of Osaka would certainly be moved and impressed by Kyōso's lectures. Then as now Osaka was an important city along with Kyoto and Edo. He felt that missionary activities in this big city would surely arouse interest throughout Japan.

He could not keep his idea to himself. On several occasions when he was in Okayama he petitioned Kyōso to spend some time in Osaka and to present his views in lectures.

"My respected Teacher, limiting your preaching to Bizen and Sakushū is not a way to spread these very precious teachings of yours very widely. Excuse me again for being forward. Osaka is a big city where people come from every province in Japan. Here they gather and they mingle. I believe missionary activities for Osaka alone might not help that much, but information and news picked up here will spread quickly throughout the country. Anything heard in Osaka will soon be heard everywhere in Japan. Although I am unworthy, thanks to our good fortune there is more than a small number of people in Osaka who have already heard about your teachings through my lectures.

"Sir, would you care to go to the trouble, without fail, of going to Osaka yourself for the express purpose of presenting your views to the people there? May I solicit your approval for this plan? Please forgive my forwardness, but even if you were to cry your voice out hoarse in this remote countryside, not a great deal of benefit can come from it. The effort will never bear much fruit. This is my deepest regret." Misawa made his petition with earnestness shining all over his face. He asked and he begged that his opinion be accepted.

The response was, "Your kind suggestion is much appreciated, and I am grateful for your wholeheartedness. I feel, however, that you must understand what is going on here just now. Not a day or a night passes without a request from people in this district to deliver lectures and per-form *majinai*. I find I can get no rest. Everyone here respects me and reveres me. They look forward earnestly and patiently to listening to my lecture and to receiving the divine blessing. As for myself, I have no time to consider whether our missionary work around here, so far from the centre of the country, is rewarding or not. So, I can't consider leaving the

107

many who are in such serious need here to go away and do that same work in the Osaka and Kyoto area.

"Misawa san, please do listen to me. Even if I end my life preaching in the countryside I feel confident that the Way of Amaterasu will spread and find its way into the three great cities of Japan, into Edo, Kyoto, and Osaka. And it will spread throughout Japan and eventually to every country in the world. Please let me be clearly and precisely understood, Misawa san. Before very long the day will come when all beings in the world, without a single exception, will hear the divine Way. It is sure to come."

This, we hear, is what Kyōso told Misawa. The last part of what he said was in a higher pitch, and Kyōso's deep and firm faith moved Misawa so much that he bowed his head down to the mat spontaneously.

74. A Pair of *Zōris* Do Missionary Work

This happened during Kyōso's pilgrimage to the Grand Shrine of Ise in 1845. On his way home after completing his worship in Ise he stopped in at Misawa san's place in Osaka. During the visit Misawa asked to be excused for some hours. He ordered his family to take good care of Kyōso and to treat him with utmost care while he was out. About the time Kyōso began to think Misawa's long absence somewhat strange, he returned home and soon came to Kyōso's room.

"My Teacher, please forgive my absence. Since I was unable to realize my desire of having you give lectures to my friends, I went around in the streets with a pair of your *zōris* hidden in my bosom, as much as I had time for. In this way I felt I was able to fulfil my long-held desire of accompanying you, sir, on your missionary work here in Osaka. I am sure the people of this city were graced with your blessings. In this way, and with thankfulness, I laid the groundwork for missionary work here in Osaka. I prepared a few paths for the opening of the Way."

75. About Okamoto Rin's *Waka*

The chapter in the *Register of Disciples*[107] for 1847 refers to a person by the name of Okamoto Mankichi, a resident of Fukumoto Village, Oku County, in Bizen Province just east of Okayama, and the chapter entitled "Unidentified Years" refers to his daughter named Riye. I believe she was usually known as Rin. Okamoto Mankichi was one of the pure-hearted disciples of Kyōso, and all three members of his family, consisting of himself, his son Ezaemon, and his daughter Rin, were devoted followers of the Way.

At one certain year-end when the family had about finished their busy preparation to welcome in the New Year, they were sitting warming themselves comfortably in their *kotatsu*.[108]

The daughter said to Ezaemon, as thoughts of New Year's resolutions were going through their minds, "I feel I owe everything to Dai Sensei Kurozumi for making it possible for us to welcome in the New Year in such a relaxed and peaceful atmosphere. His gracious teaching is the source of it all. While I was feeling full of gratitude this way, a *waka* flashed into my mind." Then she recited the following *waka*:

> If we live our lives
>   by entrusting everything
>   to the Great Kami
> Then we will feel very good
>   at the closing of the year.

Hearing her recite this poem, Ezaemon expressed his admiration. "Indeed, you are right. What a splendid *waka*!" The young pair shared stories about the various good things they had experienced because of the Way. Despite the busyness and confusion of the season, it seemed that spring had paid an earlier visit here than in other families.

When the New Year rang in and the family paid a visit to Kyōso to offer him their greetings and their wishes for the coming spring, Ezaemon mentioned to him the *waka* his sister had composed. After repeating it to himself two or three times in a low voice, Kyōso said, "Rin san, you have composed a really good poem. It conforms to the essence of the Way wonderfully. But may I suggest a change to improve the last part? The part about 'at the closing of the year' is good. Since that was what was happening when you wrote it there is no other way to say it. But let me remind you that those who read the poem might get the idea that he or she is deserving of blessings only once in the year.

"So I would suggest changing that part to 'at the closing of the day'. When we think of the hour of sunset it often gives us the thought of our hearts being busy and anxious, feeling chased around with the tasks of the day, and getting irritated, even losing patience and giving in to anger. But if we live at all times in accordance with the Heart of the Way we will feel more pleasant, more happy and joyful.[109] I would say the following version might convey your idea better. In this way we can express our gratitude for being blessed every day, all 365 days of the year.

> If we live our lives
> by entrusting everything
> to the Great Kami
> Then we will feel very good
> at the closing of the day.

The poem was introduced at different places and soon became a popular topic among people in the Okayama area. One enthusiastic admirer of Okamoto's daughter approached Kyōso asking that the girl become the bride of his son. He was not the only one, many other fathers requested the same thing. It put Kyōso in a somewhat awkward but enjoyable position.

76. Wrestling with Your Grandson

There was a person living in the city of Okayama who visited Kyōso asking for help. He was unable to solve his problem, which was his inability to overcome his anger. Kyōso responded this way. "When you get angry, I am sure your heart aches. Since your heart is a gracious gift from Amaterasu Ōmikami, acting this way is painful to it."

He then added this. "Probably you have a grandson. When you are amusing him and cheering him up, why not *sumo* wrestle with him.[110] It will surely please him. And if you let him believe he toppled you over it will make him even happier. Everything in this world is like playing pretend *sumo* with a little boy. If you are eagerly thinking about making another person happy, and if you are willing to give in on something that is your own, there isn't the slightest possibility that anger will overcome you." The man is said to have kept this teaching of Kyōso always in mind for the rest of his life. Never for an instant did he forget it.

77. Suzuki Raii's Bell

This is something that happened at a meeting that was regularly held at the Kanagawa-ya, a merchant's shop in Okayama City. In one of his lectures at that place Kyōso said, "Have you ever had a chance to enjoy the pleasant sound of the bell that Suzuki Raii treasures so much? It is so beautiful, so elegant. You should be sure to enjoy a chance to hear the ringing of this bell." In this way he advised his followers to be on the lookout for such an opportunity.

Some of those who attended this meeting took up this advice, thinking this bell must be something rather unusual. They looked for ways to be allowed to visit the Suzuki house. They thought the bell Kyōso was talking about must be the one the Suzukis kept hanging in front of their Shinto altar (*kamidana*). It was decorated with a fine piece of silk rope. But they didn't find the sound of it worthy of that kind of praise. When they reported what they found to Kyōso, he said with a smile, "Oh, the bell. "Which one is that?," do you say? It is the one with no pretty shape, one you can't see but it makes harmonious sounds everywhere in the house."

The Suzuki family was, as Kyōso had described with such praise, a home filled with harmony and cheerful satisfaction, giving a feeling like the pleasant, merry ringing of bells. Even if it became necessary to scold someone, Suzuki, the family head, was always sure to add a smile to his scolding. He would always encourage the person, never discourage him or her. A poem that Kyōso composed, that has been handed down from generation to generation of the Suzuki family, goes like this,

How auspicious here!
　Ring-a-ling and ting-a-ling!
　　In ev'ry corner,
All the people in this house
　harmonize with ringing chimes.

78. Making Use of Someone's Good Points

Kyōso had a special way of treating each of his family members and those who assisted in his house. He always praised his or her strong point, even though it might be the only strong point she or he had along with nine weak ones. If your attitude towards a person with a weak point is based not on the nine strong points he or she may have but on that one weak point and you scold that person for it, what you do will injure him or her. The nine strong points will turn into weak ones. The considerate thoughtfulness of Kyōso, vitalizing others' strength of personality by praising them, was indeed a gracious blessing.

79. Kyōso's Teaching to Hoshijima Ryōhei's Mother

Although High Disciple Hoshijima Ryōhei was a retainer who served his clan of Amaki faithfully for years with his profound knowledge of Chinese classics,[111] as a child he was not fond of reading books and learning. On his return from his teacher's classes he would throw his pack of books down in the kitchen and rush off to play, spending all his time in fun with his young friends.

His mother was at such a loss about this that she went to Kyōso's house to ask his advice. "Sir, I would appreciate it very much if you would admonish and correct my Makisaburō and guide him in the right direction towards learning." In answer to her plea Kyōso said, "It is not a good idea to force your son to read books. Instead you should make use of opportunities as they come up. Find ways to allow him to find reading interesting on his own. Then go on to encourage him in it." He taught Madame Hoshijima to put away her feeling of wanting to make the boy read books. Instead, she should rely on encouragement.

From that day she would tell him this sort of thing. "I see you are taking your books to your room. Oh, I know you are going to read them. Isn't that nice." Sometimes she gave him treats and refreshments as a reward.

Accordingly, the boy began to take his books and read them, without any particular effort or thought of pleasing his mother. The more he read, the more his mother applauded him with praise and approval. The refreshments also helped. Without his deciding anything consciously, the boy's interest in reading and learning increased. In good time his reading and study raised him up to his position as a respected scholar.

80. About Patience

Once when Kyōso visited Ohmori Busuke of Wake County, Bizen Province, he noticed a piece of framed calligraphy with two Chinese characters on it hanging over the *nageshi* of the guest room where he was staying.[112] Together the characters read *kan-nin*, meaning "patience" or "forbearance". Later he said something about it to Busuke, asking him why this motto had been placed there.

Busuke explained respectfully, "Thanks to good luck and good fortune, our family is blessed with prosperity. We are known as one of the leading families in this district. So, we are able to afford a large number of servants and maids. With this many people in the house not a day passes without a chance of someone getting angry, without some need for *kan-nin*. Every morning and every evening we look at the watchword hanging there and it helps us be more thoughtful about how we treat our workers and servants. So, to our great satisfaction the household comes to each day's end in a spirit of harmony. What a gracious delight it is!"

Kyōso's response was, "Ohmori san, you are absolutely right. *Kan-nin* is really a worthy kind of conduct. But can't you look at it this way? Wouldn't it be better and more advisable not to suppress anger?" Busuke looked at him with surprise. He said, with head tilted to one side in doubt, "Sir, are you trying to tell me that it is better not to be patient?"

"Oh, no. What I mean is this. There is no need of patience if there is no anger or rage. If you don't become angry it doesn't become necessary to be patient." With this, Kyōso composed the following *waka* and presented it to Busuke.

Rage requires patience,
  but if there is no rage, then
    nothing to endure.
  Better to have no rage at all
    and so no need for patience.

Busuke bowed his head cordially to express his sincere thanks to Kyōso for the insight he attained.

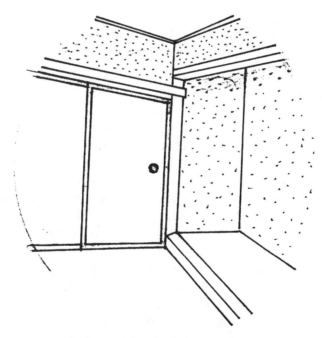

The frame above the door is the *nageshi*

113

81. The Importance of Putting Your Thankfulness into Words

There was a follower who presented this question to Kyōso. "I have to admit something. In my everyday life I've never experienced a feeling of sincere and hearty gratitude. This is the truth and I regret it deeply. How can I work myself up into having a feeling of thankfulness? Could I even achieve it when I am sleeping?"

Kyōso told him this. "Oh, is that your problem? Why not try this. The first thing to do when you get up out of bed, after washing your face and hands, is to give thanks to Kami by observing your *nippai* prayers properly. It might not come from the bottom of your heart and it might seem like lip service or imitation, but do it anyway. Offer thanks to Kami for having the occupation you have. Give thanks that you can move your arms and legs freely. And then offer gratitude to everything you see and hear. Without any difficulty your heart will gradually fill with gratitude."

The man responded to this teaching by saying, "Thank you." Kyōso said, "There. That's it. Those very words of yours show the sincere gratitude you already have, expressing itself down in your heart." This was a lesson Kyōso often used in teaching his followers and other inquirers.

82. The True Sincerity of a Sakushū Woman

In the days of Kyōso there was a woman living in Sakushū who had a serious case of a female disorder. She had this condition for more than eighteen years. She paid regular visits to Ohmoto to worship and offer prayers. During this whole time, however, every treatment and every medication suggested to her was in vain. So, she was ready to believe the worst, that her case was malignant and incurable.

On one visit to Ohmoto she listened so attentively to Kyōso's sermons that she was moved by what she heard. She asked permission to stay there for an extended time. During her sojourn she devoted herself to worship and prayer. But, alas, to her regret no blessing came in relief of her illness. She was terribly disappointed and came to think that she would never receive divine blessing. One day she spoke to Kyōso about it.

"I have devoted myself wholeheartedly in praying to Amaterasu, hoping that Great Kami would bestow on me the great blessing of restoring my health. I am deeply aware of the trouble I have caused you and I appreciate very much the prayers and *majinai* you have given for my sake. My illness must be a serious case. Despite your efforts and despite my sincerity, no hint of a blessing has shown up. There seem to be no blessings for me. If I were to keep on in this way I'm afraid I would only cause trouble, keeping others from receiving blessings. Would you please excuse my absence from any more meetings for the time being?"

Kyōso answered, "Oh yes, do as you like. But would you please listen to me. As you know, tomorrow is another meeting day here in Ohmoto. Why not spend another night here and attend tomorrow's meeting? Wouldn't it be better to leave for home just after hearing a sermon and receiving *majinai*?" This was his advice, and she obeyed it.

The next day, he made use of the following *waka* in his sermon.

When prayer's not answered
   it still is blessed with virtue,
      still it has effect.
Our inner heart, this tells us,
   is lacking true sincerity.

This *waka* moved the woman so much that she was overwhelmed with emotion, almost more than she could bear. Till then she had wondered why she was the one to whom no blessing was accorded. Now she understood that her prayer had been imperfect, lacking sincerity in the truest sense. When she had listened to Kyōso's sermons and received the healing ceremony there had always been a thought in her mind that perhaps she would not be cured. Now she understood that it was this lingering doubt that was her problem. She knew it was something for which there could be no excuse before Amaterasu and Kyōso. Deeply ashamed of herself, she offered apologies for wronging them in this way. In the depths of her heart she repented.

With this fresh outlook her heart began to renew itself, sprouting goodness and health like the leaves of a plant. As she listened to Kyōso's sermons she began to forget all about the illness she had suffered for eighteen years. In this way Amaterasu and Kyōso blessed this woman with their broad and boundless graces.

83. How to Weave a *Tatami* Mat

Here is the story of an old woman from Furumatsu[113] in Kyōso's time. She was such an earnest adherent of the Way that there was no one who did not know her or who had not heard of her. She spent her time, day after day, weaving *tatami* mats.[114] It was not an easy job, hard to do with easy progress and with good results. Making *tatami* mats is a toilsome

115

kind of work that really wears the weaver down. But she did it because her family's living expenses depended on it.

Once the old woman told Kyōso, "I have never thought of being idle in my family's occupation. This is how I was brought up and I want to work hard at what I am doing. But I am feeling tired, more than usual. My shoulder has been getting stiff a lot. Is it because I am getting older? It is keeping me from doing my work. May I ask your help in getting over this problem?" Kyōso responded, "You are feeling tired because it is you who are doing the work. Please don't perform your tasks with your own strength."

This explanation puzzled the woman and she said, "But Sensei, please understand the situation. Please remember we wouldn't be able to afford our living expenses if I didn't work."

Kyōso repeated what he had said, and added, "That is not what I was talking about. What you need to understand is that it is only thanks to Great Kami that anyone can do even the smallest bit of work at all. Your belief that it is you that is doing the work causes a weakness within you, so that the work you are doing becomes a strain to you.

"It wears you out because of the way you are doing it, relying on the strength of your own effort. That you can do even one inch of matting is already owing to divine blessing. Once you come to think about your work in this way, your shoulders will never get stiff. You will be able to do all of it easily (*kiraku ni*), without strain. When you do your work, rely on the divine strength of Great Kami. Leave it to Kami."

The old woman was much impressed with this admonition, and enlightened in her understanding. When working as she was instructed she noticed that no shoulder stiffness developed. More than that, she began to feel relaxed in a way hard to express in words, finding renewed vitality and pleasure in her work. She began to murmur prayers of thanksgiving to whatever she was working on. She gave thanks to the daybreak and to the sunset and to whatever might happen during the day. Gradually her labour had greater results, and before long everyone respected her and praised her as someone they could not do without. She enjoyed good health and long life, well into her eighties.

84. Secret Acts of Kindness

A certain man once said to Kyōso, "As a way of doing more acts of charity but without attracting attention, I make it a rule to present gifts to destitute people as I happen to meet them." Kyōso responded, "There is nothing the matter with that. But you should also take good care of your family business, never let any unfairness taint your dealings with other people, and always work for the betterment and benefit of the world."

85. One Family at Peace and Another in Discord

Kyōso once gave a sermon as follows.

"There was once a family that was well known for being very peaceful and there was another that had the opposite reputation. A certain person was curious about that and went to find out why there was that difference.

"First he visited the peaceful family. When he entered the front garden of the house he saw the grandfather sitting down in the doorway and enjoying big puffs of tobacco after putting down in the inner garden a big pot he had just bought and taken home. Not knowing the pot was there, his son threw down a bundle of firewood from the upper floor. The cracking noise of the pot told him what happened then. The son hurried down to his father and apologized humbly, bowing his head with his hands on the floor. The old man replied that it was his own fault since he had put the pot down in a bad place.

"Then his wife came, confessing that she should have put the pot away as soon as her husband came in and apologizing that she had not done it. The son's wife then came in, saying her mother-in-law's action was quite natural and she was not responsible since she hadn't known her son was upstairs. The young woman said that she herself should have put the pot away, because she had been aware of what was going on. She apologized that she had not been more thoughtful and careful.

"Then the old man broke in. 'No, no, it's not anybody's fault. Let's look at it this way. The bundle hit the pot and broke it, and so it did not land on my head instead as if to drive out an evil spirit. To our good fortune, no one was hurt. What could be better than that?' With this the incident was settled in peace and harmony and no one was left with any blame.

"Then the fellow went to the other house. As it happened, the grandfather of this home had just returned with a *shō* (about 1.8 litres) of sake in an earthenware sake bottle. He put it down in the doorway and forgot it. Minutes later his son came in from the field and accidentally kicked the bottle over and broke it. He shouted loudly, saying it was the fault of whoever left it there. The old man came out and scolded his son, 'You should have been more careful where you were walking. You should have watched your steps.'

"Soon after that the grandmother chimed in, saying her husband was to blame because he had left the bottle in the doorway in the first place. Her words made the old man angry. 'You could have watched what was happening. You should have put it away yourself.' Then the old woman called in her daughter-in-law and started saying how old she was and she couldn't see very well. The younger woman was the one who should have put it away. The young woman answered back that she had been in the back part of the house where she hadn't even known what was going on. All of this started up a big and unpleasant quarrel, adding to the disagreements in the family.

"In a peaceful family each member becomes the one at fault and takes the blame for things. Everything is settled in roundness, peace, and harmony. But in a family in discord, each member tries to look like the good person, taking liberties in trying to look better. In this way everything ends with no meaning and no favourable outcome. Any good will that might have been there dies out for lack of encouragement."

86. Ichimori Learns the Secret of Horseback Riding

Among the Okayama clan retainers was one Ichimori Hikokurō, whose family for generations had served their rulers, the Ikedas, as instructors in horsemanship. He was, needless to say, a master of the art. Still, after listening to Kyōso's sermon "On Being Initiated into the Mysteries of all the Arts", he asked guidance in being initiated into the secret art of horsemanship.

Kyōso told him to mount up and ride, and with a swing into the saddle Ichimori mounted up, touching his horse with his whip to make a round. On getting back from the round he asked Kyōso, "Sir, how do you rate my riding?" The answer was, "You are good in your art." "Good! Did you find some points lacking, or do I need correction?"

Kyōso answered with a beaming smile, "I do have to say that you are riding the horse." And he recited this poem of his,

Remember the reins
that hold you to Great Kami
in sacred oneness.
Ride with your reins holding firm
never to loosen your hold.

Ichimori was awakened spiritually by these words. He was able also to understand the real meaning of a familiar precept on horsemanship, "Up on the horse, no one; under the saddle, no horse." After that he continued his efforts in pursuing the Way. Eventually he was able to master the secret art of horsemanship.

87. The Stonemason of Man-nari

On one New Year's Day a stonemason of Man-nari donated a stone washbasin to Kyōso with these words,[115] "I have for a while been among those who listen to your sermons and lectures. I give thanks to the graces of Kami for this. My family was able to see the past year to a close with no mishap or trouble all year. We have been free from any care. Since I feel what a blessing this has been to me, I brought you this *temizu-bachi* that I sculpted out myself. It is such an inferior piece of work, but I would like to offer it as a response to you, a token that shows my sincere gratitude for your kindness."

Kyōso responded, "This is very thoughtful of you. I trust you made a good profit during the past year?" "Oh, no, no, sir," answered the stonemason.

"That's not what I mean. I am not giving thanks for making a profit in my business. My living is still quite meagre. What I mean is that after attending *gokaijitsu* and listening to your lectures now and then for about a year now, I am able to feel much more relaxed than before. I don't know exactly why it is, but I feel at peace and at ease. Poverty doesn't bother me at all, I don't feel envy towards the wealthy people of this world, and difficulties aren't problems to me any more. No matter what happens I have a sense of gratefulness.

"Others might buy fancy clothes for New Year's and get themselves up to look very handsome. For me it is enough to have old clothes so long as they have been washed clean. I am able to pay my creditors what I owe them out of the small profits I've earned by working all the time and very hard. Nobody in my family thinks inconvenience as really inconvenient, or lack of comforts as anything lacking. We were able to welcome in the New Year in peace and concord. What a blessed grace and blessing this is to us! In the past we were always tormented from outside the house by creditors pressing us, and on the inside I passed not an hour without hearing a complaint from my wife or whimpering and crying from the children. I always pitied my children when they wanted something we didn't have that others had and we couldn't afford it. Every year ended miserably in sadness and want. But since I have started listening to your lectures I have found my heart renewed. My wife's heart also has had a renewal. I owe my sincere gratitude to you for making it possible for us to welcome in the New Year in such a peaceful mind." In this way the stonemason expressed his thanks.

Kyōso was touched by these words, and without a moment's pause he composed the following *waka* and then shared it with the mason.

> The body, the self
> are totally abandoned,
>   so the heart believes;
> Now the heart must understand
> it too must be tossed aside.[116]

88. Rokuzaemon's Six Rules

This is another story about that maker of roof tiles, Rokuzaemon of Futsukaichi. He had entered the Way in his early years and was a really zealous devotee. Not only that, he was diligent in his business and put a great deal of energy into it. His shop made high quality products and he was among a small number of the most successful and prosperous businessmen in Okayama. Rokuzaemon never missed any of the regular meetings in Ohmoto and besides that he often invited his neighbours to meetings in his home. He did this with enthusiasm and he went on to encourage them to become followers of the Way. This story took place at one of those meetings at his house.

Some time before that he had requested Kyōso to give him a copy of the Seven Rules written in his own hand.[117] On the day of this meeting Kyōso presented him with a scroll with the rules. With great joy he unrolled it. But to his chagrin, one rule was missing. The fifth rule, "You shall not slacken in the work of your house except in illness", was not there. When he approached Kyōso to have the scroll rewritten, this was the answer he got.

"Since I know all about your diligence in the work of your house, without any negligence at all, I left out that rule on purpose. It isn't necessary in your case. You should understand this and accept it as an expression of divine will. I am certain there is no need of rewriting the scroll." This is what is reported to have happened. After that day, Rokuzaemon went on working with constant diligence. Among the followers he earned an even higher reputation than before.

89. A Rice Bowl and Floss Silk

Once Kyōso was giving lectures at a certain Buddhist temple. "Please, listen to me. When someone throws a rice bowl to you, don't try to catch it with another rice bowl. You should catch it softly with floss silk. In this way the rice bowl will not break or make a noise." This is what he preached.

A man who was there listening to the lecture stood up and spoke in an accusing tone of voice. "Sensei, are you sure that a rice bowl and floss silk will make no noise?" Kyōso answered, "I am positive they will make not a sound." Then the man came nearer, and said even more excitedly, "Sir, are you definitely sure there will be no noise?" Hearing this, Kyōso responded calmly with a serene countenance, "Oh yes, my friend, the two will make a sound." The man sat down again in his place satisfied, as if he was saying, "Didn't I tell you so?"

So here was a man who began by throwing a rice bowl. And here Kyōso disregarded what he had just been saying and ignored reasonable thinking to say, "Yes, sir. You are right. The two will make a sound." We see, however, that Kyōso's action in agreeing with the listener was actually a vivid demonstration of catching a rice bowl with floss silk, just as he had been preaching.

90. Distress in a Boat off Kogushi

This happened on the eighth day of the third month of 1846 when the boat Kyōso took to travel to Shodo Island in the Seto Inland Sea was passing near Kogushi, a small village on the shore of Kojima County. Sudden gusts of wind started stirring up waves. Quickly, many boats both large and small were tossed around in the rough, raging waters, and many were overturned. The boatman on Kyōso's boat understood the grave situation they were in. He knew they were in immediate danger of capsizing also. He tried with might and main, desperately, to save his boat and his passengers. Nothing he tried did any good. Among the passengers many raised their voices calling for help. Some, as a last resort, began to offer prayers. The boat was in confusion and turmoil.

For some time Kyōso had been keeping still with his eyes closed, his calmness undisturbed. But when he saw that the boat was about to tip over and he heard the boatman tell the passengers to be ready for the worst, he opened his eyes and took out his brush-and-ink case. He took out a sheet of paper on which he wrote the following *waka*.

Oh, god of the sea
  Your angry billows and waves
    ought to be at peace;
One who knows Amaterasu
  is aboard this very boat.[118]

He tossed the paper into the water. The waves of the sea tossing the boat up and down became still in that instant. The boat reached its destination safely and all those who had fallen into the water from other boats were rescued from their deaths.

Among those rescued from the stormy waters was Itō Sadasaburō, a native of Matsuzaki in today's Tottori Prefecture (to the north of Okayama along the Japan Sea). Itō was on pilgrimage to the Kotohira Shrine on Shikoku Island.[119] Both he and his son survived this distress after being tossed into the water from another boat and nearly drowned. On hearing why the rough wind and sea had calmed down so suddenly, Itō was much moved by Kyōso's personality and joined the followers of the Way. Eventually he became a teacher of the Way himself and devoted himself to many missionary activities.[120]

91. Kyōso's Dream about His Mission

Near Higashiyama Hill on the eastern side of Okayama, on top of a lower hill, is a Shinto shrine known as Tamai-gū. A regular preaching meeting (kōseki) was held here on the 18th of every month. At the March meeting in 1846 the Direct Disciple Jikihara Ihachirō accompanied Kyōso to this place and later reported the content of an unusual sermon given at that time.[121]

"Today I have something to discuss with you. Please listen to my words attentively. Some nights ago I had a strange dream. In the dream I, Sakyō, received a written summons to appear before some authority. It was not clear where to go but I left home and went to the county magistrate's office, then to the Ikeda clan office, and then to the office of the Shogunate. But the summons was not from any of these offices. Wandering around here and there, I finally came to a place where there was a huge shrine and I thought it might be the place I was supposed to go. I went through the main gate and saw beyond that a huge entrance hall. In front of it was a beautiful stretch of white sand. The person who then appeared beckoned to me that I should go up to that sanded area.[122]

"While I was waiting there, down on my knees, I could see in the distance many formally attired officers bustling around in a palace, busily attending to their duties. Then before long a samurai who seemed to be a chief appeared at the top level of the entrance hall with seven or eight other samurai accompanying him. One of them was holding a long sword and two were carrying a magnificent set of armour and a helmet. These were the words that came to my ears from the chief. 'You, sitting there, are you not Kurozumi Sakyō Munetada? The reason I summoned you here is nothing else than the serious disturbance the world is facing today. Because of my deep concern to settle the commotion the world is in, I hereby entrust you with the appointment as *Sōtoku Sōdaishō*.'[123]

"This order was something I never would have expected. It was much more than I deserve. I felt deep gratitude, for this Great Order was such a holy thing. After thinking about it and realizing my good fortune beyond my deserving I was moved in gratitude to decide on second thought to accept what was given me. I would work to put to rest the turbulences in this world so as to ease the Divine Heart of Great Kami. I would give to this mission my whole body and life, sheltering myself under the influence of Great Kami. The chief samurai was brimming over with satisfaction at my acceptance. He had his servants open the armour case and they handed me a gorgeous suit of scarlet-threaded armour, a helmet decorated with a design in gold in the shape of a hoe like a sickle moon, and wrist and knee protectors. They also gave me a gold baton with which to give my instructions and orders.

"After I was dressed in the armour and helmet as instructed, another instruction came that I was to be presented also with a long sword decorated, like the baton, with gold. I raised the gifts up to my head to express my sincere gratitude. When I looked behind me there was a saddled black horse on which I was told to mount. Mounting the horse and bowing to the eminent samurai standing by, I looked behind me and saw an army of several tens of thousands of brave men, bowing their heads to me as they came into view. It was a gallant and powerful scene.

"Then, at the moment I was about to give my whip to the horse to begin the expedition, I woke up. I realized it had all been just a dream. But it was indeed a strange dream. I thought it was most unusual and I pondered it. The chief said we are now in turbulence, but of course we are actually under the regime of the Tokugawa Shogunate, enjoying a peaceful time that is rare in the world. Pondering on this point, I came to understand that what the chief meant is not the superficial situation but the disturbance that is in the hearts of the people. What he really meant was to ease the great inner disturbance that the hundreds of millions of people living on Earth are suffering.

"I became aware that this is nothing other than the same Great Mission that Great Kami Amaterasu had already bestowed on me.[124] When I saw this, I decided to devote myself to that mission with renewed determination. From this moment on this Sakyō will put his full heart into this mission, dedicating himself solely to putting to rest the disturbance of the world in order to fulfil the gracious and divine will of Amaterasu. Since this is my firm resolution, I solicit the earnest devotees of the Way, you who are here today, to give continuous support and further guidance."

92. Introducing Shūzō of Burakuji Village to Great Kami

Once Kyōso was returning home on foot after going on pilgrimage for prayer to the Kiyama Shrine in the province of Mimasaka. He had just passed through the town of Fukuwatari when he overheard some men behind him.[125] They were leading along some horses they were offering for hire, holding the reins as they walked. They were saying, "That fellow Shūzō of Burakuji Village is so very sick. He is miserably poor and he lives all alone. And his illness is really quite serious. He is so much to be pitied for his pain and his suffering."

When these words reached his ears, Kyōso realized immediately they were words Heaven wished him to hear. He immediately decided to visit this poor old Shūzō and offer his help. He asked here and there the way to Burakuji Village. He found it was about two miles northeast of Fukuwatari, along a path that twisted back and forth over hills and mountains. "By all means, I must help him to be blessed with divine virtue." With this firm determination, he changed his course and set off to pay Shūzō a visit.

Kyōso found the man's poverty even more pitiful than he had expected. He was living in a tumbledown hut, unsightly to look at, and he was tormented by his illness and pain. After a few words of greeting Kyōso suggested, "Come on, you can receive the blessing of Kami. I will perform *majinai* on you." Then he offered his prayers most earnestly. But the man himself was only blaming Heaven for all of his problems, and cursing the kami. He had not the smallest glimmer of any kind of faith. Because he had such a closed attitude there was no chance for any opening of gracious virtue.

Still, Kyōso performed his prayers attentively. After telling the man,

124

"Shūzō, please remember that I will continue praying for you, so please look forward to the day you will receive blessings", he left the house.

When he had walked for a couple of miles he was caught in a sudden shower of rain. It made him think, "That poor Shūzō's roof is broken and there are holes in it. The rain must be leaking in and soaking him." With this thought he turned around and hurried back. "Shūzō, the roof leaking all over you must be quite a problem. I have come back because I am afraid you are in bad trouble."

The man was huddled in one corner of his room, shivering and shaking with cold. Kyōso picked up a broom he found there and praying with all his heart he threw it up to a place where the straw roof was broken near the sick man and the rain was pouring in. Miraculously, the broom stuck in the hole, stopping it up and preventing any more leaking.

Seeing what happened, Shūzō was much surprised. He was touched with a strange flash of inspiration. At this moment Kyōso blew on him a strong breath of joy (yōki), so as to perform another majinai on him. Shūzō was impressed for the first time in his life with the sincere kindness and courtesy of another person. Struck and overwhelmed by the mysterious power he had witnessed with his own eyes, he was relieved of the illness he had suffered for many years. The divine virtues blessed him with complete recovery.

93. Questioning Kyōso about the Kami Enshrined at Imamura-gū

From the town of Kamo, in Tomada County in the province of Mimasaka, hailed a Shinto priest by the name of Yuasa Satsuma. Once when a meeting of Shinto priests was being held, Yuasa happened to stay in the same inn as Kyōso. That night they shared the same room and before going to sleep they discussed different subjects. Yuasa san asked, "By the way, Kurozumi san, would you please explain to me what kami is enshrined at Imamura-gū where you serve as priest?" Since there was no response, Yuasa repeated his question two or three times.

Finally Kyōso got out of his bedding, dressed himself in his *hakama*, and said cordially, "Imamura-gū, where I serve, consists of three shrines: Tenshōkōtaijin-gū [the shrine of Amaterasu Ohmikami], Hachiman Daijin-gū, and Kasuga Daimyōjin." Because Kyōso explained this so reverently in formal dress, Yuasa was much moved. He realized he had received a lesson on the posture and attitude every priest should adopt who serves a kami; and then, having taken this mental posture, hold to it at every moment.

Later, Yuasa san (who after the Meiji Restoration joined the Matsuoka family and received the name Matsuoka Kiyomi) joined those pursuing the Way. He became one of Kyōso's best-known disciples.[126] From the Ansei period (1854–60) onward and into Meiji times Matsuoka Kiyomi devoted himself wholeheartedly to propagating the Way in Kyushu island.

94. Kimura Seiuemon Recovers His Family's Fortune

Kimura Seiuemon was a maker of Bizen pottery who practised his vocation at Inbe Village, Wake County, in today's Bizen City east of Okayama. He was also a devoted follower of the faith and often came to Ohmoto to attend Kyōso's lectures.[127] Unfortunately, one year he experienced a number of troubles and difficulties. It got so bad that his financial condition was close to bankrupt and he was finding it hard each day to make ends meet. Then he remembered one of those lectures, one in which Kyōso had taught, "Never should you become weary of anything."

Remembering this, Kimura san pulled himself together and realized, "This is the serious situation Kyōso was talking about." One day he instructed his family to tell anyone who might come to visit, no matter where they might be from, that he was not at home. With this instruction he spent the whole day in the room where Great Kami was enshrined. He offered his prayers singleheartedly to Kami from morning to night.

On the morning of the third day he was spending this way there came a traveller who asked to see Kimura san. Although the family told the visitor the master was not at home, the visitor did not give up. He explained that he was also a potter and he had come with the express purpose of showing Kimura san some fine points in the art of pottery. When he learned that the master was absent he expressed deep regret that it couldn't be helped. In great disappointment he left Kimura's house. The family reported all this to Kimura who had been earnestly offering his prayers. He was very much interested and asked a family member to call the visitor back to see him.

This is what the visitor said to him. "By trade I am a maker of pottery in the Kantō area.[128] I am just now on my way back home from a pilgrimage to Kotohira Shrine. Some years ago a secret, very excellent method of applying designs on pottery was passed on to me. This Inbe area is well known for the fine ceramics you produce. But I thought the products of this area could get even better and even more popular if I had a chance to share my method of applying designs.[129] Since I hear you are a skilled expert in the craft I came to see you to pass my method on to you."

Seiuemon san extended his heartfelt thanks to the visitor for his generous courtesy. "Such a sharing would be a great pleasure to me, but unfortunately my family is in such poverty just now that I don't have the capital to start any new venture." The visitor was a person so filled with generosity that he gave Kimura san a substantial part of his travelling money and taught him his trade secret.

The new method of design application improved the quality of Kimura's products. New outlets opened in the market and soon he was flooded with orders. Within a short period he raised himself to the position of one of the top Inbe pottery artists. It was only because Kimura san revered Kyōso's teaching and practised it so earnestly that he was blessed by divine virtues. It is said that from then on his family business enjoyed prosperity from one generation to another.

The shell-shaped *temizu-bachi* we see today at the Munetada Shrine in Ohmoto is said to be a donation of Seiuemon. He made it especially at the age of eighty-five to commemorate the enshrinement of Munetada Daimyōjin in 1885.

95. Paying a Visit to Toi's House

In the Okayama clan there served a retainer by the name of Toi Ukon. Toi was the chief magistrate of the Bizen clan, receiving an annual stipend of 4200 *koku*. For his meritorious and outstanding service to the Tokugawa Shogunate he was granted an unusual privilege of using a drum, referred to as the "Toi drum." All harbour and port authorities in Japan are said to have been instructed by the Tokugawa government that when they heard Toi's drum beating on an approaching boat, all other ships and boats were to give way. Such was the social status of the Toi family. Of course the family was also held in high esteem by the Lords of the Ikeda clan who governed the province of Bizen.

Toi san respected Kyōso very much. He often invited him to his house so he could listen to his sermons. On Kyōso's leaving the house afterward, the master, Toi san himself, was always sure to rearrange Kyōso's footwear before sending him off.[130]

In the Toi household there was a hired manservant by the name of Noro Shunpei. Once the manservant told his master, "Sir, I am afraid

Genkan, the entrance area of a house

this may not be a matter I should bring up to you but please allow me to say it. It is such an admirable thing for you to revere the sensei of Kurozumi so much and to invite him in so you and your house can hear his lectures. But sir, please allow me to remind you of your position and your status. You are a high samurai with a stipend of over 4,000 *koku*. And yet, quite often I see you rearranging the *geta* of that country priest with your own hands. You must know such behaviour is not appropriate for a samurai of your status. Sir, I fear it would not be a good idea for this to come to the ears of Lord Ikeda. I do wish you would keep yourself from turning his *geta* around."

This was Noro's suggestion, and Toi san agreed, "That is quite reasonable. You are right. Thank you for your kind advice." When Kyōso again visited the Tois, Noro was watching carefully. He saw that his master turned Kyōso's footwear around with respect as before. He was dissatisfied with this and again he brought up his advice to Toi san.

The time after that when Kyōso visited the Toi residence it was just after a spring shower. The Toi garden had been swept clean including the entryway up to where the *geta* had been placed, leaving traces of the broom's sweeping. And again, when Kyōso was leaving, Noro saw his master rearranging the footwear. The sight provoked real anger in him.

When the guest had gone, his dissatisfaction spilled over and his full anger came out. "Sir, how often have I told you! Sir, again you have turned that old priest's *geta* around!"

Seeing him reddened in anger, Toi san ordered him, "Shunpei, go out and carefully check the footpath out to the gate." "What is it you wish to tell me?" "Just go there and check the marks Kyōso's *geta* have made."[131] Grudging and grumbling, Noro went to look out in the garden. To his amazement, there was not a single *geta* mark on the path. The only marks he could see were those the broom had made. Seeing this, he was hit instantly as with a dash of cold water.

"Thank you, sir. Now I see how natural it is that you give such reverent respect to Kurozumi Sensei. Kurozumi Sensei is indeed the person who rightfully deserves the name of 'living kami'. It was my dullness and my doubt that made me so rash as to give you that advice. I am really ashamed of my bad conduct. Please allow me to beg your forgiveness."

Noro Shunpei extended his heartfelt apology to Toi san, and soon entered the Way to become an earnest devotee. His submission of *shinmon* is recorded for 1822.

96. "Never Try to Win!"

As the top swordsmanship instructor for the Bizen clan of Okayama, there served a skilled samurai by the name of Abe Ugenji.[132] One day Abe san was visited by a person skilled in martial arts, especially swordsmanship, who requested to be matched with him. He was a man who said he was from the island of Kyushu and was otherwise unknown. When Abe san crossed swords with the visitor he became aware that his challenger was a man of ability comparable to his own. The two agreed to meet again a few days later for a match.

Although Abe had confidence in his own ability, he felt a little uneasy that he might be defeated. Worrying about this and pondering on it, he decided to visit Kyōso to seek his advice. After listening to Abe's story Kyōso just said to him, "Abe san, you should never try to win."

These words gave Abe instant insight. He offered his sincere gratitude, saying, "Sensei, thank you so much." In his own mind he went on thinking to himself,

"So that is what it was. My heart was filled with the thought that I must win, I must beat him. I was just thinking that I must not be beaten, I must beat that swordsman. My mind was filled with just that thought. I kept thinking it would be a shame to me, the top swordsmanship

A *kendo* match

instructor of the clan of Okayama, that I might lose a bout to an unknown samurai. The anxiety and worry that I had the first time I met him caused my heart to be stiff. The stiffness prevented me from using my ability to the full extent that I usually do, and because of that some part of my skill couldn't show itself at the moment it was needed. I must admit I have been quite mistaken in my thinking."

With this introspection in mind Abe san faced his challenger. Not many seconds had passed before the visiting samurai threw aside his *shinai* and went to the floor at Abe's feet, admitting,

"Abe sensei, today I was really overpowered by your magical, wonderful skill. I am overcome. The level of your ability is far beyond what I could ever attain myself." The samurai looked embarrassed but he added, "Whatever it might be, I must tell you that you are, however, a sinful person. You are a cunning person because you hid your true skill when we met the first time. It seems you were just toying with me. You are *malicious*!"

With these smiling words the visitor is said to have offered his praise, extending his heartfelt admiration to Abe san.

97. A Good Person Doing a Sinful Deed

One day two ladies came to visit at Kyōso's house. One of them looked downhearted and weighed down with sorrow. She evidently had some serious concern that really troubled her heart. He instructed one of them to go outside and bring back a stone, the heaviest and biggest she could carry. To the other he handed a paper bag and told her to gather as many pebbles as she could get into it.

They were soon back, one with a large stone and the other with a bagful of pebbles. Then Kyōso gave further instructions. They were to return the stone and the pebbles to where they had been, adding that they must be put down in just the same place they had been before and with the same side up as before. It was an easy task to put the big stone back as instructed, but it was almost impossible to do this with the pebbles. Of course, there was no way to remember where every pebble had been, let alone put them back exactly as before.

Then came Kyōso's words,

"As you have found out, it isn't hard to put a large stone back where it was. In the same way, a great sin can be clearly dealt with and overcome. But trifling sins and offences are often committed unknowingly. As you have found out from the case of the small pebbles, when these sins are committed they are hardly noticed. It's hard to see where they came from. Those who do small sins don't even realize they have done something wrong. We are apt to believe we haven't done any sins at all. In this way we commit many small misdeeds without doing them on purpose. We must all be conscious of how our minds work. We must be more careful never to commit such sins, the sins that good-natured and well-meaning people do. Bear in mind that making up for them is not an easy matter."

Kyōso's advice changed the way the downhearted lady was treating her heart. It also encouraged the other lady to pursue the Way more earnestly, so as to be free of the faults that good people have without thinking. Both are said to have devoted themselves even more to deepening their faith.

98. Admonishing the Charcoal Dealer of Furugyō

On the east bank of the Asahi River that runs through the city of Okayama is a district known as Furugyō. It is located behind the famous Kōrakuen Park, well known throughout Japan. Here a large charcoal dealer had his store. For some years he enjoyed a prosperous business. But his way of running his big business was rather careless, leaving it in charge of his employees. It went on to such a state that he didn't even know the current prices of charcoal anymore. Gradually this ruined his fortune and he found himself in serious financial trouble. This affected his credit and hurt his reputation with the public and he was finding it harder every day to keep his business going. He then thought he would run away to Osaka under cover of night.

But he decided he would first go to see Kyōso whose lectures and sermons he had often listened to, in order to seek his advice on his plan to flee in the night. This is what Kyōso advised the man. "So, you are going to Osaka? But what do you intend to do there?" "Sir, since my situation is as I explained to you I just think it might do me good if I went off to Osaka instead."

"Then I will compose a *waka* for you." With this, Kyōso picked up his writing brush and wrote,

Nothing different,
    both this place and that are filled
        with anxiety.
Your body will be living
    under the same sun and moon.

"The same sun and moon shine on the place you are heading for. There could be no change because you are still the selfsame person.

"Instead of moving you should take a decisive step. Relieve yourself of all your family belongings except a pot and kettle that you need temporarily. Then get yourself up on the mountain. Buy charcoal with the money you got for your belongings, and then you must yourself be the one who pulls the cart and sells the charcoal."

The dealer was moved by this guidance. When he got home he sold everything he had, and went off into the mountains, using the money to buy charcoal. He handled the trade himself as he had done when he had started years before. He offered discounts for his goods in the amount his salesmen and clerks had secretly been putting into their own pockets. The sight of this former big businessman pulling his own cart loaded with charcoal astonished everyone who saw it. Soon orders came flooding in from many places. Before very long his business was prospering to the point that he couldn't manage it alone. He had to employ a helper and soon he hired two more employees. Within three years he was able to restore his fortune to the level it was at before.

This incident is said to have occurred in 1844.

99. The Rice-Polishing Group

As the Way began gaining favour and spreading, lecture meetings were started up in various places. Some meetings were held monthly on stated days with Kyōso invited so that people could hear him speak. Those who attended would exchange their experiences and their ideas as they pursued the faith together. This sort of meeting has been held from that day to this at various places as the members find it convenient. Such groups have been important organizations in spreading the faith.

In Kyōso's time there were a number of devoted samurai who lived in Banchō, a residential quarter for samurai. They had organized a regular meeting and they thought they should have a name for it. There were many suggestions and they couldn't decide which one to use. Finally they asked Kyōso to suggest a good name for themselves. All members of the group looked forward to getting a name that would be appropriate for them.

To their surprise, the name Kyōso gave them was "The Rice-Polishing Group" (*kome-tsuki-kai*). Noticing that they were looking puzzled, he explained why he had chosen this name.

Rice polishing with pestle and mortar

"Please listen to me. Suppose that this place of meeting is a mortar for polishing rice. I am the pestle and you are the rice grains. When rice grains are put into a mortar and pounded the bran gradually comes off and the rice gets polished and clean as the grains rub against each other. You all come to attend the meeting and you listen to my lectures and then by your mutual contact with each other you are polished and cleaned. In this way you improve your character and enhance your personality. Please understand that this is why I have named this meeting of yours 'Rice-Polishing Group'."

This explanation brought beaming smiles to the members' faces. They all felt very happy to know that their meeting was named with the idea that their bodies and souls would get refreshingly clean and polished. Since then many meetings followed this example of naming themselves. A case in point is the "Uchisange Meeting of the Rice-Polishing Group", using their location at the "foot of the castle" (*sange*) as part of their name.

100. Ishio Sensei Has His Heart Blessed with the *Majinai* Ritual

Regular meeting days at Ohmoto were the days ending in two and seven each month. The number of those attending on these days was increasing and Kyōso's house could not hold them all. Many had to sit out in the front yard to listen to the lectures. Since he performed rituals of *majinai* so wholeheartedly at these meetings, numbers of miracles occurred. Some regained their eyesight and cripples were able to stand up or walk home. So, many who came had to stand in line to be blessed by Kyōso's virtues. He treated them all earnestly and with equal attention and many who were seriously ill or who suffered disorders had to wait in line for their turn.

Among those regularly waiting in line was Ishio sensei.[133] His wife said to him, "There are so many people out there waiting to receive Kyōso's blessing. He must certainly be worn out performing *majinai* on so many people. Since you don't have any particular illness to complain about, don't you think you should refrain from standing in that line?"

"Oh, you may be right. But you must know it is my heart I am having blessed by Kyōso's *majinai*."[134] At every meeting after that Ishio was sure to be seen waiting in the line of people wishing to be blessed with the *majinai* ritual.

101. High Disciple Tokio Visits the Ise Grand Shrine on Kyōso's Behalf

In the first month of 1847 Kyōso ordered High Disciple Tokio to go on his behalf to the province of Ise on a pilgrimage to the Ise Grand Shrine, where Great Kami is enshrined. On finishing his preparations for travelling, Tokio sensei went to Kyōso to say goodbye for the trip. Kyōso said, "Tokio san, I must thank you for the trouble you are going to. Important things have been happening. Last year our new regulations went into effect. Also, our new hall will be completed this year thanks to contributions from the followers.[135] So, I ask you to be sure you are granted an audience by Great Kami." Tokio sensei set off with the words, "Yes, sir. By all means I will."

However, these instructions posed a big problem to Tokio. During his trip to Ise he constantly puzzled over the question of what he must do to be granted such an audience. Not a moment passed that he wasn't thinking about what he was charged with. Now he was in Ise, and he had paid visits to the Grand Shrine and offered his devoted prayers. To his anxiety, however, no blessing anything like a "grant of an audience" had yet appeared.

Then Tokio sensei remembered another instruction. "If you find yourself in the position of not knowing what to do, offer the purification prayer (Oharai). Let the power of this prayer clear away all the problems that puzzle you and you cannot solve. From that day on he began offering the purification prayer. One morning, not long after praying it, a *waka* flashed through his mind.

> A little story
>   told in the distant mountains
>   of far-off China
> Is something that can be heard
>   without the ears hearing it.

Tokio sensei realized, "So that was the point!" When he loudly recited, "A little story told in the distant mountains of far-off China", he felt, to his surprise, an indescribably pleasant breeze blowing from inside the Shrine building (*shinden*). It put him into a state of ecstasy, for Great Kami was bestowing a gracious audience on him.

Immediately on returning to Ohmoto, Tokio sensei was greeted by Kyōso who went with him before the altar. The two offered their prayers together singleheartedly. Kyōso then told him to go up to the pulpit, blessing him with the honour of speaking from that seat. As instructed, Tokio went up the place of speaking and from there he told the story of his trip from Okayama to Ise and back in detail. He told how he was graciously blessed with an audience by Great Kami.

Kyōso was very happy and pleased with this report and added, "In this moment, most thankfully, this Sakyō has also been accorded a most gracious audience."

102. A Blessing for a Bamboo Grove

Iwako was a place that was famous for its groves of high-quality bamboo.[136] So much was it known for this throughout the country that it was cited in a poem.

> How I wish to be
>   a bamboo that is growing
>   in old Iwako.
> Then I could serve all *daimyō*
>   hitting targets far away.

Once during the days of Kyōso all of the bamboos growing there started to bear fruit. This is a bad thing, since then those plants die back, not to sprout again for scores or even hundreds of years. In popular belief, such blooming and fruit-bearing was a sign of bad luck.

When this happened, High Disciple Kawakami Chūsho,[137] at that time serving the Bizen clan as magistrate for the county in which Iwako was located, was troubled about it. His anxiety prompted him to seek Kyōso's advice. Saying, "Since this bamboo grove is a special one reserved for Lord Ikeda, I will go with you", he went with Kawakami sensei to have a look. When they were at the place Kyōso went around the grove offering purification prayers and scattering grains of ritually purified rice (*senmai*).

Then, when they went back again the next morning, they found all the bamboo fruit had dropped to the ground, allowing the plants to keep on growing.

103. Nightsoil Buckets and Sake Kegs

During the days of Kyōso there lived in Furumatsu (a few hundred yards east of Ohmoto) a fellow who was hard to deal with when he got angry. He was a person who got angry very easily and it happened in almost any kind of situation. No one dared approach him at those times. It would only make his anger worse. Even he began to get disgusted about it, since he couldn't solve his problem.

So he went to Kyōso to talk about it. After hearing what the fellow had to say, Kyōso said, "No matter how angry you might be, just be patient and calm down. Patience is the best solution. Anyone can be a little patient, but something more than that is needed. You must know what the poem says, 'To forbear what you cannot forbear at all, that is true forbearance (kan-nin)'." In this way he admonished him firmly about the importance of being more patient. But the fellow so easily rousable to anger had no ears to listen and to follow this instruction. Kind advice of every sort fell flat with him.

Unconvinced, he headed for home. While he was walking home, grumbling, down a footpath that ran along the narrow levee above the rice paddies, he saw a farmer coming towards him. The man was carrying two heavy buckets of nightsoil balanced on the ends of a pole set across his shoulders. From the opposite direction, another man was coming, also balancing a pole on his shoulders. Slung from this man's pole were a couple of kegs of good sake.

As the grumbling man looked both ways, the thought struck him, "Which of the two will let the other pass by?" He stepped off the path to see what would happen. Then the fellow with sake kegs also stepped down into the rice field, opening the way for the farmer. After the man with the nightsoil buckets had gone by, he got back up on the footpath with his kegs and went on with his business.

The grumbler then grasped what Kyōso had been trying to teach him. He said to himself, "In this world, the person who is in the better situation is the one who should open the way for the other to pass. In this case, even one drop of nightsoil will ruin the sake." The fellow returned to Ohmoto, excited with the thought that he would report his observation to Kyōso. He wanted to extend an apology and ask for forgiveness. Again he met Kyōso, and he reported his experience.

Kyōso told him, "Oh, what happened there was very good for you. You noticed a really important point, and you thought about it well. When people get angry it is because they believe they are absolutely in the right, but something is keeping them from having their way. So, since believing one is absolutely right leads to anger, the one who gets angry is quite often the one who most strongly feels a reason for being right. When playing sumo with your grandson, you know you are stronger than he is. In ordinary sumo it is right that the stronger and better wrestler wins, but with your grandson you pretend you have lost your match to him.[138]

"If you really see how things look from another's point of view, there can be no chance of getting angry. If you would look at others in this light and treat them accordingly they would soon understand your point of view." This is how Kyōso taught the man who was once a grumbler.

104. The Scroll Kyōso Wrote for Fujita Shōsuke[139]

One of the leading retainers of Ikeda Hyōgo, second-in-command of the Ikeda clan, was Fujita Shōsuke. Fujita was a devotee of the faith. One New Year's day when he went to Ohmoto to extend his season's greetings to Kyōso he was told, "Fujita san, I have here the divine title you asked me to write for you. Please note I wrote it while I had the feeling in my heart of being eighteen years old." Fujita sensei accepted the calligraphy with heartfelt gratitude. Since it happened to be a year in which he was to be stationed in Kyoto he took it with him to be framed by an expert.

Carrying sake kegs on a pole

On his way there, while staying in the Osaka office of the Bizen clan rice warehouses, he happened to meet a talented calligraphy appraiser from Edo. By careful examination of the brush strokes and their shading and of the way spaces were filled with words or left unfilled on the page this man could evaluate the skill of calligraphers.

Fujita asked him to comment on Kyōso's work. After examining it the expert said, "This brushwork is without a doubt by an artist with very rare talent and skill. But there is a point that bothers me. This person is someone of high moral calibre and it is impossible that such a person could be only about twenty years old. This is what bothers me and I cannot understand it. I can't make it out. No doubt this person has spent sixty or seventy years of life here in this world. Yet take a good look at the brush strokes. Only a person who is around twenty years old could produce strokes such as these. What an awe-inspiring, what a gracious and powerful work of art!"

105. Praying for the Opening of the Good Fortune of Amaterasu Ohmikami

Kyōso paid six visits to the Ise Grand Shrine during his lifetime. On one occasion when he was presenting his votive offering to Great Kami through one of the priests there he was asked about the nature of his prayer. He said, "With great awe, I wish to pray for the opening of Amaterasu Ohmikami's good fortune."[140] His answer seems to have puzzled the attending priest who repeated the question with a sense of doubt.

"Humbly and respectfully, I beg to pray for the auspicious opening of Great Kami's good fortune." These words, so clear and distinct, surprised and awed the priest. It is said that this humble and sincere wish of Kyōso held him in awe and reverence.

What is meant by "the opening of the good fortune of Amaterasu Ohmikami" is that all people in this world would have their eyes opened to the divine virtues of Kami. Kyōso's goal was that each person in the world should be blessed with the divine virtue. This is what Kyōso prayed for consistently throughout his whole life.

106. Old Hishikawa Ginjibei Enters the Faith

This happened in 1821. When Kyōso was presiding over a meeting at a house in the Kobashi section of Okayama an old man was present who was much moved by the lecture he heard. He happened to be in the neighbourhood on an errand, delivering amulets for a Buddhist temple he was working for. The old man approached Kyōso and said, "Would you please hire me as one of your helpers?" Needless to say, Kyōso declined the request, saying, "Since I am not a samurai I don't keep any assistants." The old man, however, got his companion to take his amulet box back to the temple and went straight to Kyōso's house.

From that day on that is where he stayed, chopping wood and carrying water. For the rest of his life he endeavoured to follow the Way and to carry on religious practices. He never mentioned that he would be under the care of Kyōso nor did Kyōso ever bring up the fact that he had refused him. But there he was. His name was Hishikawa Ginjibei. Wherever Kyōso went, there the old man went also, carrying whatever Kyōso needed for the day. He would be always at the side of the platform when Kyōso was speaking, attentively listening to the lectures and sermons. He looked after Kyōso and really cared for him. He spent his days attending him and serving him faithfully in a manner more devoted than any servant would ever have done. The old man never stopped to spare himself nor did he spare any effort in doing whatever was for the interest and benefit of others.

Never did his own profit or loss, or his own advantage or disadvantage, have any effect on his attitude or on his work. No matter how painful or toilsome a task might be, never a word of request for any compensation ever came from him. It is related that among the villagers of Kaminanako there was a saying, when one of them would ask a fellow-villager for some kind of favour, that they would put it this way, "Would you please be my Ginjibei for a while?"

107. At the Doll Shop

One of Kyōso's sermons went as follows.

"Here is something that happened at a doll shop. An apprentice working there had an accident while dusting the doll displays, the kind used during the girls' festival that have various levels.[141] He was so busily dusting one of them, each of its levels full of dolls, that he hit it so hard with his duster that the whole display fell over.

"Now this started some big trouble. All the dolls had fallen down in confusion after they had been so carefully arranged. The apprentice was nervous and confused and put them back quickly, whichever his hands touched first, without paying attention to where they belonged. (You see, each of the dolls used in the festival has its own special place on the shelf according to the social status of the people they represent.) Now see what the apprentice had done. The prince and princess were placed on lower seats and the guardian samurai were at the top. They were sitting in positions they were not supposed to take, all mixed up.

"When the proprietor of the shop saw this he shouted fiercely at the apprentice. 'See what you have done! The dolls are all mixed up! Put them back right away where they belong!' A customer came into the shop just at that moment. After quietly watching what was happening he said to the two of them, 'Well, well. What looks like confusion may after all be the right and proper situation. It won't be long before such a time will surely come. I believe the way you have them now must be the right way.' This is the comment he made."

In those days the social status of samurai, farmers, craftsmen, and merchants, in that descending order, was strictly enforced. And it was Kyōso who taught every day that everyone is equal. The divided portion (*bunshin*) of the divine presence is equally within everyone, and the eyes of Great Kami see them so. He taught the equality of human rights every day in his preaching, using this story.

108. Feelings of Friendship among Followers at Meetings

One follower related the following story, years after it happened.[142]

"The meetings on the 'two and seven' days were well attended. We rarely failed to go, but there were others who came from even greater distances and who had to return home again on the same night. I don't know how it is now, but in those days there was a sword rack at the entrance and a number of swords were placed there. It looked very impressive, but we took off our straw raincoats and put them down next to the rack anyway before entering the house.

"The place was filled with worshippers, including some from leading samurai families in service to the Ikeda clan such as Furuta Yūjiro and Ishida Tsuruemon. There was no segregation, however, in which one person was given a seat of honour because he was a samurai, or another had to sit in a less desirable seat because he was a farmer. No matter who it was, even a merchant or an artisan, whoever arrived first got the front seats. All were seated in the order that they arrived.

"On this particular day it seemed that some important people had to sit in inconvenient places at the back, with low-born people bowing to them as they arrived. Some low-born women and children were sitting up front in the better seats. The samurai had much authority at that time

141

Display for Doll's Day festival

and were generally keen on their dignity, but at these meetings they often could not get seats near where Kyōso was preaching or sometimes even get a place inside where they could see well. In those days you would not see that happening anywhere else.

"Once the meeting began there was absolute silence. Once in a while you could hear the clap of hands (*kashiwade*) but that was all. No noise came from anyone, even the women and children. But this was not caused by any kind of rigid formality. The voice of the Founder sank into us, deep into our hearts. We were so deeply moved that our heads became heavy and we felt nothing but gratitude and the sanctity of the moment. Once the meeting was over we could not remember anything that had been said, though I had an excellent memory about everything else. Up to about the age of sixty I could remember the time at which small things happened long before. I was sometimes called a 'living diary'. But I couldn't remember anything Kyōso preached at one of those meetings. Of course, I came to understand it was not necessary to remember what was said. That was not the point. It was important simply to be filled with gratitude.

"After the sermon there was *majinai* for those who had asked for it, again on a first-come-first-served basis. Those who needed healing were lying down on the *tatami* mats with their heads on pillows, ready to be helped. Once when I was receiving help this way, Kurozumi Sensei said as he pressed my abdomen firmly, 'Oh, by the way, I do hope Kamezō is enjoying good health these days.[143] I have received letters of invitation from him. But I am sorry that various engagements and activities have kept me so busy that, to my regret, I have been unable to accept his invitation. Would you please convey the message to him, with my sincere apology, that I will arrange my schedule to fulfil his wishes?' Up to this day I can recall the message he entrusted to me, down to its minute points.

"After everyone who had asked for *majinai* had received it, we all took part in a dinner together and then the meeting was considered to be over. This was usually around ten at night. Afterwards everyone mingled together freely. Kyōso treated everyone equally in a free and friendly fashion, with the sick getting special and careful attention. As a result, whenever the followers happened to meet somewhere it was like meeting members of a family. We enjoyed a feeling of mutual closeness and care for each other.

"On one occasion as I was hurrying home from a meeting I happened to catch up with some samurai, five or six of them. They were walking ahead of me on the path and also going home from the same meeting. In those days someone of my social rank was not allowed to pass samurai on the road. I was going along behind them for a while when they turned and asked me very politely how far I had to go. When I answered that I was going to Shimoyamada in Oku County they apologized for holding me up when I had so far to go. 'Well, well. That's a long way. Don't worry about us. Please go on ahead, and be careful on your way home.' This was, I knew, because of the Way, and I felt deeply grateful."

This unadorned story of the old days says in clear and simple words what kind of atmosphere was fostered among the followers at that time, how friendly and cordial the relationship among us was. It sparkles like a pure jewel, full of the companionship enjoyed by the different members. It warms our hearts with satisfaction and gratitude.

109. How High Disciple Morishita Keitan[144] Entered the Faith

At the time when numbers of samurai of the Bizen clan were joining Kyōso's followers the reputation of the Way was rising rapidly among them. The many miracles of healing that happened were often talked about when they got together. Morishita sensei was one of those who heard these rumours. It was something he could not keep quiet about. How ridiculous, that illness could be cured by Kyōso's *majinai* and how disturbing that large crowds would gather and hear his teachings! He thought, "Is this something righteous or is it something evil? If it is evil, then by all means it cannot be allowed to go on any longer."

After mulling this over for a while this way, Morishita finally decided to go to Kaminakano to see Kyōso in person. He would cross-question him to look into the rights and wrongs of it and to contend for the right. When he arrived, a regular meeting was just being held and Kyōso was just presenting his lecture.

The thundering sounds of handclapping almost deafened Morishita. He sat up straight and listened carefully along with everyone else. Kyōso's voice could be heard clearly, even outside the meeting place. The atmosphere was so harmonious that Morishita felt a spontaneous vigour rising within himself. Without his intending it, his soul and mind were deeply moved by the lecture. His heart was filled with a feeling of gratitude.

Afterward he went to Kyōso and exchanged questions and answers with him. With each exchange he gained a clearer understanding. His doubts all disappeared. Now he was convinced that this person was a man of true virtue and the faith he preached was the true way. He was ashamed of his previous doubts and repented of them. With his irreverence gone, he submitted his formal pledge and became one of the disciples. This was in 1844.

Not long afterward he became a member of the Banchō Rice Polishers Group and devoted himself ever more deeply to the faith.[145] After the Meiji Restoration he continued to exert himself in the Way and became the head of the Headquarters administration of Kurozumikyō, and then Vice-Patriarch. The dedication of his lifetime was a great contribution to Kurozumikyō.

110. Having Kami Watch for Burglars is Irreverent

One day Kyōso was passing by the front of a particular house on his way home from a meeting. Here lived a family who were Kurozumikyō followers who often came to Ohmoto for meetings. Noticing there was no light on inside but the front door was wide open, he asked one of those who were walking with him to go up to the house and warn them not to be so careless.

Soon the person who went on this errand caught up with Kyōso and said, "Great Sensei, that family head is really a rude fellow. A man came out of the house and when I said he should be more careful, he didn't even thank me. What he said was that Great Sensei always teaches we must leave everything to follow its own course. He says all he is doing is just following your teachings. His attitude and the way he responded to me was as if he wanted to tell me my advice was not welcome. It really burns me up to think about it."

Kyōso said, "Well, well. Is that the way it is? That fellow wants Great Kami to take on the job of a night watchman? How irreverent, expecting Kami to watch for burglars! What an ignorant, sinful thing to say!"

111. Madame Kawakami and Her Son, High Disciple Kawakami Chūsho, Join in Pursuing the Way

Kawakami sensei, who was the officially appointed Confucian scholar for the Bizen clan, was held in high esteem also for observing filial piety in his own life in an outstanding way. To his great regret, however, his mother had lost her eyesight. All the medication and treatment they tried could not cure it. Kawakami was much discouraged and troubled to know that her illness was beyond the reach of medical cure. His mother had a sincere wish that they would invite Kyōso, who had such a high reputation, to their home to pray that she would be blessed. He could not do it. Because of his conscience as a scholar and because of his pride he was reluctant to do what his mother wanted.

At the time he was feeling this way, a man who was a good friend and close colleague went to him, strongly urging him to agree to his mother's request. After thinking it over carefully, he finally set off for Kaminakano. Since it happened to be a regular meeting day, Kawakami sensei had the pleasure of listening to Kyōso's lecture. He was moved, but only to the point of thinking, "That was a pretty good lecture." That was all, but the thought, "I would like another chance to hear a lecture", also lingered in his mind.

He was found there at the next time of meeting. Again he was much touched and impressed and gained a sense of respect for Kyōso's personality. But still the unwelcome thought of bowing his head to Kyōso occupied his mind.

On his third visit to Kaminakano, Kyōso started his lecture with these words, "Would you all please listen to me carefully. Today I will serve you a bottle of top quality Kamigata *sake*.[146] So, I would like you all to rinse out your *sake* bottle, that is, your hearts, and listen carefully to what I am going to say." This was the opening remark as Kyōso began speaking.

Kawakami sensei was totally startled and put back on his heels by these words. He got up and left the hall, thinking, "Oh, my. My mind and heart have been all filled up with the Chinese classics I have studied so hard all these years. I have left no room for Kyōso's words to get in. What a mistake, what a blunder I have committed! I have been wrong."[147] He admitted his mistake and repented of it quite deeply.

Then he cleansed his hands again at the *temizuya* outside. With a freshened heart he went back in to listen to the lecture. In contrast to his previous way of listening, now each word and every phrase entered into him and moved within his breast. An ecstatic feeling of utmost gratitude began moving him. Afterward Kawakami sensei waited for everyone to leave. Then he went to Kyōso to ask for a ritual of *majinai* for his poor mother. Kyōso replied, "That is very filial of you. I must visit your house at once to perform the ritual in response to your piety. But please understand that I have been very busy lately. So, would you please wait for a few days?"

146

Hearing this, he was very sorry that his own cleverness was the only reason his mother's request had been delayed until that time. With remorse, tears rolled down his cheeks. Kyōso grasped the situation and said, "What a sincere and thoughtful attitude. Allow me to convey your sincerity of this very moment directly to Great Kami. Now there is no more need for me to visit your dear mother. She will surely be blessed with the divine virtues without my visiting her. On your return home, I promise that you will see your mother has recovered her eyesight. How gracious! What could be more gracious?" He ended his words with a handclap.[148]

When Kawakami sensei got close to his house he saw his mother waiting at the gate of their home. "I was worried because you were so late and I came to the gate to welcome you home. The fact is that just a little while ago, my eyes opened! Now I can see your face! I am so very grateful." The two rejoiced, embracing each other.

There is a well-known letter, known as "The Second New Year Letter", which details in his own handwriting what the High Disciple Kawakami experienced in 1822.[149]

112. Asking Kami to Catch Fish is Small-minded

During the lifetime of Kyōso shin[150] there lived in the village of Hamano a person by the name of Hashida Usaburō. Though Usaburō was a farmer, he also eked out his income by catching fish in a nearby river. He was sure to attend the two-and-seven regular meetings to listen to Kyōso's teachings. And, he lived in accordance with these teachings so as to be blessed by the divine virtue of the Sun Kami. He was clear in his own mind that anything he did in complete singleheartedness in accordance with those teachings would have to meet with success.

So, when fishing in the river he prayed wholeheartedly to Great Kami. Then when he put his right arm down into the water he had no difficulty in getting hold of a fish. Happily he would return home with handsome baskets of sweetfish.[151] After a time Usaburō became so proud of his outstanding talent that he told Kyōso about it. "The divine virtues are so gracious that when even an ignorant person like me goes fishing and I pray singleheartedly to Kami and leave my ego behind, then I can freely get hold of any fish, as many fish as I might want. How gratifying the divine virtue is to me!"

After letting a moment go by Kyōso said, "Usaburō. Do you mean to tell me that you trouble the divine virtue for such a trifling thing as grabbing hold of river fish? What a small-minded, unworthy thing to do! Isn't it such a very small catch, if you use the divine virtue only to get hold of a fish? Don't you know that you can get hold of all of Heaven and Earth by means of divine virtue?

"You have to understand the true meaning of grasping things, in accord with the divine will. It means to grasp all things living in Heaven and Earth. Obviously, just grabbing river fish is a matter that isn't worth an argument. It is below criticism. Please broaden your heart and your way of thinking, and pursue the way of truth." Usaburō is said to have been overwhelmed with gratitude, enlightened by Kyōso's admonition.

113. Chihara Tōzaemon Enters the Faith

In Takata Village, Bitchu Province, lived a man named Chihara Tōzaemon. Chihara was by nature a very honest person, but at the age of twenty-two he was affected by tuberculosis. For three years he received hundreds of treatments and remedies suggested by physicians from different places but none had any effect. He happened to hear of a certain Ishii Sōken,[152] a physician who had studied Western medicine in the Dutch language, who was practising in the city of Okayama. Though Chihara had become quite weak in body he set off on a palanquin with the help of an attendant, wishing to have himself diagnosed by this doctor.

On the way, they took a rest at a tea-stall in the village of Taketōshi, a few hundred yards north of Imamura Shrine. It happened to be the day of one of the regular meetings at Kyōso's place and many people were seen passing by in that direction. The owner of the tea-stall asked him if he also was on his way to visit Kurozumi Sensei. "No. I am on my way to get treatment from that famous physician Ishii Sōken."

Hearing Tōzaemon's reply, the man went on, "Kurozumi Sensei has realized many miraculous graces. Many sick people who had a hard time finding a cure are coming from near and far. You should know that many go home again blessed with complete recovery. Why not pay a visit to Kurozumi Sensei and receive a blessing?" This suggestion encouraged Tōzaemon to pay Kyōso a visit. On leaving the stall he abruptly changed his direction from east to south. They arrived just as the lecture was about to begin.

In the lecture Kyōso gave this teaching. "Since we humankind are each a divided portion (*bunshin*) of the Sun-and-Moon,[153] and since humans are in oneness with Kami, all illness is subject to cure. Everyone in Heaven and Earth who lives in accordance with the ways of Providence may live vigorously without any fear of death."

As Chihara listened earnestly to the lecture, these words made him forget his illness and his anxieties. At the same time sweat came pouring down his face without his noticing it. Now and then he wiped his face with a towel. As the sermon was filling his thoughts, he became aware of his physical condition. He noticed that just as a leaf turns new he was feeling more sprightly and light-hearted. The disease that had affected him for years disappeared like a mist. Within one or two days he was able to return home on his own feet.

This was a situation that fitted exactly the saying, "coming on palanquin and returning on foot".[154] Reportedly, after this happened Chihara never missed any of the two-and-seven meetings.

114. The Kite Admonition

This story was in one of Kyoso shin's lectures.

"A child was flying his kite. To his misfortune, a strong wind began to toss the kite wildly up and down. He quickly tried to get it back from the wind, hauling on the string with all his might, facing downwind. Despite his wish and his effort the wind blew ever stronger and finally the kite crashed and was lost in a tree.

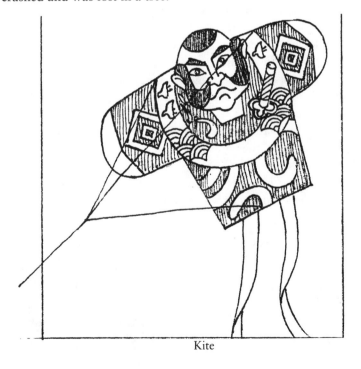

Kite

149

"I also witnessed another scene, similar to this one. Again the wind was blowing very strongly, but when the kite was about to dip down this boy didn't haul on the string. Instead, he let the string go, allowing the wind to send the kite safely down in a field."

Kyōso taught us to let things take their course, to let go of your self in relation to what you are concerned about. This was what was done in the latter case. He taught that when we let go of our strong determination to defeat our adversary at all cost, that is the moment when we put our real and strongest adversary, ourselves, at a distance.

115. Listening Attentively to Confucius' Teaching with Head Bowed

This is something that happened in High Disciple Hoshijima Ryōhei's childhood, when he visited Kyōso shin. He was to present a lecture on the Analects of Confucius, as Kyōso had instructed him to do. The moment the young Hoshijima opened the book and started to give his talk Kyōso took a lower seat and bowed his head down with both hands on the mat before him. In this position he listened attentively to every word that came from the boy.

Kyōso's attitude seemed unusual to the youngster and when he had finished his talk he felt prompted to ask, "May I ask you and hear from you, Great Sensei, why you are acting that way as you listen to a lecture from such an immature person as I am? It seems strange to me."

Kyōso explained, "No, no. You must bear in mind that the book you are lecturing on is the words of a sage. That is why I am listening to your lecture with such attention and respect. You should know this is the right way to act, the right posture a person should hold to, when you are listening to the teachings of the wise."

The admonition is said to have helped the youngster always be sensitive about respect for the teachings of the sages and those who are learned. It encouraged him to persevere in his studies.

116. Concerning Kuroda Heihachirō

About the year 1844 or soon thereafter there was a disciple named Kuroda Heihachirō. Kuroda lived in the Nodaya neighbourhood of Okayama, and he came in very close contact with Kyōso, bringing himself under his benign influence. He is remembered for his work in investigating various events and happenings related to Kurozumikyō and for

150

recording them in the many writings he left. In one of his notes there is this brief memorandum.[155]

"At the age of twenty-seven I was affected by a serious case of scrofula. The swelling grew outside my throat, but every treatment that was tried was in vain. My physician lost hope and declared my case hopeless. Around that time I happened to see Kyōso shin as he was visiting in Okayama with his daughter. I thought I should accept this as an opportunity extended to me by Kami and I went up to him and requested a ritual of *majinai*. He promptly consented and followed me home. After offering prayer he performed the ritual on me, placing his hands on the swelling.

"'I must say you are very fortunate,' he said. 'If the spot had swelled inward then water, either hot or cold, would not have passed your throat and you would not have been able to breathe. It was indeed good fortune for you. Since this is how it is, please feel at rest and feel confidence in your heart that your disease will soon be cured after this performance of *majinai*.'

"With these words he brought out, with humble respect and prayer, a packet of consecrated rice (*senmai*). He told me to go out on the veranda and put them in clean pure water. Then I should allow the Sun to shine onto the rice. After that I should eat the rice with the water. I should do this in a spirit of gratitude. I did exactly as I was told. Then to my amazement and delight I found myself in a very comfortable and vigorous mood, just as before my illness. I felt so refreshed, so invigorated, that my body and soul were exhilarated. That moment was a turning point and my condition sped towards recovery. I regained my good health. With this as the first step in showing my gratitude I was able to enter the Faith. How gracious are the divine virtues! What a blessing they are to me!"

It is reported that whenever Kuroda san recounted this experience to his fellow followers, he always was choked with tears.

At another time Kuroda said to Kyōso, "By nature I am so frightened of thunder that I spend the summer at Kanagawa in Tsudaka County (about twelve and a half miles from Okayama) to avoid all thunderstorms. This is because it is said thunder or lightning has never hit in Kanagawa." Kyōso replied, smiling, "It is most advisable that you leave all things to their natural course and not to worry about them. When you see gigantic columns of clouds rising in the south you would most naturally expect a sudden shower will be coming with tremendous claps of thunder. Although your anxiety and fear might rise up at that point there

151

is a good chance the clouds will change their direction and go east or west. Then you will feel relieved to see that your worries have vanished and your worry about the storm was not worth the trouble. Seeing that the storm cloud was not heading towards you after all would make you feel glad. But who knows whether the cloud movement might suddenly shift towards us to surprise us with rain and thunder. Then the joy you just had would also lose its meaning. It would just be a loss of time and energy. You must know that needless worry about the future and borrowing care about it leads to nothing, it yields nothing at all. This is exactly why I will keep still and not move a muscle even if I see a sword coming down from above my head."[156]

The above has been cited from Kuroda's memorandum.

117. Feeling Warm when Listening to Sermons

In the town of Okayama lived Yamamoto Kō, a devout follower of the faith. One of the family's women helpers once approached Madam Yamamoto, asking this question, "Madame, I am always wondering why I feel myself getting warm so spontaneously when I listen to sermons the Great Sensei of Kaminakano gives, even when it is a chilly day. No matter how freezing the weather may be, I feel as if I am warming myself in a sunny place with cherry blossoms in bloom. It's not the same kind of warmth as when we use a *hibachi* handwarmer. You could say it is more like a comfortable warmth that comes from the core of my body and then spreads everywhere within me. Madame, would you please explain why this is so?"

Madam Kō said, "That is just how I feel myself. You are right, I have noticed the same thing. I feel myself getting warm while listening to Kyoso's lecture. On chilly days I might notice my hands and feet getting stiff and numb from the freezing cold, but then while listening I feel my body beginning to glow with warmth. I have been wondering why this happens."

One day when the Yamamotos were visited by Kyōso, Madame Kō presented their question. His answer was, "You are exactly right. I also experience this warmth. I have no other explanation but to admit it is due to the fact that the divine virtues of Great Kami fill ourselves as well as all of Heaven and Earth. How gracious!" It is also reported that High Disciple Ishio experienced the same thing. He attended every regular meeting whenever he was stationed in Okayama. On chilly days, especially on the winter solstice, he would go out to worship, remarking to his family members as he left, "Today I am visiting Ohmoto to warm myself."

118. The Word *"Kurai"*

When Kyōso shin visited the home of Heizaemon in Iwanashi County he told the son of the family who waited on him at table, "When you take your calligraphy lessons, be sure to put forth every effort and give earnest and undivided attention. Remember, memorize and follow whatever instructions your teacher may give you. You might make remarkable advances and progress greatly in your studies but be sure you never feel puffed up and conceited, thinking you are better than others.

"As you know, the Chinese character that expresses *kurai* ('rank', 'position') consists of two parts. On the left, *hito* 'a person', and on the right, *tateru*, 'to stand up'. Together they mean 'to be held in esteem', 'to have status'. If no one holds your talent in esteem, then there is no chance for some level of rank to open for you. You must always bear in mind that your own thinking about how good you are gets you nowhere. Set your mind only on doing well."

This is what Kyōso advised the youngster. It is a very important counsel that everyone should keep in mind as they pursue the Way. As the divine virtue exhibits its goodness in the form of your accomplishments, then those who are around you begin to acknowledge you as a sensei and give you respect. It is just at this point that if one takes the wrong step one will be started on an evil way. It is an admonition of Kyōso shin that every one of us should always be mindful of. It is indeed a subject that warrants our most serious consideration.[157]

119. Ohmori Busuke Enters the Faith

Ōhmori Busuke, who lived in Shakuso to the northeast of Okayama, was infected by tuberculosis when he was about forty years old (about 1831 or 1832). Since his family was at the time one of the richest in the area, physicians were consulted and payments made to them without stint on the money. Every possible remedy was tried and the rituals of faith healers were requested. All efforts were useless and in vain. His condition only grew worse. At the point when nothing was left but to wait for the last moments of his life, a friend told him and his family about a certain Kurozumi who lived in Kaminanako. No matter how serious or hopeless a case seemed to be, sick people were cured on

153

listening to Kurozumi's lecture and receiving his wonderful *majinai* ritual.

In response to Busuke's invitation as suggested by this friend, Kyōso paid a visit of inquiry to Shakuso. At Busuke's home he offered prayers at the bedside and performed the *majinai* ritual on him. After that he gave a series of lectures.

Busuke found the lectures so beneficial that he formed a firm and deep determination to join in pursuing the Way. As should happen, this serious and incurable case turned quickly to the better. Within a period of several weeks he was completely cured and his health was recovered. Once his health was back Busuke exerted every effort without stinting, telling others about the blessings through divine virtues and exhorting others about them. In addition, he invited Kyōso to spend five days every month at his home. He gathered many to his home from near and far on those occasions, including the infirm and the sick. He asked Kyōso to let them listen to his lectures and be blessed with his miraculous *majinai*.

Every time Kyōso visited Shakuso, Busuke's home was filled with a great number of visitors and listeners. More than a few of the lectures turned into all-night sittings for those who attended. Thanks to Busuke's generous efforts, divine virtue was demonstrated and there were many miracles. Many people were encouraged to enter the faith.

120. Ohmori Busuke's Fine Horse

The family of Ohmori Busuke owned a fine horse, which had been given the name "Junpū" ("Favouring Wind"). He was a chestnut bay with an unusual build. His body was long and slim, and his beautiful tail was so long, it was said, that they had to tie it up before leading him into the barn.

Junpū was rather wild. He had such a bad temper that most people could not control him. So a certain Hayakawa, said to be the most distinguished horseman in the Bizen domain, had to come frequently to the Ohmoris to train him. One day Hayakawa came to ride on Junpū while Kyōso shin was staying there. At Busuke's suggestion Kyōso went out to the riding ground to enjoy this display of horsemanship. Of course, Hayakawa exhibited his talent to the fullest, showing his mastery of the equestrian arts.

After the exhibition ride, Hayakawa asked Kyōso to comment on his talents. What he got in response, however, was just some words of praise and admiration. Then he pressed the question, asking for something more specific.

Kyōso said, "I liked your horsemanship. You have superb skill, far beyond the ordinary. But with your permission, Hayakawa san, I must admit there is something regrettable in your way of riding Junpū. You are riding him much too hard and you are wasting his best abilities. Hayakawa san, may I suggest that you ride him in a way that makes better use of his good qualities?"[158]

Everyone there knew that Hayakawa had a stubborn and obstinate nature and they watched closely with sweaty palms to see what the outcome of this comment would be. But contrary to what they expected, Hayakawa "descended to a lower seat" and said, "Great Sensei, I have received a very instructive point in what you have said. Your suggestion is very helpful and I feel encouraged. I will never forget what you taught me. Thank you, thank you."

After that day, Hayakawa san was sure to be seen among those attending Kyōso's sermons and lectures. And, of course, he continued to develop his abilities as a horseman. Before long he had developed his talents to the point that he could ride that horse in a more easy fashion. In this sense, Junpū, Busuke's steed, joined his master in offering a *shinmon*. This was in 1833.

121. Distributing Sixty Copies of the Seven Rules in Kyōso's Own Handwriting

In 1837 Mori Bunzaemon,[159] a village head (*shōya*) living in Kohmoto Village, in Akasaka County in the Bizen domain, submitted his *shinmon* and was added to the followers of Kyōso shin. He was a gentle and courteous man of virtue, a devout and earnest follower. With enthusiasm he devoted himself to spreading the Way. He often invited Kyōso to his home, sponsoring lecture meetings there. On such occasions he was sure to invite other village heads so they could be introduced to the Way.

At one meeting of village heads held in his home Mori san said, "I have received from the Great Sensei of Nakano a copy of his handwritten Seven Rules. I love his fine calligraphy and I have put it up in our living room. It has graced me morning and evening with blessings more than I can tell. The rules also serve as guidance for our domestic helpers. We have all been refreshed and our lives have been made more lively. I am most thankful. Since I have seen from my own experience how instructive and gracious these rules are, I have come to believe that distributing them to the headmen (*nanushi*) who work under you will help your townspeople and farmers learn some very valuable lessons. They will learn some helpful guiding principles for living their daily lives. And eventually, administering the government will become easier, not to mention maintaining public order."

All present gave their consent to the idea, though with Mori's qualification in mind that since these rules were not official regulations, obedience to them could not be forced but should be left to individual discretion. No one objected to the plan, and the requested number of copies ran up to sixty. Kyōso listened to what Mori had to say and was glad to prepare for him sixty copies of the Rules to be distributed in turn to village heads and headmen.

In one village under Mori's supervision there were many followers of a Buddhist Nichiren sect, the Fujufuse group,[160] so many as to dominate the village. They kept themselves separate from others by imposing strict rules on their members. For example, they had a rule that none of their members should tie his sandal (zōri) strings while standing in front of a Shinto shrine. They were concerned that no one should misunderstand that as an act of reverence to the Shinto kami enshrined inside.

The headman of that village came to Mori, explaining that he had to return his copy of the Seven Rules. Mori drew himself up and said, "If you don't find it agreeable, I must not force you to accept the Rules. But may I ask you to think about it some more? Isn't it an act contrary to sincerity to refuse to receive what you had once agreed to accept? You must know that those who lack sincerity are not worthy to be the leaders of others. Being double-tongued is not allowed for anyone who is an official. And note this point especially. You should be aware that the Seven Rules stand above and beyond all religious differences and barriers. They are the most important observances human beings should keep to. I can hardly understand why you don't accept this. So, please give me your resignation." He gave this order in a very solemn manner.

The headman thought about it for a while and then he raised his head to say, "What you have said is quite reasonable. I am sorry for my impoliteness and I apologize. I was very much concerned about religion. Since I now understand that the Rules go beyond religion, I can now accept them back again with gratitude."

Then the headman unrolled his Rules to find, to his surprise, that where the Third Rule should read, "You shall not give way to conceit nor look down upon others", a part of the rule was repeated: "look down, look down." He asked to have his copy rewritten. Mori san responded, "Oh, no. It sounds like something you can expect. You should know that Great Sensei's brush moves freely and spontaneously when he writes.

There is no specific intention in it.¹⁶¹ Who knows whether this act of grace, this extra writing, will surely find some future use? If you understand what I am saying, accept this copy as it is."

The headman of course accepted it. And just as one might expect, soon thereafter his second son had a fishbone stuck in his throat. Since the child was an infant the physician had a hard time getting it out. It was beyond his control. Treatment was difficult. While those present were trying to think of a solution, the thought of the extra writing flashed into the headman's mind. Quickly he cut off a strip from the copy, dampened it with consecrated water, and made the infant swallow it. Then the little boy was able to swallow the bit of bone easily.

The boy was later named Taizō. It is said that as he grew up he also grew in his faith in the Way. He devoutly embraced the Seven Rules, and he spread the faith to others.

122. A Buddhist Priest is Initiated More Deeply into Buddhism

It was not a rare thing that Buddhist priests were initiated into the Way and became members of the Faith. This may be attributed to the fact that Kyōso shin's teachings helped Buddhists get a deeper grasp of their own teachings. One such priest, eminent in both learning and virtue, from a well-known temple in Jōtō County (now a part of Okayama City), became familiar with one of Kyōso's *waka* that goes as follows.

> Some call it Kami
> some even call it Buddha
> this Living Thing
> that dwells in the Sincerity
> of all of Heaven and Earth.¹⁶²

He then paid a visit to Kyōso so as to receive his teachings in person. In this way he was able to see for himself the graces and benefits of the Way. He also was able to go deeper into the essence of Buddhism. On one occasion this priest composed this *waka* and showed it to Kyōso.

> How sad it would be
> not to know our mortal life
> passing through the world
> to be scattered fleetingly
> together with the flowers.

On reading it, Kyōso's sole improvement was to change "our mortal" to "immortal."[163]

123. Kyōso Reforms a Burglar's Wretched Heart

This happened during the period Kyōso shin was observing his One Thousand Day seclusion at Imamura Shrine.[164] Early one morning he noticed some young villagers had caught a burglar who had sneaked into the building and was about to leave with some clothes and robes he was trying to steal.

On seeing they were about to beat up the thief, he stopped them and said to the villain, "Man, you have such a big body and you look so healthy. You are a full-grown man. All of us, including you, have in all humility and gratitude the gift of *bunshin* within us. We are actually in oneness with Amaterasu Ōmikami. What a fool (*baka*) you are! Don't you have any respect for this sacred truth? What a pity! How sad! You also are a child of Kami. You should have known what you are doing! What a wretched offence you have committed! You should have known better. You should realize that you could surely make this world a better place if with that healthy body of yours you put forth all your energy from this moment on in a way that respects the divine presence and power with full sincerity. Be sure to repent of your foolish mistake. Please work hard to put yourself back on the right way."

Hearing Kyōso's heartfelt and earnest admonition, the fellow bowed his head in repentance. He was choked with tears, grateful to be talked to this way. The village youngsters who at first were beating the fellow partly just for the fun of it also were much moved and impressed. They were full of youthful energy, but still they saw the man had become quite penitent and they decided to forgive him and let him go.

It is said that among the crowd of people who were watching all of this there were many who, hearing what Kyōso said to that one person, decided they also would join the Way and devote themselves to pursuing the Faith. They were that much struck with admiration and appreciation for how the incident had come out.

124. A Demon (*Oni*) is Two Tails (*Oni*)

This is what Kyōso shin said in one of his lectures. "A demon (*oni*) has a tail that splits in two. That is why it is called *oni*, 'two tails'.[165] Though *atama*, the head, remains in oneness with Great Kami, the tail splits in two, to be two pieces. Because it splits (*wareru*), it is called *ware*, 'self' or 'ego'.[166]

125. Teaching a Good Way to Practise Calligraphy

Once when Jikihara sensei was accompanying Kyōso shin back from a mission to Okayama, Dai Sensei stopped in at Manbaiya Chūbei's in Daiku. Chūbei san was practising calligraphy at the time.

Kyōso commented, "Chūbei san, your diligence in studying is so admirable. But let me remind you that if you hold to the posture of a thirty-year-old person, which you really are, you will soon find your effort is wearisome and boring. You will get tired and feel all worn out. Then it will be impossible to improve your skill in your art. You would do better if you would hold your heart in the attitude of an eight-year-old boy. This way of holding yourself will free you from boredom. Even elderly people who take this kind of attitude can show rapid progress and get reasonably good at calligraphy."

126. How to Avoid Anger
in an Extreme Circumstance

At one discussion Kyōso shin taught as follows.

"As human beings, we should never be angry. This is what every follower pursuing the Way should observe. No matter how difficult a situation is, no matter what problems others may cause, you must be sure to keep yourself calm and self-possessed. You should always have a composed attitude and never harbour any anger. Anger hurts the *bunshin* inside you. It is like chopping Amaterasu to pieces with a sword. How irreverent that would be to Great Kami!

"What in this world would most provoke our anger? On deliberation, I think no action could provoke more anger than adultery on the part of one's wife, such a thing as might happen once in ten thousand cases. It is hard to believe that anyone might stray from the Way to commit such an offence. But this is a possibility that those pursuing the Way can benefit from thinking about. The worst thing that can happen to you is to injure the divine presence within each of us. So, it is important that I teach you how you could manage yourself if you were in such a difficult situation so you can keep from becoming angry.

"The first thing to think of, if that were to happen, is 'What an unfortunate woman! I must feel sorry for her. She surely deserves to be pitied.'

159

We must pity such a woman because she would have fallen to the level of the animals despite the fact that she had been blessed with a divine soul (*mitama*) within herself, born like anyone else to be above all things in nature. What a pity! What a poor woman! We must show concern for the condition she is in.

"Invite her into a room affectionately and with a warm heart. Tell her calmly, without any anger, to think carefully about what she has done. 'Dear, please listen to me carefully. We humans owe our existence to nothing less than the divine virtue. Our bodily form as well as our soul within is a blessing from Kami. This action of yours falls below the level of humanity. It puts you down to the level of the animals. It is conduct that disgraces the divine presence within us, even lower than something animals would do. If you would only, at this very moment, feel sorry for your foolish action and regret it sincerely, you will surely be back on your path as a faithful wife and a woman to be admired'."

All of this is what Direct Disciple Jikihara Ihachirō recorded in his collection of Kyōso's teachings (*Gokōden*). In this book we see the following postscript he gave to this story.

"Since this is a lesson that Kyōso shin taught to no one else but me, it was my firm determination to keep it a secret and never tell anyone about it. It is a teaching of Kyōso, but I thought its content, referring to impropriety as it does, might be hard for people newly initiated as followers to think about. That is why I kept it to myself. But on thinking about it further I came to realize that it is in the divine will to eliminate every possible reason that can lead to anger. We might not realize our potential as humankind unless all such possibilities are erased from the world. Without that it would not be possible for us to rise to the level of kami. This is why Kyōso shin gave such deep thought to this point, with all pity and sympathy. It is because he knew that when anger is provoked within us it presents us with the greatest hindrance in observing the Way and pursuing the faith.

"He admonished us about anger using such an extreme example. This is why I have dared to include this incident in my book."

127. Kyōso shin Presents the Opening Lecture

From Kohmoto Village in Bizen Province hailed Takiyama Shuzen. In his early years Takiyama set his heart on learning the teachings of Shinto. He frequently visited Kyoto to study Shinto at the Yoshida School.[167] In later years he was appointed to a position like that of a missionary, or travelling teacher. While doing this work in Bizen Province Takiyama sensei came one day to Kohmoto since it was his home town. Kyōso happened to be there at that time, enjoying a stay at Mori Bunzaemon's place, and was going to give a lecture that night.

Takiyama sensei was scheduled to lecture in the meeting hall of a Shinto shrine at the same hour. Since this was how it happened to fall out, the sponsors of his meeting decided to propose it would be good if Kyōso and Takiyama sensei were to present their views together at the same place. Since Kyōso gave his consent to the idea, saying, "Oh yes. That would be fine", the sponsors went ahead with their preparations for a combined meeting to be held at the shrine.

One point, however, perplexed them. Who should give the first lecture? On one side was Takiyama sensei who was delegated by the Yoshidas of Kyoto, the head family of Shinto. On the other side was Kyōso, staying in Kohmoto as the guest of the leading village head of the area, Mori Bunzaemon. To solve the puzzle they went to the Sensei of Nakano to seek his consent to give the opening lecture. Kyōso agreed to the suggestion and went up to the platform and gave his lecture.

When he was through it was Takiyama's turn. He simply said, "After hearing this outstanding presentation by the Sensei of Nakano, so inspiring and so instructive, I feel I am unable to give you a lecture on Shinto. It is completely unnecessary for me to add anything to what he has said."[168] The meeting ended without his going up to the lecture table.

Notes

INTRODUCTION

1. In keeping with Japanese usage, family names of Japanese people are given first, then the individual names. Among Kurozumikyō members Kurozumi Munetada is sometimes referred to simply as Munetada. Much more often he is known to them by the reverent term "Kyōso", which may be rendered in English as "Founder". In the stories Munetada sometimes refers to himself as Sakyō, his personal name in adult life. "Sebumi" (or "Misebumi", with honorific) is an important title, suggesting one who conducts travellers across a river. Such a person seeks with his own feet for the safest way to go, and then shows others the way across.

2. Robert Bellah, *Tokugawa Religion*, 1985; Helen Hardacre, *Kurozumikyō and the New Religions of Japan*, 1986.

3. The best account of the Ise Pilgrimage is Winston Davis, "Pilgrimage and World Renewal", 1983–4. A good general account of the peasant uprisings is Stephen Vlastos, *Peasant Protests*, 1986; but as Story 91 indicates, Munetada's efforts were not political but spiritual. For Neo-Confucianism see Peter Nosco, *Confucianism and Tokugawa Culture*, 1984. However, Munetada's approach to Ise pilgrimage reflected his distinctive teachings (*KS* 95f. For abbreviations see note 7).

4. D.C. Holtom, *The National Faith of Japan*, 1965; Murakami Shigeyoshi, *Religion in Japanese History*, 1980; Harry Harootunian, "Late Tokugawa Culture and Thought", 1989.

5. "Kami" is a general term for the spirits of nature, of family ancestors, and of culture heroes, and for spirits known in mythology, worshipped in shrines small and large throughout Japan. *Oh* and *mi* are a double honorific, indicating the great reverence felt toward a Kami so designated. Kami show their purity and power by inspiring wonder and enhancing life. For orientation in Shinto see Ono, *Shinto*, 1962.

6. Note the philosopher Donald Evans' definition of "spiritual" as the *relation*

between the human spirit and the transcending Source of all (Donald Evans, *Spirituality and Human Nature*, 1993). People become spiritual as they live between the two. Munetada lays much emphasis on the relation of *kokoro*, the mind/heart of a person, to the presence within the *kokoro* of Amaterasu. This inner presence is variously referred to: as *bunshin* ("divided presence"), as *ikimono* ("living-thing"), or as *yōki* or "*daiyōki*", the positive principle; it is the expression within the *kokoro* of divine virtue, *shintoku*. His lifelong agenda was to make his *kokoro* (usually translated "heart") a reverent and stable dwelling place for the inner presence of Amaterasu. His mature spirituality has a *non-dual* character, as we shall note.

7. Kurozumikyō has perhaps a quarter million formal adherents, though its influence in many communities, especially in western Japan, is greater than this number suggests. The story of the Founder as understood from within its tradition is given by Kurozumi Tadaaki, *The Opening Way*, 1994 (OW). The author was Vice-Patriarch of Kurozumikyō. Willis Stoesz, ed., *Kurozumi Shinto*, 1989 (*KS*) contains chapters by Kurozumi Muneharu, Chief Patriarch of Kurozumikyō. Hardacre, 1986 is the most thorough study and gives information about contemporary Kurozumikyō life. Charles Hepner, *The Kurozumi Sect of Shinto*, 1935 contains much valuable information. Nobuhara Taisen, *The Brilliant Life of Munetada Kurozumi*, 1980 is an informal and empathetic study.

8. The place was also known as Ohmoto, and it has that name as a neighbourhood in the modern city of Okayama.

9. His understanding of this role had strong ethical focus from the beginning, in contrast to the loose way the term was used in some popular movements of the day. See Davis, 1983–4. And, his understanding of his goal grew as his relationship to Amaterasu deepened.

10. OW 10f.

11. Helen Hardacre surveys the background of Munetada's thought in Neo-Confucianism and Shingaku (Hardacre, 1986, 43ff.), discussing his teachings as expressions of the "core values" of Japanese culture; Alan Miller's exploration of the concept of vow in Buddhism is suggestive ("Internalization of Kami", *KS* 135–55); and a study by Janine Sawada of Shingaku, a laypersons' movement that touched many parts of Japan (Sawada, *Confucian Values*, 1993), shows intriguing parallels to Munetada's life and teachings. However, there is no doubt of his independent grounding in Amaterasu mysticism and ritual. In Story 37 Shingaku teachings are called "worldly" and "common".

12. OW 10. His respect for Confucian tradition was strong (Stories 42 and 115), and he used terms originating in Buddhism (see the poetry in *KS* 102–12), though he may have first come on them through Shingaku. Further study is needed to sort out these influences in detail, but tracing such

influences yields only partial understanding. These stories, and the account given in *OW*, show his mastery of the cultural resources he employed and his charismatic effect on his followers. What mattered to him was Amaterasu. His devotion to her, and his own experience of unity with her through ecstatic union and life-long practice, is the key to that achievement.

13. Calligraphy in Japan today survives as an art form, but before modern writing methods came into use, everyone, down to fishmongers keeping sales records, used ink and brush to write. In a time before elementary education was formalized there were many teachers who provided basic skills in reading and writing. Instruction in calligraphy was at the same time character education; skill in writing was prized and could involve lengthy study of classics of Chinese literature. See Stories 16, 25, 104, 118, and 125.

14. The *furo* is a familiar part of Japanese life. It involves first washing one's self and then getting into a tub of very hot water to soak for a time. It has a relaxing effect, but can be physically demanding if one has been ill.

15. Cited in *OW* 19.

16. *Yōki* is the positive, dynamic presence of Amaterasu. It is sometimes referred to as *daiyōki*, the great joyful power of Amaterasu, or as *shintoku*, "divine virtue". It is contrasted to *inki*, any kind of negative and gloomy influence. The contrast appears similar to that between *yang* and *yin* in Taoism, but there is a significant difference in that Kurozumi faith always looks for *yōki* to prevail and for *inki* to be overcome. See Story 45 for an especially clear example. Kurozumi faith thus does not include evil in a naturalistic balance of positive and negative factors in experience, but looks for health and positive forces to prevail over whatever diminishes life. See *KS* 110, *waka* 47.

17. Munetada used the term *issai-shintoku-kan*, which may be translated "all-encompassing viewpoint based on divine virtue". It describes his enlightened condition more exactly than does *satori*, familiar in Buddhist vocabulary (*OW* 124).

18. The Founder's term is *ikidōshi*, literally, "living in and through" each moment of time in a spirit of equanimity and joy, not keyed to any details of temporal events but keyed to the infinite Amaterasu within. A way of living constituted in complete unity with Amaterasu is immortal since physical death is no longer a concern. In *ikidōshi* Amaterasu's presence shines through each human action; to know that this is so, as Munetada clearly does, means one may still speak of spirituality in Evans' sense (n.6). It is a frame of mind explicitly aware of others; it is a relational, interpersonal spirituality. Others are "mirrors to one's self" for self-understanding. *Ikidōshi* is felt as fullness of joy and as inner freedom from temporal constraint, yet also as compassionate attention to the needs of others in fulfilment of Amaterasu's intention. It may be translated "abiding life", or "living way".

19. The term *Tenmei jikiju* refers to Amaterasu's giving and Munetada's accepting that mission. In the background of this concept lies the 'Mandate of Heaven', basic to the worldview of Confucianism. In its ancient Chinese form it referred to an imperial dynasty's moral legitimacy to rule the human realm; it is still relevant in modern political theories. Neo-Confucianism taught that Heaven makes its presence felt in each moment of every person's life; the mandate is for fulfilment of each person's moral and physical well-being. However, Munetada's experience goes beyond this background. In his ecstatic unity with Amaterasu he experienced a special case of Heaven's mission, finding himself empowered to do her work of promoting well-being and joy in the world, devoted to fulfilling her intention for sincerity and harmony in all human beings. For a discussion of the concept of recentreing see Robert Lifton, *The Broken Connection*, 1979.

20. In traditional Shinto the Great Purification Prayer (Oharai) was used only on special ritual occasions, but Munetada made frequent, daily use of it. Note Kurozumi Muneharu's comments (*KS* 67ff.); text and discussion in Hardacre, 1986, 57f., 196–8.

21. *OW* 67; *KS* 70ff., 143; Hepner, 149.

22. Munetada made use of many forms of religious practice (*shugyō*) found in traditional Shinto, such as pilgrimages and prayers, but his most important practice was the effort in each moment to be receptive to her inner presence and action. Kurozumi Muneharu indicates the distinct difference made in Munetada's use of Shinto tradition by his ecstatic union with Amaterasu (*KS* 95f.), keyed to receptivity to her presence rather than to ethical striving. The new state of mind was seen as a restoration of the "age of kami" (*Michi no Kotowari*, Appendix B).

23. Kurozumi Muneharu lays emphasis on the Rock Cave myth about Amaterasu, whereby her emergence from the cave, enabling light and life to return to the world, expresses a commitment to universal harmony and well-being (*OW* 94).

24. The Founder's usual manner of healing (*majinai*) was to lay his hand on the affected part of an ill person's body, and then to blow a vigorous breath on that part. The blown breath communicated awareness of the healing presence of Great Kami. The *inki*, or negativity of egoism and self-concern, would be overcome by the *yōki* of Amaterasu's presence. The stories also show other means Munetada used, such as saying a sudden loud word that surprised a hearer into the beginnings of understanding. Consecrated water (*shinsui*) is a staple of Kurozumikyō pastoral ministry.

25. Munetada is worshipped in Kurozumikyō as a high Kami, one who definitively enables others to realize the vivifying and healing presence of Amaterasu within themselves.

26. The best example of the relation between preaching and healing is given in Story 37. See also the way an ill woman's disease could be cured only when

every trace of her doubt and self-concern was gone (Story 82). Twenty-seven of the stories refer to healings.

27. The term is familiar in Japanese society for those who are accepted as disciples by a master (a scholar, or potter, or other master of a skill or craft), so that they may be schooled in his accomplishments. The term is more intense than in general usage, however, in that the Founder showed his followers the way to the Great Kami (Amaterasu Ohmikami), and was himself Kami for them.

28. Cited in *OW* 54.

29. To "leave all in Amaterasu's hands" is an act of total trust, in grateful receptivity to her energizing presence. In this act the spiritual dimension of life is established. It does not mean inaction on one's own part, but rather participation in Amaterasu's spontaneous Way of things as they happen. See Stories 18 and 83 for an introduction to what he meant.

30. See Appendix A. For a discussion of the rules see *OW* 56–9. See also Willis Stoesz, "The Universal Attitude of Kurozumi Munetada", *KS* 248f., for alternative translations.

31. Such alternate-year service was an important feature of the Tokugawa Shogun's governance, required of all provincial lords (*daimyō*) in the country.

32. *OW* 76, 91. The Founder insisted that some of the donated money be given to the poor, and the record shows that about 245 beggars received alms of two pieces of silver each.

33. See the Index for names and dates of followers, and for the year in which they made their pledges (*shinmon*) of membership.

34. A Daimyōjin is a high-ranking kami. The Yoshida family was the official agency for the regulation of worship in Japan.

35. Note his *waka* (*KS* 102):

> Ah, how grateful
> to be born here in the land
> of the Rising Sun,
> And to know that in the Sun
> I continue to abide.

The term "age of kami" is used in the *Michi no Kotowari*, a summary of his teaching (Appendix B). For discussion of the Shinto Restoration movement see Peter Nosco, *Remembering Paradise*, 1990.

36. *OW* 48ff., 67f. Gratitude is a ubiquitous motif in Japanese culture and spirituality, but Munetada has a distinctive view, emphasizing the practice (*shugyō*) of gratitude (*arigatai*) to Amaterasu as a means by which one habituates one's self to her energizing presence within.

37. *OW* 92f. The first of these *waka* recalls a haiku by the Zen poet Issa published in 1819 about the death of his daughter, but the conclusion to which Munetada came is clearly his own. See Robert Hass, *The Essential Haiku*, 1994, 228.

38. Edited by Kamiya and Stoesz.
39. This is in contrast to metaphors of changelessness in western religion; for example, the Psalmist's reference to God as "my rock and my salvation" (Psalm 62).
40. See Hepner 104ff. for a discussion of how several such names and terms approach each other in meaning. See also Hardacre 53ff.
41. An example is the occasion when the Founder's story of the man who was utterly honest and trusting, to the point of foolishness, stimulated the High Disciple Akagi's insight into sincerity so that he was healed of his blindness (Story 37).
42. This point is discussed more fully in Willis Stoesz, "The Universal Attitude of Shinto", 1992, 215–29. See comments by Kurozumi Muneharu in *KS* 50f., 97f. This universal attitude distinguishes Kurozumi spirituality from Japanese spirituality as described by D.T. Suzuki (D.T. Suzuki, *Japanese Spirituality*, 1972). Suzuki's discussion asserted Japanese cultural superiority.
43. Worshipping the sun at the moment it comes over the horizon while being able to see the whole circle of the horizon enhances the meaning of the experience, says Kurozumi Muneharu (*KS* 243).
44. Ono, 1962, 21.
45. *KS* 112.
46. Among numerous such stories, see especially Stories 22, 80 and 127.
47. Instances of his beaming smile are in Stories 5, 6, 19, 50, 51, 58, 65, and 86. See Story 10, where a physiognomist diagnosed his facial features as those of a fool, and he took it in high good humour. See also Stories 18 and 53. Laughter has a healing effect, as we see in Story 45.
48. See Story 18 for an excellent example, showing the difference between appropriate and inappropriate flexibility.
49. Cited in *OW* 60. See Story 89 for an example of flexibility. See also Stories 62–68, and discussion by Kurozumi Tadaaki (*OW* 59–61). He referred to his state of mind as *mushin*, "no-mind", and as *munen*, "no-thought".
50. *OW* 69ff.; see also Stories 52, 18, 105. The same insight applies to following requirements of a healthy lifestyle, as some contemporary Kurozumikyō members advocate; and to following the teachings of other religions successfully.
51. An example is in Winston King, *Zen and the Way of the Sword*, 1993.
52. See Appendix C for a listing of Kurozumikyō literature.
53. Hardacre, 1986, 77–88; and Stories 46, 28, 29, 78, and 45.
54. *KS* 92–101; Stories 11, 29, 108, and 107.
55. *KS* 50.

THE STORIES

1. "Kyōso" may be translated as "Founder" but in Kurozumikyō Shinto it is familiarly used as an affectionate and intimate personal name. In this respect it is similar to the way "Christ" is commonly used in Christian faith as a personal name, though strictly speaking it too is a title. Kyōso is often referred to as "Dai Sensei" ("Great Teacher"). Other individuals are sometimes given the title "sensei", but in these stories the term is capitalized only (except in titles of chapters) when referring to Kyōso.

2. The tray (sanbō) was the kind ordinarily used in Shinto worship, about eight inches high and a foot square at the top.

3. He was a yamabushi or mountain ascetic. For many centuries these mountain ascetics, centred in a number of sacred mountains throughout Japan where their training took place, had treated people's physical and spiritual ills according to an ancient system of teachings. This particular yamabushi had his home base on Norikura mountain in central Japan.

4. The ryō was generally equated with the value of a koku of rice, about five bushels. However, comparing monetary values of the time to today's prices is difficult because of the greatly different social and economic circumstances.

5. The temizuya is a covered place with clean water near the entrance of a shrine, where worshippers stop to rinse their hands and mouths before entering. It is a place for purification preparatory to worship. The Imamura shrine in Ohmoto (sometimes referred to as Kaminakano) is where Munetada served as a priest until his retirement in 1841 at the age of 62.

6. In Japanese usage "wet clothes" means "a false charge". "Wearing wet clothes" is a way of saying the wearer is unjustly accused.

7. The reference is to the Zen priest Hakuin (1686–1769), famous for reviving the Rinzai tradition of Zen. Stories by him and about him were a familiar part of popular culture during the late Tokugawa period.

8. The reference is to a calendrical system of good luck and bad luck days, days on which it is considered good or bad to engage in various kinds of activities. Almanacs listing these days were familiar in traditional Oriental households.

9. Moxa treatment is a part of traditional Oriental folk medicine. It involves placing a small amount of a dried herb (moxa) at one of a number of places on the body, each believed to be connected with a different specific illness, and setting it to smouldering.

10. This household ceremony is held on the day before the beginning of spring, according to the ancient solar calendar still familiar in Japan. In the modern calendar the date is 3 or 4 February. It remains today a joyful, light-hearted ceremony in which the whole family participates.

11. The relationship of Munetada to his wife Iku was close and warm, as all the

stories indicate. See especially Stories 7 and 62. She nursed him in his serious illness, questioned him closely about what he meant when she did not understand, and gave him a supportive home. In this story the affectionate good humour of their relationship is fully clear.

12. Familiar talking between husband and wife in the home traditionally uses honorific terms of address. Japanese language is rich in many levels and variations of such terms. "My master" translates *danna-sama*, a term that varies in form according to social class and family occupation. O is often used before a female name as an honorific. Both terms imply consideration and affection for one another, not necessarily the subservience western readers might at first assume them to have. Certainly they were used affectionately by Munetada and Iku. Japanese language lacks such terms as "my dear", or "darling", or "honey".

Adding such prefixes as *o-*, *go-*, and *mi-* indicates a great sense of respect (though in this story that respect is mingled with affectionate humour). For instance, in the case of the name of Amaterasu Ohmikami, the double honorific before "kami" indicates the highest possible reverence. For other terms indicating recognition of social status, see Stories 61 and 113.

"San" after a name is a personal title that would be translated "Mr", "Mrs", or "Miss" etc., depending on who is being referred to. "Sama" is a much more rarely used title, indicating extremely high respect (Story 13).

13. It was a small bridge (*dobashi*) of a type no longer seen in most of Japan, roughly made of lumber and pieces of wood and covered with twigs and branches over which dirt and clay were laid to provide a smooth surface.

14. The *haori* is a short formal coat. In this period of Japanese history feudal law and custom prescribed what clothing the different social classes should wear. The *haori* was worn only by higher class or wealthy people. Though the Kurozumi family had been priests for generations, they had always held samurai rank. The *hanten* was a coat worn by merchants, craftsmen, townsmen, and their employees and helpers, but never by samurai, who were the highest class. Today the *haori* is in general use.

15. I.e., one who does not conform to ordinary expectations of common sense. *Aho* does not have the derogatory sense of *baka*, another term in common usage translated "fool". Munetada's experience of ecstatic unity with Ameratasu in 1814 gave him extraordinary perspective and insight.

16. *Hakama* are men's formal skirts, divided so that they appear somewhat similar to trousers.

17. Bizen province (*kuni*) was the domain of the Ikeda clan (*han*). All of Japan was divided into such provinces in the Tokugawa period (1600–1867). The next smaller jurisdiction was the county (*gōri*, *kohori*; modern term: *gun*), then the town (or neighbourhood in a city: *chō*, or *machi*) or village (*mura*, or *son*).

18. *Geta* are wooden platform footwear (clogs), elevated from the ground by

two pieces of wood, useful for walking in muddy streets or in wet gardens. *Taka-geta* are high *geta*. *Zōri* are sandals woven of straw or of cloth.

19. In traditional Japanese reckoning a child is one year old at birth (i.e., it is in its first year of life). At each New Year everyone is considered a year older. For example, in a rare case, a baby born on the last day of the year would be reckoned as two years old two days after being born. Thus, six or seven years old could correspond closely to a Western concept of five years old. The Founder was born on the day of the winter solstice, not long before the end of the year.

20. He was a secretary or amanuensis (*yūhitsu*) whose work included writing out the fair copies of the Lord's formal letters and pronouncements.

21. The Tōsho-gū Shrine is where Tokugawa Ieyasu, founder of the Tokugawa Shogunate, was enshrined. The main shrine is the famous one located at Nikko, northwest of Tokyo, but there were branch Tōsho-gū shrines scattered throughout the country. The one in Okayama is in the eastern part of the present-day city.

22. That is, the oar was fastened on the back of the boat slanted to the left. When the boatman pushed on the oar it would push water to the left; pulling it towards him would push the water to the right. The back-and-forth 'figure eight' motion would get the boat across the river, whose current was coming from the left as this was happening.

23. *Makase* means to leave a matter entirely to someone, to entrust someone fully with something; *sute* means to abandon, to throw away; *maru* means "totally, entirely". Munetada uses *maru makase* to mean leaving every aspect of one's life, body and mind, totally to the care of Kami. See Stories 110, 112 and 116.

24. *Miyako* ordinarily means the capital of a country, or a large city. Here it is used as a metaphor for "the main thing", the "core" of the matter.

25. Miyata was also a Confucian scholar.

26. Tokio Katsutarō was one of the Four High Disciples, one of those closest to the Founder.

27. The "High Plains of Heaven" according to ancient Japanese mythology. From Takamagahara came the original movement to create the world and all living things, according to this myth contained in the *Kojiki*. The relation of Shinto and Confucian concepts and practices was in active discussion among scholars in the Tokugawa period.

28. "Miyauchi" means "in the precinct of the shrine". In those days the Ikeda clan had strict rules designed to promote thrift and diligence. No entertainment quarter was allowed in the city of Okayama. So, such facilities were established outside the city, about three miles to the west in the neighbourhood of a Shinto shrine. After the Meiji Restoration (1868) these facilities were abolished. The modern Okayama City now includes this area.

29. Most Chinese characters have a left and a right half; and of course are writ-

ten using a writing brush and India ink. A brush holds enough ink to write a number of characters, each composed of a number of separate strokes. The steadiness and art with which one puts a brushful of ink on paper is an expression of one's character. See also Stories 104, 125, 16 and 121.

30. A model textbook he had written for use in teaching children calligraphy (*Miyako Meisho*; *Places of Interest in the Capital*) was rediscovered in the 1920s. Everyone who could read and write would use such calligraphy.

31. Faith healers whose powers were drawn from their mastery of a number of different religious disciplines ministered to the ills of the people in these times. Kurozumi Munetada differed from their practice in grounding the goal of healing in a changed spiritual attitude of the ill person and in basing his understanding of that goal in his own experience of healing through union with Amaterasu. See Appendix B, the *Michi no Kotowari*.

32. The handclap (*kashiwade*) is an expression of reverence in Shinto worship, acknowledging the presence of a kami or a moment of high significance. It is similar to an "Amen" sometimes said in the course of Christian worship.

33. The "Eight Million Kami" (*yao-yorozu-no-kami*, i.e., an uncountable number of kami) includes the people of Japan who have died in the past and are venerated as ancestors. There is an altar to them in the Main Shrine (Daikyōden) at Shintozan in Okayama. In Kurozumi teaching, they all derive from Amaterasu and all are created equal. Each is a "divine child of Kami".

34. *Zōris* usually are woven from straw or reeds, and so don't last as long as modern sandals. Anyone walking long distances had to carry an extra pair or buy them as they travelled.

35. See Hepner 227 for a discussion of membership statistics in the late nineteenth century. Between three and four million followers and their family members, in addition to seekers, were reported to the government in these years.

36. In 1843 at the age of 22 he took the place of his father as deputy priest at the Imamura Shrine, leaving Munetada free to devote himself full-time to teaching. At his father's death in 1850 he became the leader of Kurozumikyō (as the organization came to be known).

37. Sano is short for Sanokichi, Munenobu's childhood name.

38. *Yōki*, the positive spiritual power deriving from Amaterasu's presence within, overcomes *inki*, the weakness in a person that has led to illness. In this case Ginjibei served as a proxy in the ceremony.

39. *Makoto*, sincerity.

40. He was from the small hamlet of Kamiachi in Oku county, in the present Saidai-ji area just east of Okayama. His family was wealthy and to this day has a respected place in that vicinity.

41. There was less conflict of this sort in Okayama than elsewhere in Japan because of the enlightened rule of the Ikeda government, but it remained a risky thing to do.

42. It was the Great Purification Prayer (Oharai) that was being chanted; the handclappings were also, of course, expressions of Shinto prayer.

43. Together with Tokio Katsutarō he became one of the Two Principal Disciples, and of the Four (sometimes given as Six) High Disciples who were the Founder's inner circle.

44. Nishimura was village head of Inambo Village, Mimasaka Chō, Aida County, of the same province.

45. The chests (*nagamochi*) were each about a metre high, a metre wide, and 1.8 metres long. The reference is to Chinese classics and Buddhist scriptures, which usually had blue covers.

46. His name within the family at that time.

47. I.e., leprosy, or Hansen's disease.

48. If Nishimura Saisuke was Akagi's cousin and not his uncle, then the elder person saying these things to him would have been Saisuke's father, Nishimura Fusao.

49. Or, the Isle of Eternal Youth, *Hōrai-ga-shima*, well known in Chinese Taoist mythology.

50. Parts of today's Yamagata and Akita Prefectures.

51. Munetada's story employs a play on words. The word "follow" (*fumu*) has multiple meanings: to trample, to step on, to go through, to keep on, to finish completely, to appraise, to put a price on, etc. It is also part of the word *misebumi*, applied to the Founder of Kurozumikyō. A *misebumi* is one who with his own feet finds the way to walk through a river, to find the other side by the best route, so that those who follow may cross more easily. Of course, what the rice dealer was saying was that the honest fool should follow his directions by stamping down on the treadle of a rice-polishing machine for three years. Kyōso here uses *fumu* to refer to both levels of meaning. The dishonest rice dealer is speaking more truly than he knows.

52. The name of the shrine is the Battai San Jinjya (Battai Mountain Shrine). The Chinese character *batt* (or *batsu*) can also be read *ikada*, meaning "raft". *Tai*, in this case, means "group", so that the name of the shrine may refer to a string of rafts going downstream. It may be for this reason that the hermit was called the "raft hermit". Or perhaps the cloud was called a raft ironically, in recognition of his wish to go to the Isle of the Blessed.

53. Later in his career Akagi was instrumental in establishing Kurozumi faith in Kyoto. His spirit is enshrined in the Munetada Shrine in Kyoto along with that of the Founder.

54. The Kurozumi organization used a banner with a red ball on it to identify itself until the national government adopted such a flag during the Meiji period. The red ball stands for the sun.

55. Japanese *innen*.

56. In earlier days when traditions were stronger than now, members of families in which a death had occurred were regarded as impure. Until a period

of mourning was over – up to a year when it was a parent who had died – they were not allowed to visit public places that could be defiled by their presence.

57. A parallel is being drawn between Kurozumi Munetada and Confucius. See also Story 44 below. Sōshin is another name for Tseng Ts'an (Tseng Tzu). The Kokumin were the two High Disciples Akagi and Tokio (OW 84). Hoshijima made many scholarly contributions to the Kurozumi cause, including a short biography of Munetada.

58. Rai Sanyō was a prominent Confucian intellectual and patron of the arts from the Hiroshima area, living in Kyoto after 1811. He was the author of a popular history of Japan and of widely circulated historical poems whose tone was critical of the Tokugawa shogunate. He contributed significantly to the broad movement in Japanese society favouring the Imperial Office that led to the Meiji Restoration (1867).

59. A *kago* is a palanquin, or covered litter, carried by two men and commonly used for personal transportation at the time. The man's complete sincerity (*maru makase*) is evident.

60. They would not need to make any more stops to catch their breath before getting to Kaminakano.

61. He was chanting the Oharai prayer, the traditional Great Prayer of Purification.

62. See Confucius, *The Analects (Lun yü)*, translated and introduced by D.C. Lau (New York: Penguin Books, 1979), XI. 3, VI. 8.

63. *Confucian Analects*, translated by James Legge (Hong Kong: Hong Kong University Press, 1960; reprint of 1893 edition), VI. 8.

64. The title of this story in Japanese is "Saki-Mitama no O-Hataraki". It draws on traditional Japanese beliefs in the nature of the spirits (*tama*; *mi* is an honorific), both of humans and of kami dwelling in nature or enshrined in various shrines. Each *tama* has two functions, a rough (*aramitama*) and a peaceful (*nigimitama*); or, frequently, *tama* are said to have four functions, with the *nigimitama* being divided into the *kushimitama* (wonder-working) and the *sakimitama* (happiness-bringing). Japanese scholars' opinions vary as to whether the functions of *tama* are two-fold or four-fold.

However, it is clear that in traditional belief any one of the functions of a *tama* (of a human being or of a kami) could act separately from that *tama* as a whole. In ancient history there are instances of separate shrines being built for the different functions of a single kami. The distinction between kami and human is never a sharp one, particularly in the case of an outstanding person like Kurozumi Munetada. In this story Munetada Sensei good-humouredly employs these beliefs in crediting his *sakimitama* with appearing to the sick man in Ohkuradani many miles to the east. *Hataraki* refers to the effects distinctive to some agency; in this case, the divine blessing of Amaterasu through Kyōso.

65. A *koku* was equivalent to 5.119 bushels, or 150 kilograms. Retainers of feudal lords were paid in *koku* of rice; the more rice, the higher the rank. The *koku* is no longer in use in modern Japan.

66. An important feature of the Tokugawa Shogunate (1600–1867) headquartered in Tokyo (Edo) was a requirement that the feudal lords (*daimyō*) of the various provinces be in residence every other year in Tokyo. When the *daimyō* went to fulfil this requirement they took with them many of their retainers. Among the samurai serving as retainers of Lord Ikeda, Daimyō of the Bizen Province, were a number of followers of Kurozumi Munetada.

67. Tuberculosis of the lymph glands in the throat.

68. Literally, "within his abdomen", i.e., his *hara*. The *hara* is regarded as the physical seat of the inner person (*kokoro*). Keeping a "stiff upper lip" was expected of honourable samurai. See Takeo Doi, *The Anatomy of Self* (Kodansha International, 1985) for discussion of this concept important in Japanese culture. However, as this story shows, for Kurozumi spirituality it is the sincerity of the heart in its trust in Amaterasu that is even more important than this aspect of outer expression.

69. Gratitude (*arigatai*) for the experience of divine benefit is at the core of Kurozumi spiritual experience. *Arigatai* and *Arigato gozaimasu* are words spoken as a religious discipline (*shugyō*) in Kurozumi Shinto practice, cultivating an attitude of receptivity to divine blessing and of thankfulness for it. Here, however, Ishida's words express ecstatic, spontaneous joy, like "Hallelujah!" and "Amen!" in Christian devotion.

70. The *Hōzuki* (*Physalis alkekengi*), Japanese bladder cherry or Chinese lantern plant, has a red lantern-shaped pod with a single round fruit inside, similar to the ground cherry familiar in western gardens. It is commonly used in traditional Japanese folk medicine.

71. See OW for discussion of the contributions made by these two most central followers of Kurozumi Munetada.

72. *Taiki seppo*; fitting the specific lesson to the specific situation being addressed.

73. As one would before a kami in a shrine.

74. He was also referred to as Shikata. Futsukaichi is on the west bank of the Asahi River just south of Okayama City. Rokuzaemon, the owner of the factory, made important contributions to the early development of Kurozumikyō.

75. Literally, "severe, quick-swelling boil", or "carbuncle".

76. *Ikimono* (literally, "living-thing") is Munetada's vivid term for the presence of Amaterasu within each person. We see how he expressed this concept at the level of ordinary people's understanding; or, at what level he sometimes was understood. Nevertheless, Madame Hata clearly was a happy person who benefited from his care for her.

77. Though born a merchant, he had been given special permission by the Bizen

Daimyō to use the surname Nozaki and to wear swords (ordinarily allowed only to samurai). He developed many large salt farms along the coast of the Seto Inland Sea, enabling him to earn a large fortune. He became the wealthiest merchant in Bizen Province, and his descendants are among the wealthiest in the area down to the present day. Some years ago these descendants opened a museum where the many precious objects of art Buzaemon collected are on display. The *Register of Disciples* is part of the *Kyōsho*, the collected canonical writings of Kurozumikyō.

78. Sanuki Province, known today as Kagawa Prefecture, is across the Seto Inland Sea on the island of Shikoku.

79. By one estimate a *ryō* of those times is worth about 55,000 *yen* in today's purchasing power in Japan. At any rate, only the highest samurai and the most wealthy merchants had access to such goods. The price was high because it was imported from the West.

80. Pieces of good quality paper, about a foot long and a few inches wide, would have been furnished, of a kind used for writing poetry or for making small paintings.

81. Of course, behind the navel is the *hara*, the abdomen, in Japanese usage the seat of understanding, of the heart/mind. It was Munetada's witty way of teaching this man so prone to gloom and anger. "Remember this message where it is most needed."

82. Munetada insists that reliance on one's own power (*jiriki*) cannot accomplish what is needed; that one must rely on the presence of Amaterasu and seek unity with her.

83. A double delight is expressed: each being in oneness with Kami, and being together in this oneness.

84. A *bu* in Tokugawa period money was a fourth of a *ryō*. The next smaller unit of money, the *shu*, was one fourth of a *bu*. Tradesmen in Japan used to keep a running account of what their regular customers owed them, and then collect twice a year (at the time of the *O-bon* festival in July or August when the spirits of ancestors visit their families, and at year-end). Occasional customers would pay at the time of receiving the goods or services.

85. This advice is in accord with the Confucian concept of reciprocity, a version of the Golden Rule. But, whereas class differences could co-exist with the practice of reciprocity in traditional Confucian society, for Munetada the fish peddler was in his religious insight his equal.

86. Compare the saying of Confucius at Analects 17.19: "What does Heaven ever say? Yet there are the four seasons going round and there are the hundred things coming into being. What does Heaven ever say?" (D.C. Lau translation).

87. In Kurozumi belief, one's character stems from the moral character of the family one is born into. The concept is a Japanese adaptation of the Buddhist idea of karma. See Kurozumi Muneharu's comments in *KS* 74.

88. The "don" suffix to a name identifies a person as having low status.

89. The respect in which he came to be held can be seen from the fact that Munetada allowed Ikeda to use the Chinese character given in *romaji* spelling as *tada*, part of his own name, as part of Ikeda's formal name. See OW 81, 85 for other instances of this practice.

90. Kyōso would have then have been only a few feet away from her, seated up on a low platform about two feet high (see portrait on p. xxxvii).

91. Consecrated water has a purificatory effect since it communicates the power and presence of Amaterasu Ohmikami. Containers of it are available at the entrances of Kurozumi Shinto shrines, and may be served to guests or to anyone in need of a blessing from Kami.

92. See Kurozumi Tadaaki's discussion (OW 26, 59f.).

93. The direct guidance of Heaven within the human spirit attunes a person to use whatever skills they have, or faith-practices they adhere to, in fullest effectiveness and in fullest harmony with others. See Stories 83, 86, 96, 120, 121 and 122.

94. Tsuyama, then the seat of the Matsudaira clan who were rulers of most of Mimasaka Province, is today within the bounds of Okayama Prefecture.

95. *Narukana* is an emphasis term: "I believe so", or "Yes, this is so", or "It certainly is so".

96. I.e., in five phrases or lines, with a 5–7–5–7–7 pattern of syllables. The sermon was about to end with *megumi*, which would, with the previous phrases having a 5–7–5–7 pattern, leave a *waka* with a fifth line only three syllables long. *Narukana* supplies the last four syllables of the final line, felicitously producing an excellent poem.

97. See Story 29. The Eight Million are understood to have contributed blessing and virtue to their presently living descendants, as the large limbs of a tree bring life from the trunk of the tree (Amaterasu) to its twigs and leaves. Reverent gratitude is due to them.

98. The rushes (*igusa*) were soaked in clay-water to preserve their colour and flexibility and then dried. The whole process had to be finished in a few days. Then the same ground had to be prepared for rice cultivation immediately afterward. The Okayama area still produces these rushes and the *tatami* made from them, but leadership in making mats has passed to Kumamoto and Oita Prefectures in Shikoku Island where modern machinery is in greater use. The Okayama area still prides itself on the quality of the *tatami* it produces.

99. The *tokonoma* is a standard feature of Japanese homes. It is a shallow alcove, raised above the floor a few inches, in which flower arrangements and seasonal art objects or important scrolls are placed.

100. The Bizen area east of Okayama is one of the most important pottery-producing areas in Japan. Bizen *yaki* has a traditional style that is well known and widely appreciated.

101. I.e., Kyōso himself. It is a polite way of referring to one's self. The "secrets" here referred to are the techniques of the mending trade, not the "secrets of all the arts" that are part of the fundamental life-attitude every person should have.

102. This chronology is the sixth section of the *Kurozumikyō Kyōsho*, the official compilation of the teachings of Kurozumikyō. See Appendix C.

103. The castle was the headquarters and residence of the Ikeda Daimyō, ruler of the Bizen *han*. The Ikeda were among the most prestigious of the vassals of the Tokugawa clan. With the castle tower covered with burned boards, it was known as the "crow castle" after its black colour. A modern replacement stands today on the site, the original having been destroyed in 1945.

104. Under Edo period law only samurai were allowed to carry swords. They could at their own initiative act like freelance policemen, using their swords.

105. I.e., *seppuku*, ritual suicide by disembowelment (*harakiri*). The offence was so seriously regarded that his whole family line (*Oie-no danzetsu*) could also be destroyed as punishment.

106. That is, there is no more attachment to one's body, one's self, even to the movements of one's *kokoro*, one's inner thoughts and awareness. No ego (*jiga*) remains. In such a state of emptiness (*mushin*) the heart is completely sincere (*makoto*). It is grounded solely in the *bunshin*, in Amaterasu's inner presence. See also Stories 18, 44, 56, 70, 72, 82, 111, 122 and 123.

107. The *Monjin Nadokoro-ki* is Part Five of the complete compilation of Kurozumikyō teachings. It is a book of the names and addresses of those who had presented their pledges (*shinmon*) to practise the Way as taught by Munetada. Collectively the *monjin* were called the *Shinmon Shū*, "Vowed Group".

108. A low table with a heat source under it, covered with a quilt down to the floor. People can sit around it with their legs underneath, warming themselves and having close familiar conversation. The New Year Festival (*Saitan Sai*) is perhaps the most important festival in the Japanese calendar, emphasizing a fresh start in reliance on divine blessing. In addition to visiting the shrine of a kami, people go to one another's homes during a ten-day period to offer good wishes for the coming year.

109. Munetada seems to have been thinking also of the closing of his life. See *OW 95*.

110. *Sumo* is a popular sport in Japan. Two wrestlers stand in a ring, each trying to push the other out or force the other to fall to the ground.

111. Amaki, ruled by relatives of the Ikeda clan based in Okayama, was located south of Kurashiki City. Makisaburō was his childhood name.

112. The *nageshi*, a decorative wooden beam partly covering the upper frames of the sliding partitions (*fusuma*) between rooms, is wide enough to allow a framed piece of calligraphy or a painting to rest on it, fastened to the wall above the *fusuma*.

113. Furumatsu was a quarter-mile east of Ohmoto.

114. *Tatami* are used as floor covering. They are made using *igusa* rushes, a narrow-leafed plant growing in the area (see Story 69). The rushes are tightly woven and placed over an inner core that is made by hand out of straw. Any imperfection in the weaving would lead to a mat wearing out much too fast. *Tatami* are made in standard sizes, about six feet by three feet and about two and a half inches thick. They must be made precisely since they are set into prepared spaces in the floors of houses. Single mats can be replaced as needed. Sizes of rooms in many kinds of buildings are ordinarily indicated in numbers of mats used to cover the floors.

115. The *temizu-bachi* is a basin in which people ceremonially rinse their hands and mouths before entering a shrine. Man-nari's gift still stands at the former headquarters shrine at Ohmoto in Okayama.

116. This *waka* reads as an apology for a bit of worldliness that had crept into Kyōso's words when he asked if the stonemason had a good profit the previous year. Kyōso had thought he had tossed aside ("abandoned") his body and mind, but his heart (*kokoro*) that had thought so still had its own traces of attachment to that which is not Amaterasu – financial profit. See the discussion at Note 106.

117. See Appendix A.

118. A deep and intimate knowledge is implied in the verb *shiru*. Munetada was in complete oneness with Amaterasu; her full virtue was resident within him.

119. The Kotohira Shrine, in today's Kagawa Prefecture on Shikoku island, dates from the eleventh century. The kami enshrined there, until the Meiji period known as Kumbira (Konpira) Daigongen, is worshipped as a protector of sailors and fishermen. Munetada, Ito has found, is greater than that kami.

120. Details of the incident are documented in his diary, now in the possession of his descendants. See also O W 130.

121. Jikihara made a record of a number of Munetada's sermons and discussions, available today in the archives at Kurozumikyō headquarters.

122. It was a kind of "sand bar" where one stood to be tried by a judge.

123. I.e., Governor-General and Commander-in-Chief.

124. The Great Mission (*tenmei jikiju*) was the Mandate of Heaven conferred by Munetada's ecstatic experience of unity with the Sun Kami at the winter solstice of 1814. This was the chartering experience that set him on his course as healer and teacher and as the founder of Kurozumikyō. See O W 15ff.

125. Fukuwatari is located about eighteen miles from Kiyama and from Okayama, halfway between.

126. See Story 42.

127. After Munetada's death Kimura played a role in encouraging the followers not to lose hope but to continue faithful to the Way. See O W 96.

128. The area around Tokyo, including Tokyo, Kanagawa, Chiba and Saitama Prefectures. The term "Kantō" originally meant that area east (tō) of the checkpoints (kan; sekisho) set up on the main roadways by the watchful Tokugawa regime to regulate the flow of information in the realm; in this case, the checkpoint in the Hakone area.

129. Since Bizen pottery uses no glazes, the method probably had to do with some way of applying ash to the surfaces during the firing process.

130. Everyone takes off their shoes when entering a Japanese home. Visitors leave them in the entrance area (genkan) at the door. Footwear would be left with toes pointing into the house, as taken off before stepping from the entrance into the house. The polite host would switch the direction the footwear were facing so the visitor could more easily put them on when leaving. Ordinarily this humble courtesy would be performed by a servant or by the wife of the house.

131. The wooden cleats of the geta would ordinarily make distinct marks in the wet ground.

132. Swords (shinai) in the kind of swordsmanship (kendō) referred to were made of strips of bamboo instead of the traditional steel swords. They are without a blade, but they are about four feet long and a good clout can be administered to one's opponent. The bamboo sword, and protective clothing and rules about scoring points, were introduced in the course of the 18th century as the older training in the use of the long sword (kenjutsu) was deemphasized during the long period of Tokugawa peace when few battles between samurai were fought. Skill in the use of the long sword was still valued, though the use of both types was increasingly regarded as a spiritual discipline ("martial art"). The Bizen domain, with its annual income of 325,000 koku of rice, was one of the most prestigious provinces in the country. Abe was from the Asakusa section of Edo and had been trained in one of the leading schools of kendō. He was a nationally recognized master of the art.

133. Ishio was a boyhood friend of Munetada and one of the Four High Disciples. He was a samurai who had to go to Edo with the Daimyō on alternate year service, and many letters between the two have been preserved. See OW 37f., 64.

134. Majinai on kokoro has the same purpose as majinai performed with some physical illness in mind: to bring the person into unity with the bunshin, with the inner presence of Amaterasu. In either case, egoistic mists and clouds preventing the full light of that presence from enabling happy, healthy life are swept away or dissipated.

135. The Regulations of 1846 and the group's decision to build a house for Munetada in which to live and conduct his work were important steps in establishing the following as an organization. See OW 74–76.

136. Bamboo is an important crop in Japan, attentively cultivated for its many

uses. It is an important source of food and building materials and has countless other uses. The variety growing in Iwako was especially straight and strong, useful for making excellent military weapons. Iwako was in a place then known as Takashima Village, within today's Okayama City.

137. Kawakami was a leading scholar of Chinese classics before becoming a follower and served prominently thereafter as a writer. Among other things, he wrote an important biography of Munetada.

138. See Story 76.

139. This was a scroll in Kyōso's own calligraphy, containing the name ("title") of the Ise Grand Shrine (Tenshō Kōtai Jingū) where Amaterasu Ohmikami is enshrined.

140. The opening (kaiun) of "good fortune" happens when Amaterasu can act directly in human events through receptivity to her inner presence. Such action opens the way to bring all together for good. When that "all" is focused on an ill individual, healing happens; when that "all" is the worldwide scene, as is here intended, it is a step in the direction of the whole world being brought together in harmony and sincerity.

141. The dolls' festival is held each year on the third day of the third month, a very popular and happy time of the year. The platform has a series of shelves resembling a stairway, perhaps three or four feet high, with dolls at the top level representing a prince (always seated on the right) and princess, the attending samurai below them, then court ladies and musicians in descending order according to their rank in traditional society. A full set of such dolls is displayed in homes and in schools on the festival day. The ceremony annually reminds everyone of the traditional understanding of social status in Japan.

142. The follower who recounted the story was Imada Esaji from Shimoyamada in Oku county. It was recorded from his reminiscences at the age of 90.

143. Kamezō was from the same village as Imada Esaji.

144. At the time Morishita was a minor samurai in service to the Bizen Daimyō, but later, just before the Meiji Restoration in 1867, he organized a group of farmers fighting against the old shogunal regime. He was appointed governor of Oita Prefecture (in Kyushu) in 1872 by the Meiji government. After retiring in 1876 he served as Vice-Patriarch (Fuku-Kanchō) of the Kurozumikyō organization. See OW 88–90.

145. See Story 99. The increase among samurai followers occurred during a period of three years after Munetada gave himself to teaching full-time in 1843.

146. "Kamigata" refers to the area of Kyoto and Osaka, known for the brewing of fine sake. "Kami" suggests "high" or "upper" (in this case the Emperor as the highest person in Japan), and gata indicates "in the direction of".

147. Kawakami was an adherent of the Wang Yang-ming school of Neo-Confucianism, which emphasized the personal realization of truth through

181

existential practice. The *sake* metaphor reminded him that he had not involved himself personally in what he had studied as a scholar.

148. I.e., *kashiwade*, the normal way of reverently acknowledging a kami, or a kami's action.

149. The letter reads, in part: "I am grateful to have been initiated into the teaching of Amaterasu Ohmikami. I would never have been able to enjoy this salvation of mine without the teaching of Kurozumi Sensei. I understand the grace of Kami much more because of the benevolence and virtue of the Sensei. You guided me kindly so I may know for myself the blessings of Great Kami. As I sit quietly in meditation in my study on this rainy day, my tears flow down my cheeks in my feeling of gratitude. Please accept the deep sincerity of my heart and bestow your generous understanding upon me." Cited in *OW* 40.

150. Kyōso shin is a term of great respect, which might be translated "The divine Kyōso" or "Kyōso Kami". Here we leave it untranslated in order to signal the great reverence with which he is regarded by Kurozumi followers.

151. *Ayu*, or *ai*, prized as a delicacy.

152. Ishii Sōken was a student of Philipp Franz von Siebold, a German in Dutch government service. From 1824 to 1828 he conducted a school for physicians in the Dutch settlement of Dejima at Nagasaki. Von Siebold later was a major figure in introducing Japanese culture to the west.

153. Another way of referring to Amaterasu. To live in an ego-less, unattached way, not separate from (*funi*; "not-two") Amaterasu's inner presence, is to be in accord with what she provides; this is to live in Heaven's Way (*tendō*), in accord with divine providence. To live in this way is to have abiding life (*ikidōshi*); death is not a concern in this way of living.

154. This saying is a quotation from a formal Chinese poem by Kawakami Chūsho (*OW* 80).

155. Kuroda's letters and memoranda are preserved in the Kurozumikyō archives. What is cited here is in a collection of materials relating to the topic of *ikidōshi*.

156. As in Story 72 about the drunken samurai who threatened Munetada with a sword.

157. *Manshin*, conceit, is the subject of the third of the Seven Household Rules by which every Kurozumikyō follower measures himself or herself every day.

158. See Stories 86 and 105.

159. He was an important village head in Akasaka County, Bizen Province, with the medium-level rank of *chū-shōya*. Under him would have been a number of lowest-rank *shōya*, who along with headmen with the rank of *nanushi* were in immediate contact with the village people. Village heads, entrusted by the Tokugawa regime with many tasks of direct governance, were quick to see the value of Munetada's teachings, as this story demonstrates.

160. This was a sect of the Nichiren tradition of Buddhism who made a point of not giving any alms for charity, nor of begging for any. They had a strict attitude about their rules and were well known for their resistance to government controls. They were numerous in the Bizen domain, though they were treated rather harshly.

161. Often when Munetada spoke and wrote it was in an ecstatic mood, with conscious intention absent and in direct reliance on the inner presence of Amaterasu. Words said or written in this way were called *tengen*, "words from Heaven". Their special value is evident. See Story 62, and *OW* 59ff.

162. *KS* 103.

163. Though both deplore spending one's self in busyness and mere ado without understanding life's true nature, there is a clear difference in emphasis. The Buddhist priest's concern is for the transient character of life, dwelling on awareness of its limits. Munetada is aware of life's transience, but his attention is on its limitless character within each moment. To "live through" (*ikidōshi*) each moment with such awareness is to have "abiding life" that is vital and harmonious in the here and now.

164. He was holding his personal thousand-day retreat (*sen-nichi-sanro*) for prayer and rededication. See Story 31.

165. I.e., *ni*, "two", and *o*, "tail". The two terms are spelled with different Chinese characters, though with the same *romaji* letters. Such word-play, or serious punning, is a common way of bringing out meaning in Japanese discourse.

166. I.e., ego, or selfishness, causes a separation between Kami and one's self. Whereas in its origin human life is one in being based in the divided presence of Amaterasu within, egoism leads the heart astray as one's identity develops. It is because our hearts' attention becomes scattered that we have "two tails" like the demons.

167. The Yoshida family in Kyoto were the appointed, hereditary standard-bearers of Shinto tradition, holding that position until the Meiji Restoration in 1868. They were in charge of appointments to the various ranks of Shinto priests throughout the country. They also maintained a school in which a theoretical, ritualized form of Shinto was taught deriving from Yoshida Kanetomo. See Alan Grapard, "The Shinto of Yoshida Kanetomo", *Monumenta Nipponica* 47 (Spring, 1992) 27–58.

168. He acknowledged that he could not speak from his own experience but only as a scholar of Shinto.

Appendix A

Daily Rules for the Whole Family

1. Born in the Land of the Gods, you shall not fail to cultivate faith.
2. You shall neither get angry nor worry.
3. You shall not give way to conceit nor look down upon others.
4. You shall not follow another's evil while increasing evil in your own heart.
5. You shall not slacken in the work of your house except in illness.
6. While pledged to the Way of Sincerity, you shall not lack sincerity in your own heart.
7. You must never stray from the spirit of gratitude.

The rules must never be forgotten.

> Standing before you
>   others hold up mirrors
>   as their own hearts
> And there within you can see
>   your own heart being reflected.

Appendix B

Michi no Kotowari*

(What has been taught about the Way of Great Kami by Munetada Kami, our Kyōso.)
The origin of all that live and thrive in Heaven and Earth is Amaterasu Ohmikami. She is the Parent Kami of all beings and the source of all life. The whole world is brimming over with her shining essence. Our growth, our flourishing, and our enjoyment of the fulness of life are all due to her ceaseless graces within us. How great a blessing this is! Know that the warmth in our bodies is the heart (*kokoro*) we receive from the Kami of the sun. The word *kokoro* has the meaning "to condense" (*kogoru*); the divine energy of Amaterasu has condensed to become the heart within us. When we leave behind all cravings and are fully sincere, our hearts become one with the heart of the Sun Kami. When the heart is enlightened, it is the master and the body the servant. Then the heart controls the physical form. But when our hearts are confused, the servant becomes the master. So, entrust everything to the Kami of the sun. Tune your heart to every inward blessing. Savour every sight and every sound.

Breathe the sun's divine essence into your lower abdomen and keep it active there. When you live in oneness with Kami your bodily form is enlivened and all your illness cured. Your heart will then be warm and bright. When your heart is kept constantly warm and joyous, your whole life will be joyful and active. To live this way is to follow the Way of Kami. Your cheerful joy is what the heart of Great Kami desires. These teachings come from Heaven, and the Way is what Heaven shows us directly everywhere.

* This summary of the teachings of Munetada was prepared by Hoshijima Ryōhei and the other High Disciples.

Never stray from sincerity.
Entrust everything to Heaven.
Abandon every selfish desire.
Be filled with the positive spirit of Kami.
Grasp firmly the living presence within yourself and put it to active use.

The hearts of the ancients had no form, and neither do our hearts today. When we dwell only in the heart and forget about the body, then is the age of kami. The age of kami is in the present moment, and the present moment is the age of kami.

Everything in life depends entirely upon the heart. When the heart becomes one with Kami, then indeed we are one with Kami.

Appendix C

Kurozumi Literature

A. *Kurozumikyō kyōsho*, ed. Kurozumi Muneyasu (Okayama: Nisshin-sha, 1974). The *Kyōsho*, the official compilation of the teachings of Kurozumikyō, consists of the following:

1. *Outa Waka*: Poems composed by the Founder to convey his teachings; *Den Uta*: those that survive only as copies;
2. *Gobun*: letters he sent to his followers; *Den Gobun*: those that survive only as copies;
3. *Zasshū*: (*Miscellany*); Munetada's diaries and accounts of his pilgrimages to Ise; memoranda, notes and comments on various things he experienced or heard; and other writings and documents of Munetada written from time to time;
4. *Michizure Toshi Oboedome*: *The Register of Followers*, including the traditional calendar year in which they were born, and, in the case of samurai, their rank as measured by their yearly stipends (in *koku* of rice);
5. *Monjin Nadokoroki*: *The Register of Disciples*; names and addresses of those who had given their vows (*shinmon*): the "Vowed Ones" (*shinmon shū*);
6. *Gonenpu*: the *Chronology of The Founder's Life*, from birth to his ascension to the Heavens.

B. *Other Kurozumi literature*
"Akagi's Evening Talks". Copy of manuscript in Kurozumikyō Headquarters.
Biography. Kawakami Chūsho, *Biography of the Great Deity* (*Munetada Daimyōjin Godenki*). Okayama: Nisshinsha, 1965.

189

Chronology of Kurozumi Documents. Kyōsho 413–482.

Denshū Kikigaki; Goshōden Denshu Kikigaki. Notes by Miyake Jūzō on lectures by Hoshijima Ryōhei on his book, the *Goshōden.*

Gokōkoden. Jikihara Ihachirō, *Gokōden; Munetada Shin Gokōden (Memorandum of the Founder's Sermons and Letters).* Okayama: Ohmoto Gakuen, 1965 (mimeographed).

Gokōshakuden. A compilation of notes made by various people on the Founder's lectures and sermons.

Hoshijima Ryōhei, *Kyōso Munetada shin Goshōden (Short Biography of our Founder).* Okayama: Kurozumikyō Headquarters, 1877, and successive recent printings by Kurozumikyō Nisshinsha.

Ito Sadasaburō, *Kenbundan Kikigaki* ("Memorandum of What I have Seen and Heard") (original preserved by the Ito family of Tottori Prefecture).

Kawakami Chūsho, *Daishi no Setsu (The Teaching of the Substitute Instructor).*

————, *Dendō Shinpen (Texts for a Mission).*

————, *Dōtai Tai-i (Outline of the Way).*

————, *Michi no Hokori (Prides of the Way).*

————, *Munetada Daimyōjin Godenki) (Biography of the Great Deity Munetada.*

————, *Nyūmon Tai-i (Outline for Initiation into the Way).*

————, *San Tai-i ("The Three Great Outlines"); Nyūmon Tai-i Dōtai-i,* and *Shinseki Tai-i.*

————, *Shijun Tenmei no Maki (Book of the Reverent Observance of the Divine Mission).*

————, *Shinseki Tai-i (Outline of the Deity's Accomplishments).*

Kurozumi Church Regulations (Kurozumikyō Kyōki). Current name of a document frequently revised; originally prepared as "Kurozumikyō Kōsha Kisoku" ("Regulations for the Kurozumi Association"). All revisions on file at Kurozumikyō Headquarters.

Kurozumi Tadaaki, *Chibyō to Shinkō (Therapy and the Quest for Faith).* Okayama: Nisshinsha, 1969.

————, *Kansha to Yōki no Seikatsu (To Live with Gratitude and Yōki).* Okayama: Nisshinsha, 1969.

————, *Kuromon Kōtei; Yūkō Monjin Ryakuden (Brief Biographies of High Disciples and Worthy Followers of Kurozumi Kyōso).* Okayama: Nisshinsha, 1994.

————, *Kurozumi Kyōso to sono Shūkyō (Kurozumi Kyōso and His Faith).* Okayama: Nisshinsha, 1970.

————, *Kurozumikyō Kyōsoden* (*Biography of the Founder of Kurozumikyō*). Okayama: Nisshinsha, 1964. 5th ed., 1974; published as *The Opening Way; Kurozumi Munetada, Founder of Kurozumikyō*. trans. Julie Iezzi and Harold Wright, with assistance from Kamiya Sumio, ed. Willis Stoesz (Lanham, Md.: University Press of America, 1994).

————, *Kurozumikyō Shinto no Kokoro* (*The Heart of Kurozumikyō Shinto*). Okayama: Nisshinsha, 1939.

————, ed. Kohmoto Isshi, *Kyōso sama no Go-Itsuwa* (*Stories of the Founder*). Okayama: Nisshinsha, 1960. 2nd ed. 1974.

————, *Ogami-ai no Shinjin* (*Mutual Support Through Prayer*). Okayama: Nisshinsha, 1971.

Morishita Keitan, *Jikiju Go-kōden* (*Kyōso's Lectures and Sermons, as I Have Heard Directly*).

Nisshin. Okayama 1– (1914–). The journal was originally named *Kuni-no-Oshie* (*Teachings of the Nation*), renamed *Keisei Zasshi* (*Leading Your Life Magazine*) in 1909, and again renamed *Nisshin* (*The New Sun*) in 1914. It continues under that name.

"Ohmoto House Regulations" (*Ohmoto-ke Hōsoku*). Preserved at Kurozumikyō Headquarters.

"Record of Gifts Received". *Kyōsho* 464–467.

"Rules for the Group Studying the Divine Teachings". Original rules for the Tenshinsha (Heaven-Heart Society) preserved at the Nagasaki Kurozumikyō Church.

Stories of the Founder (*Kyōsosama no oitsuwa*). ed. Kohmoto Isshi (Okayama: Nisshinsha, 1960. rev. ed, 1974). *Itsuwa* were first published in *Kuni-no-Oshie*, official journal of Kurozumikyō at that time, between 1896 and 1906. In 1949 these were published under the title *Kurozumi Kyōso Itsuwa-shū* as part of the centenary commemoration of the death of the Founder. Between 1937 and 1944 Kohmoto Isshi had published his modern versions of many of the originally published stories in Nisshin. These were collected and published in 1960 as *Kyōsosama no Go-Itsuwa.* Seventy-five of these, plus twenty-six more not used by Kohmoto, were rewritten in modern Japanese by the Kurozumi School of Theology under the leadership of Kurozumi Tadaaki and published in 1974 under the same title as the 1960 edition. For the English edition twenty-seven more of those originally published have been rewritten by Kurozumi Tadaaki.

"A Written Memorandum Concerning Missionary Work". *Kyōsho* 427.

Further Reading

Beardsley, Richard, *et al*. *Village Japan*. Chicago: University of Chicago Press, 1959.

Befu, Harumi. *Japan: An Anthropological Introduction*. Rutland, Vt. and Tokyo: Charles E. Tuttle Co., 1981.

Bellah, Robert. *Tokugawa Religion*. New York: The Free Press, 1985.

Davis, Winston. *Japanese Religion and Society; Paradigms of Structure and Change*. Albany: State University of New York Press, 1992.

————. "Pilgrimage and World Renewal: A Study of Religion and Social Values in Tokugawa Japan", *History of Religions* Part I: Vol. 23, 2 (November 1983) 97–116; Part II: Vol. 23, 3 (February, 1984) 197–221.

Evans, Donald. *Spirituality and Human Nature*. Albany: State University of New York Press, 1993.

Fu, Charles Wei-hsun, and Steven Heine, eds., *Japan in Traditional and Postmodern Perspectives*. Albany: State University of New York Press, 1995.

Grapard, Allan G. "The Shinto of Yoshida Kanetomo", *Monumenta Nipponica* 47:1 (Spring 1992) 27–58.

Hall, John W. *Government and Local Power in Japan*. Princeton: Princeton University Press, 1966.

Hardacre, Helen. *Kurozumikyō and the New Religions of Japan*. Princeton: Princeton University Press, 1986.

————. *Shinto and the State*. Princeton: Princeton University Press, 1989.

Harootunian, H.D. "Ideology as Conflict", in *Conflict in Modern Japanese History*, ed. Najita and Koschmann, 25–63.

————. "Late Tokugawa Culture and Thought", in *The Cambridge History of Japan*, Volume 5, ed. Marius B. Jansen. Cambridge: Cambridge University Press, 1989, 168–258.

————. *Things Seen and Unseen; Discourse and Ideology in Tokugawa Nativism.* Chicago and London: University of Chicago Press, 1988.

Hashimoto, Mitsuru. "The Social Background of Peasant Uprisings in Tokugawa Japan", in *Conflict in Modern Japanese History*, ed. Najita and Koschmann, 145–63.

Hass, Robert, *The Essential Haiku; Versions of Basho, Buson, & Issa.* Hopewell, N.J.: Ecco Press, 1994.

Hepner, Charles W. *The Kurozumi Sect of Shinto.* Tokyo: Meiji Japan Society, 1935.

Holtom, D.C. *The National Faith of Japan.* New York: Paragon, 1965.

Keene, Donald. *World Within Walls; Japanese Literature of the Pre-Modern Era, 1600–1867.* New York: Holt, Rinehart and Winston, 1976.

King, Winston, *Zen and the Way of the Sword.* New York: Oxford University Press, 1993.

Kitagawa, Joseph. *On Understanding Japanese Religion.* Princeton: Princeton University Press, 1987.

————. *Religion in Japanese History.* New York: Columbia University Press, 1966.

Kodansha Encyclopedia of Japan, ed. Itasaka Gen *et al.* Tokyo: Kodansha International Ltd., 1983.

Kurozumi, Tadaaki. *The Opening Way; Kurozumi Munetada, Founder of Kurozumikyō (Kyōsoden).* Trans. Julie Iezzi, Harold Wright and Kamiya Sumio, ed. Willis Stoesz. Lanham, Md.: University Press of America, 1994.

Lifton, Robert. *The Broken Connection.* New York: Simon and Schuster, 1979.

Maruyama, Masao. *Studies in the Intellectual History of Tokugawa Japan.* Trans. Mikiso Hane. Princeton: Princeton University Press, 1974.

Murakami, Shigeyoshi. *Japanese Religion in the Modern Period.* Trans. H. Byron Earhart. Tokyo: Tokyo University Press, 1980; *Nihon Hyakunen no Shūkyō.* Tokyo: Kodansha, 1968.

Muraoka, Tsunetsugu. *Studies in Shinto Thought.* Trans. Delmer M. Brown and James T. Araki. New York: Greenwood Press, 1988.

Najita, Tetsuo, and J. Victor Koschmann, eds. *Conflict in Modern Japanese History: The Neglected Tradition.* Princeton: Princeton University Press, 1982.

Nobuhara, Taisen. *The Brilliant Life of Munetada Kurozumi; A Philoso-*

pher and Worshipper of the Sun, 2nd ed., trans. Sakai Tsukasa and Sasage Kazuko. Tokyo: PC Publications, Inc., 1982.

Nosco, Peter, ed. *Confucianism and Tokugawa Culture*. Princeton: Princeton University Press, 1984.

————. *Remembering Paradise; Nativism and Nostalgia in Eighteenth-Century Japan*. Cambridge: Harvard University Press, 1990.

Ono, Sokyo. *Shinto: The Kami Way*, in collaboration with William P. Woodard. Rutland, Vt. and Tokyo: Charles E. Tuttle Co., 1962.

Ooms, Herman. *Tokugawa Ideology; Early Constructs, 1570–1680*. Princeton: Princeton University Press, 1985.

Picken, Stuart. *Essentials of Shinto; an Analytical Guide to Principal Teachings*. Westport, Ct: Greenwood Press, 1994.

————. *Shinto; Japan's Spiritual Roots*. Tokyo, New York: Kodansha International Ltd., 1980.

Ross, Floyd. *Shinto, the Way of Japan*. Boston: Beacon Press, 1965.

Sansom, George. *Japan: A Short Cultural History*, 2nd rev. ed. Stanford: Stanford University Press, 1978.

Sawada, Janine. *Confucian Values and Popular Zen; Sekimon Shingaku in Eighteenth-Century Japan*. Honolulu: University of Hawaii Press, 1993.

Spae, Joseph, *Shinto Man*. Tokyo: Oriens Institute for Religious Research, 1972.

Stoesz, Willis, ed. *Kurozumi Shinto; An American Dialogue*. Chambersburg, Pa.: Anima Books, 1989; New York: Columbia University Press, 1995.

————, "The Universal Attitude of Shinto as Expressed in the Shinto Sect Kurozumikyō." *Journal of Ecumenical Studies* 29, 2 (Spring 1992), 215–29.

Suzuki, D. T., *Japanese Spirituality*. Trans. Norman Waddell. New York: Greenwood Press, 1972.

Tucker, Mary Evelyn. *Moral and Spiritual Cultivation in Japanese Neo-Confucianism; The Life and Thought of Kaibara Ekken (1630–1714)*. Albany: State University of New York Press, 1989.

Varley, H. Paul. *Japanese Culture*, 3rd ed. Honolulu: University of Hawaii Press, 1984.

Vlastos, Stephen. *Peasant Protests and Uprisings in Tokugawa Japan*. Berkeley: University of California Press, 1986.

Walthall, Anne. *Social Protest and Popular Culture in Eighteenth-Century Japan*. Tucson: University of Arizona Press, 1986.

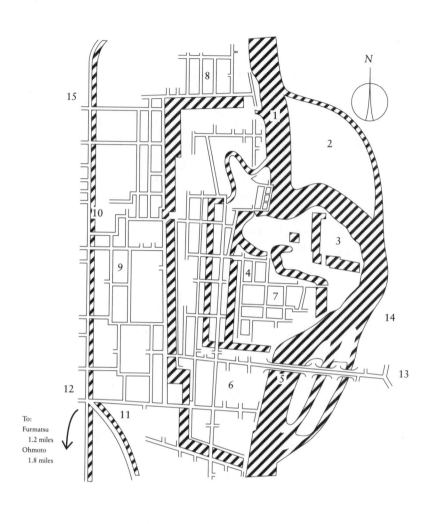

1 Asahi River   5 Kyōbashi Bridge   9 Tamachi   13 Tamai-gū River
2 Korakuen Garden   6 Saidaiji-chō   10 Nishigawa   14 Furugyō
3 Okayama Castle   7 Uchisange   11 Kawaramachi   15 Man-nari
4 Nakanochō Gate   8 Banchō   12 Daiku

Map 1 Okayama Castle Town (Edo Period)

1 Kamo	7 Shimoyamada	13 Okita Shrine	18 Kurashiki	24 Asahi River
2 Ohzasa	8 Kamiyamada	14 Ohmoto	19 Okayama City	25 Takahashi River
3 Tsuyama	9 Achi	(Kaminakano)	20 Fukuwatari	
4 Ohmachi	10 Kohmoto	15 Mishima	21 Ochiai	
5 Shakuso	11 Saidaiji	16Ajino	22 Kuse	
6 Sayama	12 Kogushi	17 Amaki	23 Burakuji	

Map 2 Okayama Prefecture

HOKKAIDO

Akita

HONSHU

Okayama

Kyoto

Edo (Tokyo)

KYUSHU

Ise

Ohita

Naniwa (Ohsaka)

SHIKOKU

Map 3 Japan

Map 4 Edo Period Provinces and the Modern Prefectures

199

The Editors and Translator

Kohmoto Isshi (1877–1947) was born at Saidaiji-chō in Jōtō County just east of Okayama City. As a young man he entered Waseda University in Tokyo with high expectations, but due to circumstances had to leave before graduation. For some years he was active in the Farmers' Movement, but at the age of thirty contracted a case of pulmonary tuberculosis which soon became critical.

At that point he was introduced to the teachings of Kurozumi Munetada by Kobayashi Inokichi (1837–1922), a native of a village near his own birthplace. Kobayashi had been for many years a dedicated minister in the Saidai-ji area. After receiving a single ritual of *majinai* Kohmoto was on the road to a complete recovery from his illness.

It was a turning point in his life, a conversion to the teachings of Kurozumikyō, and he became an earnest follower of the Way. His flowing eloquence and fine literary art soon placed him in the front rank of Kurozumikyō leaders, and in 1935 he joined the headquarters staff. His talents were especially evident as the editor of *Nisshin*, the monthly denominational journal.

In that capacity he wrote many fine articles, including the first seventy-five Stories of the Founder (*Go-Itsuwa-shū*) contained in this book. His story-telling talent and his broad knowledge are clearly visible, even in translation. Readers in his own time were captivated by his writing ability. His personal name was Masaji, but he adapted the Chinese characters used to write it to make his pen name of Isshi, or "one-stop", suggesting his determination to see his projects through to completion.

Kurozumi Tadaaki was born in Okayama, Japan, in 1919. He graduated from Tokyo Imperial University in 1943 with a major in Occidental Philosophy, and then served as an instructor in Ethics and in English Language at the Naval Academy then located on Etajima Island offshore from Kure, near Hiroshima.

In 1945 he joined the Kurozumikyō headquarters staff. In 1953 he became the Rector of the Kurozumikyō Institute, and also served as head of several other departments of the headquarters office. He was Director of the Educational Bureau and Chief Priest of the Munetada Shrine in Okayama from 1981 to 1989. In 1989 he began serving as Vice Patriarch of Kurozumikyō. He has published eight books, including *Kurozumikyō Kyōsoden* (*Biography of the Founder of Kurozumikyō*; Okayama, 1964), translated as *The Opening Way* (Lanham, Md., 1994); and *Kyōsosama no Itsuwa* (*Stories of the Founder*; Okayama, 1960). (See the bibliography for a complete list.)

Kamiya Sumio, the translator, was born in Los Angeles in 1921 and received his early education there through the fifth grade. He then moved to Okayama with his family in 1932. He studied at Keijō Imperial University in Seoul and then was called to the Imperial Army, serving as an Army Quartermaster Officer with the rank of Second Lieutenant. After receiving his Bachelor of Laws degree he joined the Hayashibara Company in Okayama in 1947. During his career he served as the head of several departments of this major pharmaceuticals corporation. He was a member of its Board of Directors from 1965 to 1988, rising to the rank of Executive Director of the Board of Directors until his retirement in 1990. He has also earned a certificate to be a Museum Curator, receiving that recognition from Okayama National University in 1993.

Mr Kamiya has been for a number of years a close partner with the Reverend Kurozumi Tadaaki in various translation projects.

The Editor of the English translation, *Willis Stoesz*, was born in Mountain Lake, Minnesota, in 1930. His undergraduate education was at the University of Minnesota, and his graduate degrees are from Union Theological Seminary (1958) and Columbia University (1964) in New York City. He is Emeritus Professor of Religion at Wright State University in Dayton, Ohio, after serving on its faculty from 1970 to 1993.

His association with Kurozumikyō dates from 1983 while working as an exchange professor at the Okayama University of Science. In 1985 he organized a Conference on Kurozumikyō Shinto in Dayton, co-sponsored by Wright State University, the University of Dayton, United Theological Seminary, and the Ohio Program in the Humanities. *Kurozumi Shinto; An American Dialogue* (1989) included presentations at that conference by the Reverend Kurozumi Muneharu, Patriarch of Kurozumikyō, and papers by several American scholars of Japanese religion. He also edited the translation of the *Kyōsoden*, the authorized biography of Kurozumi Munetada, published as *The Opening Way*. He has visited Kurozumikyō headquarters a number of times.

Indexes

173, 174
Four High Disciples xxviii, 50, 171
Six High Disciples xxviii, 62
meeting days (*kaijitsu*) xxvi, 25, 58,
 100f., 119, 134
meetings xxvii, 13, 16, 31f., 34,
 38f., 52, 54, 57f., 60f., 75, 85,
 93, 94, 95, 96ff., 98f., 100f.,
 110, 111, 115, 120, 122, 133f.,
 134, 139, 141ff., 144, 145, 146,
 147, 148f., 152, 155, 161
Three Distinguished Ladies 44, 63
vow, pledge (*shinmon*) xxvi, 5, 91,
 129, 155, 167, 178
vowed group (*Shinmon Shu*) 178
fool (*ahō*) xviii, 14, 52, 168, 170, 173
furu (bath) xxiv, 165

grandson story 110, 137f.
gratitude xvii, xxiv, xxvi, xxvii,
 xxviii, xxxv, 14, 18, 26, 28, 33,
 38, 40, 41, 48, 54, 60, 61, 70,
 72, 74, 77, 80, 81, 87, 89, 95,
 96, 98, 102, 109f., 114, 119f.,
 123, 129, 130, 143f., 144, 146f.,
 148, 151, 156, 158, 175, 177,
 182, 185

hakama 125
handclap (*kashiwade*) 37f., 39, 40,
 47, 60, 61, 77, 143, 144, 147,
 172, 173, 182
haori (formal dress) 13f., 86, 170
hara xxiv, xxv, xxxiv, 59, 84, 175
hardships xix
harmony xix, xxv, xxx, xxxi, 25, 48,
 111, 113, 117f., 144, 165, 166,
 177, 181, 183
healing xix, xxvi, 45, 54, 57, 63f., 64,
 69, 75, 77, 86, 87, 115, 144,
 147, 149, 154. 166, 167, 172,
 181
 (*see also majinai*)

health xix, xx, xxvi, 28, 32, 57, 61,
 67, 114, 115, 116, 151, 154,
 165, 168, 180
heart, all depends on the xxvi, xxvii,
 xxix, xxxiii, 18, 28, 43, 54, 73,
 77, 185
heart/mind (*kokoro*) xxv, xxxiv, 138,
 164, 175, 176, 177, 178, 179,
 180
Heaven (*Ten*) 11, 25, 29, 35, 42, 53,
 54, 87, 92, 94, 98, 103, 176, 179
 (*see also* Takamagahara)
 Heaven's approval 92
 Mandate of Heaven xxv, 179
Hell 22
honorifics 163, 170, 174, 177
humour xxxiii, 75, 168

ikidōshi ("abiding life") 165; xxiv,
 xxxi, xxxiii, 182, 183
ikimono ("inner power") xxv, 79,
 157, 175, 185
intellect xxxiii
intention xxxi, xxxii, 26f., 94, 101,
 129, 157, 183
 (*see also* spontaneity)
Ise Pilgrimage xxi, xxix, 108, 139,
 163
Ise Shrine 135, 181
Isle of the Blessed 52f., 173

jiriki 176
joy xxv, xxxv, 54, 59, 61, 185, 187

kami 163
 age of kami xxix, 82, 166, 188
 become kami (humans) 40
 divided kami 174
 Hachiman 125
 healing kami xxiv, xxvi, 69
 Japan, divine land 48, 66, 68, 167,
 168, 185
 kami/Kami 166, 167

207